The Foundations of Vulnerability Theory

This volume is the first collection of Martha Albertson Fineman's most important and influential work. Feminist legal theorist Martha Albertson Fineman has spent decades pushing the boundaries of law, questioning and reconceptualizing legal and social definitions of family, dependency, vulnerability, and state responsibility. The pieces collected in this book trace the arc of Fineman's scholarship, from gender equality; to the role of the family as a social institution; to dependency; to autonomy; to the legal subject and vulnerability theory.

This book reflects a lifetime of radical reimagining of the relationship between the state, individuals, families, and other social institutions that is just as relevant today as when it was written, if not more so. In this book, Fineman offers a foundation for the achievement of true social justice, through the centering of our shared human vulnerability and dependency, grounded in the recognition of the ontological body and its material needs. Arranged in sections, and introduced by leading scholars in the field, these pieces ask us to re-examine our legally enshrined commitment to formal equality and the "mythological" autonomous independent legal subject; recognizing instead that we must call for an active and responsive state that meaningfully provides resilience through its social institutions. This collection demonstrates an evolution of heretical thought that has always pressed for a deeper understanding of the foundations of law and society, offering a model for other scholars on how to keep pressing through the hard work of thinking and rethinking the conceptual basics of language, law, society, and justice.

This book will appeal to academics, policymakers, lawyers, activists, and students in law and politics theory with interests in law and society, human dependency and vulnerability, state responsibility, and feminism and the family; as well as others who have applied Fineman's vulnerability theory to issues in the fields of bioethics, artificial intelligence, and policing, to name just a few.

Jennifer Hickey is a Postdoctoral Fellow with the Vulnerability and the Human Condition Initiative at Emory University School of Law, USA.

Gender in Law, Culture, and Society

Series Editor
Martha Albertson Fineman, Emory University School of Law, USA

Gender in Law, Culture, and Society will address key issues and theoretical debates related to gender, culture, and the law. Its titles will advance understanding of the ways in which a society's cultural and legal approaches to gender intersect, clash, and are reconciled or remain in tension. The series will further examine connections between gender and economic and political systems, as well as various other cultural and societal influences on gender construction and presentation, including social and legal consequences that men and women uniquely or differently encounter. Intended for a scholarly readership as well as for courses, its titles will be a mix of single-authored volumes and collections of original essays that will be both pragmatic and theoretical. It will draw from the perspectives of critical and feminist legal theory, as well as other schools of jurisprudence. Interdisciplinary, and international in scope, the series will offer a range of voices speaking to significant questions arising from the study of law in relation to gender, including the very nature of law itself.

Other titles in the series

Feminism, Law, and Religion
Edited by Marie Failinger, Elizabeth Schiltz and Susan J. Stabile

Critical Queer Studies: Law, Film, and Fiction in Contemporary American Culture
Casey Charles

Gender, Vulnerability Theory and Public Procurement: Perspectives on Global Reform
Edited by S.N. Nyeck

Law, Vulnerability, and the Responsive State: Beyond Equality and Liberty
Edited by Martha Albertson Fineman and Laura Spitz

The Foundations of Vulnerability Theory

Feminism, Family, and Fineman

Edited by
Jennifer Hickey

Routledge
Taylor & Francis Group
a GlassHouse Book

First published 2024
by Routledge
4 Park Square, Milton Park, Abingdon, Oxon OX14 4RN

and by Routledge
605 Third Avenue, New York, NY 10158

Routledge is an imprint of the Taylor & Francis Group, an informa business

a GlassHouse book

British Library Cataloguing-in-Publication Data
A catalogue record for this book is available from the British Library

ISBN: 978-1-032-52219-7 (hbk)
ISBN: 978-1-032-52221-0 (pbk)
ISBN: 978-1-003-40562-7 (ebk)

DOI: 10.4324/9781003405627

Typeset in Sabon
by Taylor & Francis Books

For Martha

Contents

List of Contributors ix
Acknowledgments x
List of Credits xi

Introduction 1
JENNIFER HICKEY

PART I
Gender Equality **9**
DEBORAH DINNER

1 The Equality Ideal (1983) 13

2 Challenging Law, Establishing Differences (1990) 20

3 Equality Discourse and Economic Decisions Made at Divorce (1991) 33

4 The Individualization of the Family: Child Advocacy (1991) 52

5 The Illusion of Equality (1991) 60

PART II
The Sexual Family **63**
TEEMU RUSKOLA

6 The End of Family Law? Intimacy in the Twenty-First Century (1994) 67

7 A Claim for Justice (1995) 78

PART III
Dependency 81
MICHAEL THOMSON

8 A Dystopian Fantasy (2000) 85

9 Dependency and Social Debt: Cracking the Foundational Myths (2000) 87

10 The New Tokenism (1999) 97

PART IV
Autonomy 103
MARTHA T. MCCLUSKEY

11 Equality and Autonomy (2005) 107

12 Posing the Philosophy for an Active State (2005) 112

13 What Place for Family Privacy? (2003) 114

PART V
Vulnerability 125
AZIZA AHMED

14 Vulnerability and Inevitable Inequality (2017) 129

15 Equality and Difference – The Restrained State (2014) 141

16 The "Still Face" of a Compassionately-Challenged Society (2017) 146

17 Injury in the Unresponsive State (2018) 151

18 Vulnerability and Social Justice (2019) 158

19 Conclusion: Resilience is the Watchword 174
LUA KAMÁL YUILLE

20 Afterword 178
ATIENO MBOYA SAMANDARI

Index 181

List of Contributors

Aziza Ahmed is Professor of Law at Boston University School of Law.

Deborah Dinner is Professor of Law at Cornell Law School.

Martha T. McCluskey is Professor Emerita at State University of New York, University at Buffalo Law School.

Teemu Ruskola is Professor of Law and Professor of East Asian Languages and Civilizations at Penn Carey Law, University of Pennsylvania.

Atieno Mboya Samandari is Professor of Practice at Emory University School of Law.

Michael Thomson is Professor of Health Law at University of Technology Sydney and Chair in Health Law at University of Leeds.

Lua Kamál Yuille is Professor of Law and Business at Northeastern University School of Law.

Acknowledgments

I would like to thank Dr. Patricia Richards at University of Georgia for early review and feedback. I would also like to thank Dr. Stu Marvel and Payton Laskaskie of Emory University for their thoughtful contributions.

List of Credits

All excerpted material was written by Martha Albertson Fineman, Robert W. Woodruff Professor of Law at Emory University School of Law and Founder of the Feminism and Legal Theory Project and the Vulnerability and the Human Condition Initiative.

- Martha L. Fineman, *Implementing Equality: Ideology, Contradiction and Social Change-A Study of Rhetoric and Results in the Regulation of the Consequences of Divorce*, 1983 Wis. L. Rev. 789, 816–26 (1983). Copyright 2013 by The Board of Regents of the University of Wisconsin System; Reprinted by permission of the Wisconsin Law Review.
- Martha L. Fineman, *Challenging Law, Establishing Differences*, 42 FLA. L. REV. 25, 25–41, 43 (1990).
- Essays used with permission of The University of Chicago Press, from The Illusion of Equality: The Rhetoric and Reality of Divorce Reform, Martha Fineman, 2nd Edition, 1994; permission conveyed through Copyright Clearance Center, Inc.
- Martha Fineman, *The End of Family Law? Intimacy in the Twenty-First Century*, 5 DRAKE L. REV. 23 (1994).
- Essay used with permission of Taylor & Francis Group LLC, from The Neutered Mother, The Sexual Family, and Other Twentieth Century Tragedies, Martha Albertson Fineman, 1995; permission conveyed through Copyright Clearance Center, Inc.
- Martha Albertson Fineman, *Cracking the Foundational Myths: Independence, Autonomy, and Self-Sufficiency*, 8 AM. U. J. GENDER SOC. POL'Y & L. 13, 15–29 (2000).
- Martha Albertson Fineman, *The New Tokenism*, 23 VT. L. REV. 289, 290–96 (1998).
- Martha Albertson Fineman, *The Social Foundations of Law*, 54 EMORY L.J. 201, 222–230 (2005) is reprinted with the permission of Emory Law Journal.
- Essay used with permission of Columbia University Press, from *What Place for Family Privacy?*, Martha Albertson Fineman, *in* Women and the United States Constitution: History, Interpretation, and Practice (Sibyl A. Schwarzenbach

and Patricia Smith, Eds.) 2003; permission conveyed through Copyright Clearance Center, Inc.

- Martha Albertson Fineman, *Vulnerability and Inevitable Inequality*, 4 Oslo Law Review 133, 134–35, 139–149 (2017). The article is licensed under the CC BY 4.0 license (https://creativecommons.org/licenses/by/4.0/). © 2017 Martha Albertson Fineman.
- Martha Albertson Fineman, *Equality and Difference – The Restrained State*, 66 ALA. L. REV. 609, 609–14, 625–26 (2014–2015).
- Martha Albertson Fineman & Silas W. Allard, *Vulnerability, the Responsive State, and the Role of Religion, in* H. Springhart and G. Thomas (eds.), Exploring Vulnerability 185, 186–91 (2017).
- Martha Albertson Fineman, *Injury in the Unresponsive State, in* A. Bloom, D. Engel, & M. McCann (Eds.), Injury and Injustice: The Cultural Politics of Harm and Redress 50, 50–53, 66–72 (2018). © Cambridge University Press 2018. Reproduced with permission of the Licensor through PLSclear.
- Martha Albertson Fineman, *Vulnerability and Social Justice*, 53 VAL. U. L. REV. 341 (2019). Available at: https://scholar.valpo.edu/vulr/vol53/iss2/2.

Introduction

Jennifer Hickey

Feminist legal theorist Martha Albertson Fineman began her career at a time when few women were in law school and even fewer were law professors and legal theorists. Representing the generation that made a shift from focusing on "women and the law" to exploring the possibilities of developing a feminist approach to legal theory, she has spent decades pushing the boundaries of law, questioning and reconceptualizing legal and social definitions of family, dependency, vulnerability, and state responsibility. She began the Feminism and Legal Theory (FLT) Project at the University of Wisconsin in 1984 shortly after she received tenure in order to give a "safe space" to scholars wishing to explore the use of feminist theory in law. Since then, she has published a series of collections applying feminist theory to legal issues and institutions, including the first anthology of feminist legal theory: *At the Boundaries of Law*.[1] The FLT Project is still going strong, evolving and growing to include the Vulnerability and Human Condition Initiative after Fineman moved to Emory.

While the FLT Project's history is an interesting one and well worth exploring, this volume is focused on Fineman's individual work and her role as a theoretical innovator. As early as the 1980s, she began to challenge the dominant feminist approach rooted in concepts of non-discrimination and sex neutrality, arguing these ideals failed to realize socio-economic security for women and children in the divorce, child custody, and social welfare arenas. In the 1990s and early 2000s, she broadened her scholarship to a critique of the liberal fixation on autonomy as an ideal in US legal culture. In the last decade and a half, she has

1 AT THE BOUNDARIES OF LAW: FEMINISM AND LEGAL THEORY (Martha Albertson Fineman and Nancy Sweet Thomadsen eds., 1990). Other collections include: MOTHERS IN LAW: FEMINIST THEORY AND THE LEGAL REGULATION OF MOTHERHOOD (Martha Albertson Fineman & Isabel Karpin eds., 1995); FEMINISM CONFRONTS HOMO ECONOMICUS: GENDER, LAW, AND SOCIETY (Martha Albertson Fineman & Terence Dougherty eds., 2005); TRANSCENDING THE BOUNDARIES OF LAW: GENERATIONS OF FEMINISM AND LEGAL THEORY (Martha Albertson Fineman ed., 2010); EXPLORING MASCULINITIES: FEMINIST LEGAL THEORY REFLECTIONS (Martha Albertson Fineman & Michael Thomson eds., 2013), FEMINIST AND QUEER LEGAL THEORY: INTIMATE ENCOUNTERS, UNCOMFORTABLE CONVERSATIONS (Martha Albertson Fineman, Jack E. Jackson, & Adam P. Romero eds., 2013).

DOI: 10.4324/9781003405627-1

shifted decisively from critic to constructive theorist, arguing that the law should respond to universal vulnerability, creating an alternative legal framework to both a social contract and rights-based paradigm for thinking about state responsibility.

This compilation of some of her most influential work is the first collection of published work by Fineman, spanning the arc of her over 45-year career as a legal scholar. This work, reflecting a lifetime of radical reimagining of the relationship between the state, individuals, and social institutions, shows how crucial it was to foreground gendered experiences in developing Fineman's theoretical approaches to politics and law. Interestingly, the reader may well find that many of the insights Fineman developed in those early days are just as relevant today as when first published. For example, the Supreme Court's recent overturning of *Roe v. Wade* has sparked a renewed interest in matters of motherhood, gender, and family law. The failure to secure meaningful access to abortion care within the liberal framework of individual rights and bodily autonomy has left scholars and activists struggling to define new approaches to the legal regulation of reproduction and sexuality beyond a formalistic focus on gender equality and discrimination.

In addition, since we live in a time of rising political misogyny and "culture wars," Fineman's work suggests an alternative, fiercely feminist method with which to approach the politically and societally polarizing gender issues that divide us. It unites, rather than divides, across categories of difference. Increasingly, progressive legal scholars as well as the political left more broadly are recognizing the limits of prevailing antidiscrimination frameworks. Fineman's work can offer guidance in formulating new analytic tools better suited to meet humanitarian, environmental, and democratic crises. Her approach also suggests possibilities for building coalitions between progressive social justice movements and some of those disillusioned with liberalism's failings and struggling to imagine alternatives.

It is important to emphasize that this collection is much more than a retrospective appreciation of Fineman's contributions to the growth of feminist legal theory. Her early work shows Fineman's keen eye for unresolved tensions and gaps in standard analysis, as well as her ability to bravely wrestle with such omissions constructively. Interestingly, it also reveals the tensions and challenges that resulted in productive changes to Fineman's own analysis over the decades. For example, her early work reveals a lack of faith in law as a vehicle for change, while the more recent vulnerability work suggests engagement with law is not only possible, but fundamentally essential in order to broadly achieve social justice.

In addition to offering an example of how effective scholarship anchored in the law and society tradition can be, this book will make an important contribution to feminism and women's studies as an intellectual history that shows the changes in key debates over the years, with Fineman often highlighting or drawing attention to what has been minimized or missed. This collection will be a resource for critical theories of law, politics, and society, showing the necessity of incorporating the insights gained from reasoning from realities of our embodied and inevitably embedded lives. Finally, the arc of Fineman's work is extraordinary for showing the process whereby a theory grows and evolves over time and the importance of having a scholarly collaborative community. Fineman's distinct feminist method is also likely to engage readers interested in other books critical of neoliberal law and policy impacts on the family, gender, and sexuality, while going further to challenge the liberal framework dividing state and market, or individual from society.

The book is organized into five main parts that represent the major themes of Fineman's work, ordered roughly chronologically. Each part is introduced by a different scholar. This design aims to reflect the collaborative and generative networks of scholarship that Fineman has created over her decades of work. It demonstrates how this work does not exist in isolation, but lives in conversation with scholars and theories of gender, sexuality, work, family, politics, and law both inside and far beyond the legal academy.

Part I: Gender Equality

1980–1991, Introduced by Deborah Dinner

This section contains excerpts from some of Fineman's earliest work, in which she critically examines the practical consequences of divorce reform, specifically the implementation of no-fault divorce and concomitant abolition of gendered custody rules. In a series of articles written throughout the 1980s, culminating in the book publication of *The Illusion of Equality* in 1991, Fineman thoroughly exposes the detrimental effects of the dominant rhetoric of formal gender equality that pervaded divorce reform efforts. Boldly challenging hegemonic discourse, Fineman argues that liberal feminists' commitment to equal treatment ignored the reality of most women's economic dependency, a result of socioeconomic factors that disadvantaged women in the marketplace while simultaneously motivating primary assumption of domestic duties.

In particular, the stigmatization of dependency as antithetical to the idealized notion of equality prevented adoption of legal rules that addressed the material needs of most women who would carry with them unequal caretaking responsibilities postdivorce. These needs, Fineman argues, should instead be the conceptual basis of property distribution law. Fineman also addresses the practical harms of gender equality and neutrality ideals in custody decision-making. She criticizes the assumption of equal responsibility underlying the legal preference for shared parenting, arguing that it motivated a harmful devaluing of roles typically associated with "mother," such as nurturing and caretaking, and a tendency to pathologize and ignore mothers' legitimate opposition to joint custody.

This section also highlights the development of the methodological and theoretical underpinnings of the fledgling field of feminist legal theory. Fineman begins during this time to explore how feminist theory might be incorporated into legal discourse. She criticizes existing work as being too concerned with "grand theory" and advocates for a "middle range" approach to scholarship that blends theory with concrete stories and empirical information. This approach has informed subsequent decades of Fineman's work.

Additionally, Fineman aims her critical lens at feminist theorists' adoption of formal equality rhetoric. Instead, she asserts that feminist legal theory must be based on a "theory of difference," grounded in the recognition that women lead socially "gendered lives," experiencing society differently from men. Further, she cautions against overemphasis on differences among women and their identity characteristics, arguing that such a focus fails to capture the complexity of women's lives and creates a "competition of the oppressed" that impedes reform efforts. This early grappling with equality eventually leads to her ideas about "inevitable inequality" in vulnerability theory.[2]

In the foundational works included in this section, Fineman deftly demonstrates the harm of uncritically incorporating dominant rhetoric into law and policy. These works explore a broader concept of the law as a reflection of social and cultural values (though not always a timely one), rather than a catalyst for societal change. They highlight the harm caused by an overemphasis on the symbolic aspect of law rather than a practical concern for those affected. They also foreshadow Fineman's later work focusing on the familial institution as the repository for dependency and the appropriate subject of legal regulation, rejecting the individualism inherent in liberal theory. While some are focused on a specific legal reform, these early pieces lay the groundwork for the development of decades of subsequent critical legal theory.

Part II: The Sexual Family

1990–1995, Introduced by Teemu Ruskola

This part highlights the next phase of Fineman's scholarship, in which she expands her critique of formal equality in divorce reform by examining how the commitment to gender neutrality between "sexual affiliates" (husbands and wives) harmfully altered both the social and legal construction of the role of "Mother." This emphasis on motherhood (and indeed the institution of the family generally) was unusual in feminist scholarship at the time, which was constrained by the ideals of formal equality and also tended to focus on reproductive rights and workplace issues. Through her focus on the inevitability of dependency and need for caretaking, Fineman articulates feminist legal goals that bring the nurturing role of "Mother" back into the conversation, independent of the sex of the person fulfilling that role or the familial structure.

This part includes excerpts from Fineman's revolutionary 1995 book *The Neutered Mother, the Sexual Family and Other Twentieth Century Tragedies*,

2 See Martha Albertson Fineman, *Vulnerability and Inevitable Inequality*, 4 OSLO LAW REV. 133, 134–35, 139–149 (2017).

which called for complete transformation in our conceptualization of family and intimacy and a "radical reform" of family law. Fineman criticizes the legal and social primacy of the nuclear family, which serves to reinforce gender inequality within the family and to label non-conforming familial arrangements as "deviant," thus requiring patriarchal intervention. Instead, she asks us to reimagine a society organized around caretaking and nurturing rather than the sexual relationship between two individual adults. She argues that the Mother/Child is the proper dyad of legal regulation, rather than two adult partners, and the primary role of family law should be subsidizing the caretaking that occurs within this unit. This shift in legal focus would expose and center the work of the private family as an "assumed institution" and establish collective and state responsibility for the dependency that is inevitable in the human condition. This focus on dependency and state responsibility would inform Fineman's work for decades to come.

Part III: Dependency

1996–2000, Introduced by Michael Thomson

This part includes pieces that highlight the development of Fineman's theories of dependency. With a continued focus on the social role of the private family as an assumed institution, Fineman's theory centers the inevitable and universal dependency that results from human embodiment. She asserts that this dependency and the caretaking work required to manage it should be the primary rhetorical and legal focus of state subsidy. This obligation, she argues, stems from the collective debt owed to caretakers for their role in societal reproduction and for the public function they serve. In this work, Fineman reminds us that this obligation and debt do not solely belong to the state. She argues that market institutions reap the benefits of caretaking and should be required to structure workplaces to accommodate such work.

Of course, Fineman is not the only feminist theorist to criticize the undervaluing of domestic labor and unpaid care work. However, rather than argue from a position of gender discrimination or neutrality, Fineman invites us to value caretaking for its fulfillment of a public function. Rather than dismissing domestic labor as a mere obstacle to female market participation, Fineman establishes the universal nature of dependency and the critical importance of the care that we will inevitably need at some point in our lives. As such, she unites us in a critical examination of the discourse of dependency and invites us to question the vilification of dependency as anathema to the valorized American ideals of independence, autonomy, and self-sufficiency. Similarly, she asks us to consider our stigmatization of subsidy, noting that we all, in fact, lead subsidized lives as a necessary aspect of the human condition.

This material forms the origins of what Fineman would later develop as vulnerability theory. Here we see the beginning of her arguments for a more active and responsive state that properly addresses the material needs of its subjects.

Part IV: Autonomy

2001–2007, Introduced by Martha T. McCluskey

This part includes excerpts from Fineman's articles which later inform her 2004 book, *The Autonomy Myth*. In them, she critiques the US "foundational myths" of autonomy, independence, and self-sufficiency, arguing that these ideals shape our misguided demands for a limited and restrained state and negatively influence the rhetoric and ideology surrounding economic and social policymaking. She demonstrates the political, economic, and social injustice resulting from our focus on individual autonomy and independence and the resulting impoverished notions of equality. Further, she argues that the "myth" of autonomy masks the reality of our dependency, which should be the primary focal point of a state response.

Within this analysis, Fineman continues to center her conceptualization of the family as a social institution deserving of subsidy for its role in managing dependency. She explores the friction between notions of parental autonomy and state responsibility and the tensions that might arise within the family if children are legally treated as autonomous individuals, pitting their "rights" against those of their parents. She grapples with the proper allocation of familial privacy and autonomy and the line between proper fulfillment of state responsibility and intrusiveness.

These critiques of autonomy, individualism, and rights-based discourse, as well as her early conception of the responsive state, would be central to Fineman's subsequent vulnerability theory. Decades after publication of *The Autonomy Myth*, Fineman continues to expose the fallacy and negative consequences of our relentless focus on the autonomous individual.

Part V: Vulnerability

2008–Present Introduced by Aziza Ahmed

The final part illuminates Fineman's highly influential vulnerability theory. After publication of *The Autonomy Myth*, Fineman further considered the concept of derivative dependency, shifting from a more individualized analysis based on gender to a broader focus on the social role of caretaker and the place of that role within our societal structure. She also began to shift theoretical focus from dependency to the universal and constant human vulnerability that inevitably gives rise to dependency throughout the life course. Thus, Fineman introduced her vulnerability theory in the groundbreaking 2008 article, 'The Vulnerable Subject: Anchoring Equality in the Human Condition.'[3] This article remains Fineman's most cited work.

Vulnerability theory begins with the recognition of our shared human vulnerability by nature of embodiment. It argues that the current liberal legal

3 Martha Albertson Fineman, *The Vulnerable Subject: Anchoring Equality in the Human Condition*, 20 YALE J.L & FEMINISM 1, 2 (2008).

subject, autonomous and self-sufficient, should be replaced by the more realistic vulnerable legal subject, reflecting the human condition. It calls for a state that is responsive to this vulnerability by providing the resources needed for its citizens to achieve resilience. The responsive state provides these resources through social institutions, which it must monitor for inequitable allocations of power and privilege because institutions, as well as humans, are vulnerable.

Vulnerability theory continues to expand to new areas and attract further scholarly attention and engagement, particularly as the Covid-19 pandemic has highlighted our shared human vulnerability and the urgent need for a more responsive state. Once again, Fineman has asked us to imagine a better world and demonstrated that it is within our grasp, if we only shift our rhetorical and legal focus. The chapters in this part show that by moving beyond the individual and focusing on our shared vulnerability and responsibility for collective welfare, we can achieve meaningful social justice.

Together the pieces excerpted in this collection ask us to re-examine our legally enshrined commitment to formal equality and the "mythological" autonomous independent legal subject, recognizing instead that we must call for an active and responsive state that meaningfully provides resilience through its social institutions. Fineman's work demonstrates an evolution of heretical thought that has always pressed for a deeper understanding of the foundations of law and society, offering a model for other scholars on how to keep pressing through the hard work of thinking and rethinking the conceptual basics of language, law, society, and justice. By centering human material needs, Fineman destigmatizes and unites us in a quest for social justice. Her work emphasizes a broader analysis of social institutions, including the family, and the role of the state in ensuring their equitable and just operation, rather than a privileging of formal equality and individual autonomy.

Part I

Gender Equality

Deborah Dinner

In her 1990 piece, "Challenging Law, Establishing Differences"[1] Fineman posed a provocative question. Did feminism have the power to transform law to improve women's lives? Or did the "law, when it bec[ame] the battleground … transform feminism"? Fineman warned about evidence of the latter. Indeed, the richness and importance of Fineman's early scholarship derived, in part, from her resistance to law's hegemony, as both the conceptual framework that defined justice and as the site for feminist mobilization. Fineman called for attention to the ways in which the political and social realms constructed gender relations and hierarchies, influenced, but not wholly determined, by law. She also admonished feminist activists to engage in these fora with as much energy as they did courts. Today, Fineman's words ring even more true, when extreme, conservative federal judges and the Supreme Court pose one of the largest threats to women's freedom.

Fineman wrote her prescient early scholarship in feminist legal theory, from the early 1980s to the early 1990s, at a time when a regime of explicit sex discrimination was beginning to yield. Ruth Bader Ginsburg and the American Civil Liberties Union (ACLU) Women's Rights Project, along with other feminist attorneys, had won recognition for women's personhood under the Equal Protection Clause of the Fourteenth Amendment. Federal statutory law had prohibited sex discrimination in employment, and many states passed laws that guaranteed equal access to public accommodations. Legal reforms were eroding the legacies of coverture in family law. Yet gender justice – a regime that both freed women from constraints and met their material needs – remained a distant ideal. Fineman investigated why this was the case and the role that liberalizing legal trends had played in maintaining, or even exacerbating, gender subordination. My goal in this short introduction is to offer some historical background situating Fineman's analysis and briefly comment on the pioneering qualities of her scholarship.

In the mid-sixties, multiple constituencies began to advocate the liberalization of divorce law. This was not entirely, or even primarily, a feminist project.

1 Martha L. Fineman, *Challenging Law, Establishing Differences*, 42 FLA. L. REV. 25, 30 (1990).

DOI: 10.4324/9781003405627-2

Several factors contributed to the rising social demand for divorce: the economic and political forces that lowered the real value of men's wages – globalization, automation, and the conservative assault on unions; increases in middle-class mothers' labor-market participation; and enhanced cultural expectations of companionate marriage. Many couples circumvented legal restrictions on divorce. Some, for example, staged extra-marital affairs. In the face of the widening gap between formal legal rules and social reality, legal scholars and reformers grew increasingly committed to shoring up the crumbling legitimacy of family law. Their interests aligned with those of men's rights activists who opposed fault-based restrictions on marital dissolution. Such laws enhanced married mothers' bargaining power at divorce. Male-dominated state legislatures were sympathetic to men's interests in gaining freedom from alimony and child support obligations. California passed the first no-fault divorce in 1970. That same year, the National Conference of Commissioners on Uniform State laws recommended a Uniform Marriage and Divorce Act (UMDA), which focused almost exclusively on eliminating fault-based grounds for divorce.

As both facilitators and critics of family-law reform, feminist activists pursued both the freedom to exit marriage and protections for divorcing women. Betty Blaisdell Berry, the Chair of the National Organization for Women Family Relations Task Force from 1968 to 1973, was a leading advocate. Berry embraced a partnership theory of marriage, premised on the entitlement of wives who performed caregiving and housekeeping labors in the home to the couple's joint economic product. Many feminist activists argued that states should only adopt UMDA if they also enacted affirmative protections, giving wives' financial control within marriage and property entitlements upon divorce. Berry argued that acting as a "housewife" was an occupation, though it lacked the remuneration, overtime pay, and public and private benefits that accompanied professional jobs. Berry and National Organization for Women (NOW) activists, including Tish Sommers, Chair of the NOW Task Force on Older Women, advocated Social Security credits for so-called homemakers. Such credits would directly protect married mothers who worked solely in the home, rather than making their entitlement to benefits derivative of their status as widows or divorcees.

Feminists met with far greater success, however, advancing their liberalizing agenda rather than their protective aims. By 1974, the American Bar Association adopted UMDA and 45 states legislated no-fault divorce. Only small percentages of divorced women had ever actually received alimony. Yet, the no-fault trend made such awards even more rare. In recognition of a socio-legal shift to view women as wage-earners, too, courts began to substitute time-limited maintenance in lieu of lifetime support awards. These states made only modest reforms to protect the economic security of divorcing women and their children. Common-law states ended title-based systems of property distribution and adopted contribution-based models. But they adopted narrow definitions of what constituted property, which largely exclude husbands' professional degrees and other forms of human capital. As a result, purported "equitable distribution" was based on a distorted economic accounting of particular marriages and their assets. Although Congress made minor reforms to enhance benefits for divorced women and widows, it never implemented homemaker credits. The 1970s thus witnessed the advent of neoliberal family law: a regime that in its formal sex neutrality reinforced gender subordination.

It was against this context that Fineman authored landmark critiques of family law. Fineman's early work in this arena challenged liberal equality ideals and advanced new methodologies in feminist legal theory. Fineman criticized liberal feminists for advocating formal sex neutrality in the home, even as they pursued gender-sensitive remedies to disadvantage, including affirmative action, in the workplace. Fineman was sympathetic to feminist fears of reinforcing gender stereotypes and to the aspiration for legal rules to model an egalitarian division of child-rearing labor. Ultimately, however, she concluded that formal equality ignored the ways in which gender continued to shape both the labor market and familial care work. In the face of these realities, formal sex neutrality produced only "The Illusion of Equality," as Fineman titled her piercing 1991 book. Fineman's analysis was courageous, as it challenged dominant civil rights ideals.

Fineman's normative goals were intertwined with her methodologies. Drawing on Robert Merton's concept of the "middle range," she insisted that feminist legal theory mediate between the universal and the particular. The iterative process of moving between data and structure took at least two forms in Fineman's work. To start, it meant keeping in mind both empirical accounts of how law affected women on the ground and grand theory. Empiricism without a theoretical analysis did not hold potential to inform legal change. Yet sweeping theorization without sociological analysis could lead reforms astray. In addition, Fineman's commitment to the importance of both the universal and particular shaped her understanding of difference within the category "women." Fineman recognized that race and class shaped women's disparate experiences. Yet she argued that other differences, too, were formative, including age, disability, orientation, maternal status, and among siblings. She cautioned against an intense, and sometimes divisive, focus on ever-expanding categories of difference that might undermine a coherent struggle for gender equality. The dilemma of how to handle difference within universal justice commitments persisted as a theme in Fineman's later work, as she transitioned from a critique of equality to an affirmative theory of vulnerability.

Fineman's ideas interrogating equality have been enormously influential to my own development as a scholar. I became Professor Fineman's colleague as I embarked on turning my dissertation into my first monograph. The book traces the evolution of sex equality ideals in law and policy from the Civil Rights Act of 1964 to welfare reform in the mid-1990s. Fineman was a historical actor in this process, shining a light as a dissenting voice. Her theorization of the legal changes that did take place, and their limits, helped me to analyze those feminist voices and legal paths that were lost in the rise of what I call "neoliberal sex equality." In addition, Fineman pushed me to move from historical detail to broader structural analyses – to perform my own interpretations of the "middle range." Fineman's commitment to gender justice has led her to take significant intellectual and professional risks in challenging legal liberalism over the course of her career. In this way and many others, she serves as a model.

In conclusion, let me return to the crucial questions with which I began. What does Fineman's work teach us about law and social change, writ large, beyond the scope of the specific historical processes she criticized? It may be helpful to understand Fineman's work in relationship to critical legal studies, which provided one context for its academic development. Fineman shares with this movement a cynicism about formal neutrality as well as the capacity for legal reform to disrupt socio-economic power. At the same time, however, embedded in Fineman's work is an idealism about what she terms the "roots" of law. Perhaps influenced by her years as a civil procedure teacher, Fineman wrote with hope about legal institutions even as she embraced a healthy skepticism about them. It is this productive tension, too, that we need to hold, wrestle with, and articulate, as we navigate difficult times for feminist legal theory.

Chapter 1

The Equality Ideal (1983)[1]

In this early piece, Fineman challenges the "ideal" of formal equality that pervaded liberal feminist rhetoric and family law reform efforts. She criticizes the feminist movement's myopic focus on inequality within the market and political sphere, treating the family as a mere obstacle to women's participation in the market rather than as a site of injustice necessitating remediation. In exploring the material inequalities of marriage and divorce, Fineman urges consideration of the practical consequences of uncritical adoption of egalitarian ideology and rhetoric.

Rule equality, or sameness of treatment of individuals, has been an ideal throughout American history, but for the most part, early expositions of the concept failed to encompass women's position. Classical liberal theory, while opposing the idea that status follows birth, did not pull the family, with its historical sex-based division of roles and rights, into its ambit because the family was considered part of the private sphere and thus beyond the reach of public political theory.[2]

The concept of rule equality was early employed by feminists in the public sphere, however. It became a banner under which feminists organized to demand access to political and public institutions. Equality of access was one answer to the oppression exemplified in their portrayal of the woman as victim.[3] The latest manifestation of this use of the concept is the recent movement behind the Equal Rights Amendment.[4]

Application of the rule equality concept may be easy to comprehend when the questions are relatively straightforward, as with the right to vote. Problems arise,

1 This essay originally appeared in: Martha L. Fineman, *Implementing Equality: Ideology, Contradiction and Social Change-A Study of Rhetoric and Results in the Regulation of the Consequences of Divorce*, 1983 WIS. L. REV. 789, 816–26 (1983). Copyright 2013 by The Board of Regents of the University of Wisconsin System; Reprinted by permission of the Wisconsin Law Review.

2 GORDON S. WOOD, THE CREATION OF THE AMERICAN REPUBLIC 1766–1787, 70–75 (1969).

3 *See* NORMA BASCH, IN THE EYES OF THE LAW (1982).

4 *See* Phyllis A. Dow, *Sexual Equality, The ERA and the Court-A Tale of Two Failures*, 13 N.M. L. REV. 53 (1983).

DOI: 10.4324/9781003405627-3

however, when the concept must be integrated with prevailing assumptions about women's different physical, emotional, or social characteristics. At some periods in our history, there has been general agreement that significant differences existed between men and women in one or more of these areas, which justified different treatment. For example, protective legislation for women was part of the progressive movement. This legislation was encouraged by reformers who sought to require that employers treat women unequally. These reformers wanted such laws in order to protect women from being victimized by existing working conditions, which some believed would affect them differently and more severely than men.[5]

Conceptual barriers to the imposition of a pure rule equality solution are also evident in the twentieth century, and affect the current debates generated by feminists about needed law reform. While some contemporary feminists tend to accept the notion that equality can be achieved merely by the adoption of rules which either eliminate gender as a basis for distinguishing between people or impose sanctions in situations where gender is such a basis, other feminists have urged more recently that the object of equality extends beyond mere formal treatment. The rules, they would argue, should be developed explicitly to achieve equality of result, and gender may be important to such a consideration.

Such calls for explicit gender consideration in fashioning rules differ from the progressive era's arguments for special or different treatment of women. They focus on an analysis of existing institutional structures and their historical inadequacies in incorporating women, and not on the different and therefore implicitly "deficient" characteristics of women as a group. Difference of treatment is therefore desirable not because of women's inherently different internal qualities, but because of the discriminatory qualities of the institutions with which they must deal. The significant question of differences between men and women are externalized. Because such arguments identify the significant differences as those of treatment – the result of institutional failures – and do not concede an inalterable biological or physiological basis for such treatment, it follows that the disadvantages will disappear if the institutions can be changed. Under this approach, the protection that women are perceived as needing is in assuring them access to these institutions and the opportunity to function within them without being disadvantaged by institutional inadequacies.

This modern perception of a need for "protective-" or result-oriented legislation has been at the base of many recent battles in the public arena. As women have moved into new market and political spheres during the last several decades, women's rights advocates have broadened their focus beyond the more obvious manifestations of inequality for women, such as denial of the right to vote, hold

5 *See Muller v. Oregon*, 208 U.S. 412,422 (1908) (limited working hours for women upheld because of their weaker physical nature and their need to be protected). *See also* Leo Kanowitz, *"Benign" Sex Discrimination: Its Troubles and Their Cure,* 31 HASTINGS L.J. 1379 (1980).

office, or engage in certain occupations where injustice can be rectified by simply treating women the same as men. Feminists are now grappling with new problems, and their solutions reflect the belief that some problems are not likely to be resolved by simple rule equality without reference to characteristics statistically related to gender and to the socio-economic disadvantages of women in this society. For example, they observe that more women work today than ever before in this country's history but point out that they earn much less than men. Feminists recognize that women are often clustered in a few occupations, and have moved from demands for equal pay for equal work to demands which raise difficult legal questions of comparable worth.[6] They show a growing awareness that even women who achieve access to "male" occupations do not "have it made" since sociological studies of businesses and professions have begun to reveal subtle forms of sex discrimination in promotions and delegation of responsibility.[7]

This progression from concern with the obvious to concern with the more hidden manifestations of discriminatory or unequal treatment of women has created a need for feminists to develop a coherent concept of equality with which to address these problems. In some areas a difficult choice must be made between two potentially conflicting equality models, that of gender-neutral rules as a matter of principle (rule equality) and that of individualized justice for women (result equality). This potential conflict is at the heart of the issue of affirmative action, for example, when society is asked to formulate a rule which is not neutral (demonstrates a preference) to achieve social equality or equity (hiring more women). It is also at the heart of many issues in family law. Feminists have not always recognized this, however, and the failure to do so may be damaging to many women's interests in that area.

6 *See* Ruth G. Blumrosen, *Wage Discrimination, Job Segregation and Women Workers,* 6 WOMENS RTS. L. REP. 19, 22 n.7 (1980) (25 percent of working women work in occupations which are more than 95 percent female; 50 percent in occupations that are more than 70 percent female).

For a discussion of comparable worth, *see Lemons v. City & County of Denver,* 17 Fair Empl. Prac. Cas. (BNA) 906 (D. Colo. 1978), *aff'd,* 620 F.2d 228 (10th Cir.), *cert. denied,* 449 U.S. 888 (1980); Comment, *Equal Pay for Comparable Work,* 15 Harv. C.R.-C.L. L. Rev. 475 (1980).

7 *See* Harlan & Weiss, *New Curbs Arise for Female Execs,* CHICAGO TRIBUNE, 1982. Wellesley College Center for Research on Women studied subtle forms of sex discrimination in promotion patterns, which included a lack of supervisory feedback for women. The study also indicated that resistance to the presence of women becomes overt as they reach a "critical mass" of 15 percent of the total number of employees. *Id.*

One author concludes that job discrimination is the result of men's collective domination over women in all spheres of life including unions, and legal actions. Heidi Hartman, *Capitalism, Patriarchy and Job Segregation by Sex, in* WOMEN AND THE WORKPLACE: THE IMPLICATIONS OF OCCUPATIONAL SEGREGATION 137–70 (M. Blaxall & B. Reagan eds., 1976). *See also* Harlan & Weiss, *supra;* Brigid O'Farrell & Sharon L. Harlan, *Office Workers and Clerks: The Effect of Male* Co *Worker Hostility on Women's Statistics with non-Traditional Jobs,* 29 SOC. PROBS. 252 (1982).

Feminist Concepts in the Family Area

In general, feminist reformers are more likely to vigorously advocate the application of formal, result-oriented affirmative action principles in the market, but call for application of a pure rule equality model within the family context. The feminist metaphor for marriage is found in the terminology of business association, a "partnership."[8] In addition, there are efforts to make decisions concerning the family gender neutral. In the family law area, formal gender-specific rules have been virtually abolished either by legislation or by court decisions in the past several years, often as a result of reforms initiated by feminists.[9] Concern with more subtle inequalities has not yet

8 *See* Doris Jonas Freed & Henry H. Foster, *Marital Property Reform in New York: Partnership of Co-Equals?*, 8 FAM. L. Q. 169, 176 (1974) (supporting the notion of marriage as a "partnership of co-equals with division of labor that entitles each to a one-half interest in the family assets ... such a system reflects the contemporary understanding of marriage, and the reasonable expectations or the parties"). *See* SEX DISCRIMINATION AND THE LAW: CAUSES AND REMEDIES (B. Babcock, A. Freedman, E. Norton & S. Ross eds., 1975) for a distinction between commercial and marital partnership. In Walter Weyrauch, *Metamorphoses of Marriage,* 13 FAM. L. Q. 415, 418–24, 435 (1980), the author asserted that the incidents of marriage are governed increasingly by notions of equality of spouses, with spouses viewed as persons entering a voluntary association with equal rights, duties, and contributions. He noted that small business case law aided evolution of the partnership concept of marriage. Underlying this conception, however, is a fundamental assumption of freedom of will that is not always born out in reality as noted by Weyrauch. There are problems, also, with how one views children if marriage is a contract. There seem to be conflicting views: they are seen as chattels, assets, or products of the marriage, or as persons who are consumers of marriage and entitled to protection. An additional problem, not mentioned by those advocating the partnership concept, is that expectations which may be reasonable at the time of marriage or during a functioning marriage may appear substantially unreasonable at time of divorce when ongoing benefits of support and mutual cooperation are terminated.

The partnership model has long been urged as a way of limiting judicial discretion. In criticizing judicial discretion, one author commented that the "greatest evil is not so bad when certain." Harriet Daggett, *Divisions of Property Upon Dissolution of Marriage,* 6 LAW & CONTEMPORARY PROBS. 225, 229 (1939). Daggett recommended the concept of partnership based on community property principles and mandatory equal division. She also believed that community property states were far ahead of common law property states. With an economic partnership it would make "no difference whether one contributes more energy to the task with better material results than the other; nor does it matter if one makes no contribution at all." *Id.* at 223.

The partnership idea is a concept which also can be traced to 19th-century feminist theory. John Stuart Mill observed the parallels between partnership and marriage in his essay. J. MILL, THE SUBJECTION OF WOMEN IN THREE ESSAYS 427–548 (1975), at 472–84.

9 *See, e.g., Orr v. Orr*, 440 U.S. 268 (1979) (invalidating on equal protection grounds a state statute permitting alimony awards only to wives).

For the origins of the "tender years" doctrine, *see* Jamil S. Zainaldin, *The Emergence of a Modern American Family Law: Child Custody, Adoption, and the Courts, 1796–1851,* 73 NW. U. L. REV. 1038, 1072–74 (1979).

evolved in the family context, nor have affirmative action concepts been proposed. It is clear that feminist discussion of family relationships has not evolved in the direction of affirmative action. One possible explanation for the focus on gender-neutral rules and formal equality within the family is that the liberal feminists' goals for women in the family context are formulated from the perspective of their fundamental objective of ensuring women's ability to function as equals in the political sphere and in the marketplace.

The early themes concerned with problems of equal access to political and market institutions have been carried through to some extent in addressing the problems in the family sphere, because the family is viewed as affecting access to political and economic power. The early feminist dialogues on the family centered on changing role expectations within marriage and on the notion of shared domestic responsibilities between spouses. The goal appeared to be the breakdown of gender stereotypes associated with the family's division of labor. The family was represented as an adjunct to the primary market functions that women would ideally perform, and it consequently had to be restructured.[10] Women could not be expected to function as equals in the marketplace if they could not free themselves from their traditional family responsibilities. Rhetoric in the family context, then, has been consistent with and complementary to equal access issues raised in relation to the market and politics.

Although equality in the ongoing family seems to be viewed as a key for women's entry into the market, feminist theory has for the most part neglected divorce as a distinct subject of inquiry and has failed to recognize that divorce presents the same sort of access questions as ongoing marriage, except that problems associated with combining work and family are exacerbated. The circumstances that would make equal access to market institutions a viable reality for a divorced woman are more complicated than those presented in the context of an ongoing family with both spouses present. The idealized feminist solution of shared, equal responsibility for domestic chores is hard to implement when the unit is broken. The chores still have to be done, children must be cared for, and a home must be established and maintained, but there are no longer two adults to divide the burdens. If women assume these responsibilities after divorce, as they do in the overwhelming majority of cases, they may need more assets or financial resources than their ex-spouses to have effective access to market opportunities. This need is further complicated by the fact that a woman is statistically likely to earn far less than her ex-spouse after divorce

10 *See, e.g.*, Sandra L. Benn & Daryl J. Benn, *Women's Role in American Society: Retrospect and Prospect; Training the Woman to Know Her Place: The Power of a Nonconscious Ideology, in* WOMEN'S ROLE IN CONTEMPORARY SOCIETY, THE REPORT OF THE NEW YORK CITY COMMISSION ON HUMAN RIGHTS SEPTEMBER 21–25, 101, 107–12 (1970); Pat Mainardi, *The Politics of Housework, in* SISTERHOOD IS POWERFUL: AN ANTHOLOGY OF WRITINGS FROM THE WOMEN'S LIBERATION MOVEMENT 447–54 (1970).

even if she is working.[11] To achieve equality of result, it might thus be necessary to treat the spouses differently when distributing the assets of the marriage.

Divorce, it would seem, presents the ideal situation for feminists to argue for solutions which move beyond rule equality, in the same direction as do affirmative action solutions in the market context. In fact, the juxtaposition of the affirmative action arguments in the market with those for the equalitarian marriage model in divorce points out an underlying inconsistency between the alternative views of the public and private positions of women within society.

The feminists argue for the employment of concepts of affirmative (or protective) action in the public sphere as part of the response to the perceived structural inadequacies of economic institutions. In addressing the economic questions in divorce, however, they have adhered, for the most part, to the ideal of egalitarian marriage. The question, therefore, is why gender, which feminists perceived as fundamental in formulating idealized rules to structure women's dealings with employers and other outside economic forces, is not likewise perceived as fundamental in formulating idealized rules for the structuring of economic relationships at divorce?

There may be several related reasons why feminists have not made these arguments. First, such arguments would cast doubt on the ideal of family equality. If at divorce different or preferred treatment for women were to be demanded, it could not be justified as consistent with the goal of an egalitarian family in the ongoing marriage and would therefore frustrate desired social change. Second, although the family is distinguishable from the market, result-oriented arguments that women should be treated differently in the family area because of their gender-related social characteristics might be transferred with very different symbolic connotations into the market. Such differential treatment in the family sphere may be used to perpetuate discriminatory beliefs already operating to disadvantage women at work. Feminists may sense that gender-specific rules in the family area, whether implicitly or explicitly formulated, afford the danger of generally stigmatizing or calling into question the abilities or commitment of the "protected" sex on a wider, work-related scale.[12]

Third, even if only the issue of divorce is considered, generalized result equality rules may not help to improve the disadvantaged position of women at divorce, but rather may actually perpetuate it. Explicit gender-specific rules, such as the "maternal preference" for the custody of children of "tender years," may assist women who are more prone than men as a group to seek custody of their children, but at the same time reinforce the notion that biology is destiny. Perpetuating the notion that motherhood comes first for women in general may make an individual

11 Robert Hampton, *Marital Disruption: Some Social and Economic Consequences, in* FIVE THOUSAND AMERICAN FAMILIES-PATTERNS OF ECONOMIC PROGRESS 163, 172 (1974).

12 *See generally,* Peter Westen, *The Empty Idea of Equality,* 95 HARV. L. REV. 537, 575–82 (1982).

woman's decision to relinquish custody of her child to her husband more difficult.[13]

Finally, to the extent that the feminists' overriding objective is the affirmation of the ideal of equality, result equality rules which concede that equality does not in fact exist may create an impression that it cannot exist. The recognition that women may be in need of protective rules could be viewed as an admission that women as a group are dependent, and as a suggestion that they will be dependent forever. Such rules might not be viewed as merely necessary corrective measures for institutionally disadvantaged women.

To be satisfied with or to insist upon rule equality in divorce, however, is to overlook the serious toll that an egalitarian ideology may take on women who must function in an unequal world which requires that they meet greater demands with fewer resources. It also elevates a simplified ideal to the status of a rule of decision and obscures the real issues in divorce. Feminists, consistent with their desire to assist women, should be advocating the need for unequal treatment – for result equality – in divorce.

13 *See* SUSAN GETTLEMAN & JANET MARKOWLTZ, THE COURAGE TO DIVORCE 194 (1974). *See also* JUNE NOBLE & WILLIAM NOBLE, THE CUSTODY TRAP 120–22 (1975) recounting a case in which a mother was ostracized by friends and family because she failed to seek custody.

Chapter 2

Challenging Law, Establishing Differences (1990)[1]

Here, Fineman lays the groundwork for the emerging field of feminist legal theory, calling on theorists to consider the reality of women's "gendered lives" and urging them to ground their scholarship in the concrete experiences of women rather than "grand theory."

This chapter concerns the complex, difficult, and perhaps impossible goal of introducing feminist theory into legal discourse. In it I analyze existing and emerging themes that dominate contemporary feminist legal discourse and that concern me because of their limited usefulness in developing a theory of women's experience within law and legal institutions.

On the broadest level feminist legal thought seems unanchored. It drifts between the extremes of "grand theory," which is totalizing in its scope and ambitions, and personal narratives, which begin and end with the presentation of one individual's unique experience. Neither of these extremes does much to further the discussion of feminist issues because they obscure more than they illuminate. Between these extremes, in that space between something so exclusively personal as to be beyond generalization or political content, and something so general and abstract as to be removed from the everyday realities of women's lives, lies fertile ground for feminist methodology.

In my efforts to assess the future of feminist legal scholarship, I am not concerned with discussions that focus merely on including women in the legal profession, nor with those directed at ensuring that, once included, women in law share power and positions equally with men. Women's presence in the legal profession has not caused feminist theory to follow. In fact, all too often in order to be successful, women have adopted assimilation as their intellectual strategy and equal treatment as their substantive principle.

My version of feminist theory is decidedly antiassimilationist. It does not adopt existing legal norms and merely require equal entitlement for women to the benefits and burdens distributed throughout our system of legal regulations. Rather, my version of feminist theory questions both the asserted universal

1 This essay originally appeared in: Martha L. Fineman, *Challenging Law, Establishing Differences*, 42 FLA. L. REV. 25, 25–41, 43 (1990).

DOI: 10.4324/9781003405627-4

"ideal" of equality espoused in dominant legal thought and the existing distributions of power and economic benefits held in place by the structure and nature of law. It goes beyond considerations of gender and addresses questions of value (what we deem worthwhile) and knowledge (how we construct truth).

I begin with my version of the ideally antagonistic interaction of feminist theory with the law. I locate my discussion between the extremes of grand theory and unique experience. I consider the central, pressing task of feminist theory to be challenging existing law and legal doctrines through the articulation and establishment of a theory of difference. In this chapter I divide my discussion of the theory of difference into two sections. The first section concerns the theoretical and political necessity of establishing the differences between men and women. Articulation of the extent of this manifestation of difference illustrates that the law primarily represents and reflects male experiences and norms. Critiquing the law from a feminist perspective requires understanding how women's perceptions and experiences differ from men's and how such differences are relevant to the development and implementation of legal doctrines and theories.

The second theoretical consideration involved in developing a theory of difference is the realization that important differences exist among women. Feminists must overcome these differences in both practice and theory because the existence of these differences is misused to divide women. The task of feminist theory in this regard is to encourage women to work together, across differences, so that the similar, shared gendered aspects of our lives do not continue to be invisible and unspoken in law.

Finally, I will address questions about the notion of "representation." I focus on the concept of representation as a legitimating selection criterion that affects our acceptance of an individual possessing an identified characteristic as "typical" of a class or group. Representation implies that an individual can typify a group or class merely by possessing a shared characteristic that serves the functions of both distinguishing him or her from the whole and unifying him or her with an identifiable subgroup. In this regard, representation is a totalizing concept even though its premise initially lies in the recognition of difference. Representation depends upon identifying and privileging one characteristic from among the many that an individual may possess. The characteristic thus serves to identify the individual as well as the group that the individual represents. The characteristic, so designated, publicly becomes the most politically, and perhaps socially, salient feature that the individual possesses. The theme of representation is integrally related to and is an outgrowth of my earlier considerations of differences.

Feminist Theory and Law

Recently, the interest in feminist scholarship has increased. Law has been an area relatively untouched by the postmodern currents that have washed through other disciplines, but it now appears to be caught within tides of critical methodologies and conclusions that threaten its very roots. An examination of the concept of feminist legal theory reveals both a subject and a methodology that are still in the process of being born. There are no "right" paths, clearly defined. The scholarship, however, can be described as sharing the objective of raising questions about women's relationships to law and legal institutions.

Theory and Practice

Given the newness of the inquiry, many "practitioners" of feminist legal theory may prefer to describe their work as examples of feminist "methodology" rather than as expositions of "theory." In fact, in regard to feminist scholarship, it is appropriate to conclude that method *is* theory in its most relevant form.

My approach has been to reject the resort to abstractions and to concentrate on understanding why little relation exists between women's lives and material circumstances and the specific doctrinal representations of those lives and circumstances. My choice has been to "do" feminist theory as an exercise in the concrete, both by focusing on a specific area of law and by using empirical information and stories of specific lives. This emphasis on specifics relates to my understanding of the insights feminist methodology has produced for scholars. The real distinction between feminist theory (legal and otherwise) and more traditional legal theory is this belief in the desirability of the concrete. Such an emphasis also has had rather honorable non-feminist adherents. For example, Robert Merton coined the term "theory of the middle range" to describe work that mediated between "stories" and "grand theory." He described such scholarship as being superior to mere storytelling or mindless empiricism, as well as superior to vague references to the relationships between ill-defined abstractions.[2] Clifford Geertz[3] and James Boyd White, among others, have noted that language or rhetoric itself is specific and tied to given material concerns. White has stated,

> Like law, rhetoric invents; and, like law, it invents out of something rather than out of nothing. It always starts in a particular culture and among particular people. There is always one speaker addressing others in a particular situation, about concerns that are real and important to somebody,

2 ROBERT K. MERTON, *On Sociological Theories of the Middle Range, in* ON THEORETICAL SOCIOLOGY: FIVE ESSAYS, OLD AND NEW 39, 68 (1967).

3 Geertz stated in regard to grand anthropological concepts:

"If anthropological interpretation is constructing a reading of what happens, then to divorce it from what happens - from what, in this time or that place, specific people say, what they do, what is done to them, from the whole vast business of the world - is to divorce it from its applications and render it vacant. A good interpretation of anything – a poem, a person, a history, a ritual, an institution, a society – takes us into the heart of that of which it is the interpretation." Clifford Geertz, *Thick Description: Toward an Interpretive Theory of Culture, in* THE INTERPRETATION OF CULTURES 18 (1973).

> and speaking a particular language. Rhetoric always takes place with given materials. One cannot idealize rhetoric and say, "Here is how it should go on in general" .... [R]hetoric is always specific to its material.[4]

At least in nonlaw areas, feminist scholarship has tended to focus on specifics. Feminist legal scholarship, however, seems to be drifting toward abstract grand-theory presentations. Carol Smart recently warned that feminist legal theorists are in danger of creating the impression that one specific form of feminist jurisprudence represents the "superior" (or true) version as opposed to various other feminist legal theories. Smart labeled this totalizing tendency, evident in the work of many of the most well-known North American legal feminists, the construction of a "scientific feminism" and was explicitly critical of such grand theorizing.[5]

While I agree with Smart's assertion, I am aware that the tenure, hiring, and promotion committees, in addition to the law reviews of elite American law schools, often prefer grand theory over middle-level theory: the grander the feminist theory, the more it resembles mainstream scholarly format and content. Grand theorizing represents the creation of a new form of positivism in a search for universal truth discoverable within the methodology of critical legal analysis. In contrast, middle-range theory mediates between the material circumstances of women's lives and the grand realizations that law is gendered, that law is a manifestation of power, and that law works to the detriment of women. These realizations previously have been hidden or ignored in considerations of the laws that regulate women's lives. They are best exposed by referencing and emphasizing those lives.

Increasingly, I have become aware of the difficulty of trying to use middle-range feminist methodology within the confines of legal theory. Not only does the pull toward grand theory categorize less grand scholarship as non-theoretical, but I fear that feminist sensibilities become lost or absorbed into the morass of legal concepts and words. I have lost faith. Feminism, it seems, has not transformed, and perhaps cannot transform the law. Rather, the law, when it becomes the battleground, threatens to transform feminism. This result stems from the obvious power of the law as a "dominant discourse" – one which is self-contained (though incomplete and imperfect), self-congratulatory (though not introspective or self-reflective), and self-fulfilling (though not inevitable nor infallible).

4 James Boyd White, *Law as Rhetoric, Rhetoric as Law: The Arts of Cultural and Communal Life,* 52 U. CHI. L. REV. 684, 695 (1985).

5 C. SMART, FEMINISM AND THE POWER OF LAW 70–71 (1989); *see also* Robin West, *Jurisprudence and Gender,* 55 U. CHI. L. REV. 1 (1988) (the need for a more experience-based jurisprudence). *But cf.* Frances Olsen, *Feminist Theory in Grand Style,* 89 COLUM. L. REV. 1147, 1166–77 (1989) (a defense of grand theorizing in the context of reviewing the work of Catharine MacKinnon).

The transformative potential of feminist thought is blunted because in order to be incorporated into and considered compatible with legal theory, feminist thought must adapt, even if it does not totally conform, to the words and concepts of legal discourse. Feminism may enter as the challenger, but the tools inevitably employed are those of the androphile master. And the character of the tools largely determines the shape and design of the resulting construction. Therefore, the task of feminists concerned with the law and legal institutions must be to create and explicate feminist methods and theories that explicitly challenge and compete with the totalizing nature of grand legal theory. Such a feminist strategy would set its middle-range theory in opposition to law – outside of formal legal categories.

Feminist Methodologies

In my opinion, there are several characteristics that, in various permutations and combinations, provide the ingredients for feminist legal analyses that effectively can challenge existing legal theory and paradigms. First, feminist methodology should be critical. This critical stance is developed by adopting an explicitly woman-focused perspective, a perspective informed by women's experiences. Feminist theory cannot be "gender neutral" and often will be explicitly critical of that paradigm as historically having excluded the woman's perspective from legal thought. "Gender-sensitive" feminism, however, cannot be viewed as lacking legitimacy because of an inappropriate bias. Rather, it is premised on the need to expose and correct an *existing* bias. "Gender-sensitive" feminism seeks to correct the imbalance and unfairness in the legal system that result from implementing perspectives that exclude attention to the circumstances of women's gendered lives, even on issues that intimately affect those lives.

Feminist analysis, if recognized at all, often is seen as marginal to legal thought. Traditional legal scholarship tends to view the status quo as unbiased or neutral. This belief in the possibility of a neutral stance is the logical place for feminist analysis to begin: as an explicit challenge to the use of the concept of bias, as contrasted with the concepts of perspective and position, when introducing previously excluded voices into legal discourse and analysis.

Feminist theory can demonstrate that the status quo is *not* neutral; that it is as "biased" as, and certainly no more "correct" than, that which challenges it. And there can be no refuge in the status quo. Law has developed in the context of theories and institutions which are controlled by men and reflect their concerns. Historically, law has been a "public" arena, and its focus has been on public concerns. Traditionally, women have belonged to the "private" recesses of society: in families, in relationships controlled and defined by men, and in silence.

In addition to exposing the inevitability of bias, feminist analysis critically evaluates not only outcomes, but also fundamental concepts, values, and assumptions embedded in legal thought.[6] Results or outcomes in cases decided under existing legal doctrines are relevant to this inquiry but criticizing them is only a starting point. Too many legal scholars end their inquiry with a critique of results and recommendations for "tinkering"-type reforms without considering how the conceptual structure of legal thought condemns such reforms merely to replicating injustices. When, as is often the case, the basic tenets of legal ideology clash with women's gendered lives, reforms based on those tenets will do little more than the original rules did to validate and accommodate women's experiences.

From this perspective, feminism is a political theory concerned with issues of power. It challenges the conceptual bases of the status quo by assessing the ways that power controls the production of values and standards against which specific results and rules are measured. Law represents both a discourse and a process of power. Norms created by and enshrined in law are manifestations of power relationships. These norms are applied coercively and are justified in part by the perception that they are "neutral" and "objective." Appreciating this phenomenon, many feminist scholars have focused their attention on the legislative and political processes rather than on the judiciary.[7] The recognition that law is power also has led many feminists to concentrate on social and cultural perceptions and manifestations of law and legality rather than to focus narrowly on formal legal doctrinal developments.[8]

Implicit in my assertion that feminism must be a politically rather than a legally focused theory is my belief about the relative powerlessness of law, as compared to other ideological institutions within our culture, to transform society. While law can reflect, and even facilitate, social change, law can seldom, if ever, initiate it. Regardless of the formal legal articulation, legal rules will tend to track and reflect the dominant conclusions of the majority culture. Thus, while law perhaps highlights the social and political aspects it reflects, it is more a mirror than a catalyst in regard to enduring social change.[9]

6 *See* Catherine MacKinnon, *Feminism, Marxism, Method and the State: An Agenda for Theory?*, 7 SIGNS: J. WOMEN IN CULTURE & SOC'Y 515, 534–36 (1982) (discussing the political implications of method); *see also* Martha Fineman & Anne Opie, *The Uses of Social Science Data in Legal Policymaking: Custody Determinations at Divorce*, 1987 WIS. L. REV. 107 (1987).

7 *See, e.g.*, AT THE BOUNDARIES OF LAW: FEMINISM AND LEGAL THEORY (M. A. Fineman & N. S. Thomadsen eds., 1990).

8 For two excellent illustrations of works analyzing the interplay between formal legal developments and their application in practice, *see* Linda Girdner, *Child Custody Determination: Ideological Dimensions of a Social Problem, in* REDEFINING SOCIAL PROBLEMS 165 (1986); Kathryn McCann, *Battered Women and the Law: The Limits of the Legislation, in* WOMEN IN LAW: EXPLORATIONS IN LAW, FAMILY & SEXUALITY 71 (1985).

9 No-fault divorce reform illustrates this phenomenon. Prior to these statutes, lawyers often would counsel clients on how to "create" divorce grounds. *See* L. FRIEDMAN, A HISTORY OF AMERICAN LAW 438–40 (1973). Thus, rather than representing any legal "change," no-fault reforms actually mirrored existing practice.

An additional characteristic of feminist legal methodology is that it seeks to present alternatives to the existing order.[10] The construction of alternatives may be, of course, a natural outgrowth of other characteristics of feminist legal thought, particularly that feminist legal thought is critical and political. I place the construction of alternatives as a separate characteristic, however, because an independent goal of much of feminist work is to present oppositional values.[11] Feminist analysis often is radically non-assimilationist, and it resists the mere inclusion in dominant social institutions as the solution to the problems in women's gendered lives. In fact, the larger social value of feminist methodology may lie in its ability to make explicit oppositional stances vis-a-vis the existing culture. The task of the moment for feminism may be to transform society by challenging dominant values and defiantly refusing to assimilate into the status quo. The point of making women's experiences and perspectives central factors in developing social theory is to change "things," not merely to change women's perspectives on their positions within existing power relationships. To many feminist scholars, therefore, assimilation is failure, while opposition is essential for feminist methodology applied to law.[12]

It seems to me important to emphasize that feminist theory that effectively challenges existing paradigms will be characteristically evolutionary in nature. Feminist legal theory, therefore, will not represent doctrine carved in stone or even printed in statute books. Feminist methodology at its best generates contributions to what is recognized as a series of ongoing debates that start with the premises that "truth" changes over time as circumstances change and that gains and losses, along with recorded wisdom, are mutable parts of an evolving story. As feminist legal theory references women's lives, it must define and undertake the "tasks of the moment." The tasks of the future cannot yet be defined, and each piece of feminist legal scholarship is only one step in the long journey feminist legal scholars have begun.

Feminist legal thought contains explicit criticism as well as implicit disagreements about the wisdom of pragmatic uses of law, the effectiveness of law as an instrument of social change and, most broadly, the importance of law as a focus for feminist study. Some feminist scholarship reveals antagonistic, even violent, disagreement with other feminist works.[13] Disagreements aside, however, feminist legal theory has lessons for all of society, not just for women or

10 *See* Robin West, *Jurisprudence and Gender*, 55 U. CHI. L. REV. 1, 72 (1988) (discussing the construction of present goals in light of a feminist utopian vision).

11 *See, e.g.*, AT THE BOUNDARIES OF LAW: FEMINISM AND LEGAL THEORY (M. A. Fineman & N. S. Thomadsen eds.,1990).

12 In the context of family law, for example, many scholars refuse to accept the dictates of formal rule-equality. *See* Martha Fineman, THE ILLUSION OF EQUALITY: THE RHETORIC AND REALITY OF DIVORCE REFORM (1991).

13 *See, e.g.*, Wendy Williams, *The Equality Crisis: Some Reflections on Culture, Courts, and Feminism*, 7 WOMEN'S RTS. L. REP. 175 (1982).

legal scholars. Ultimately, the members of our audience will judge the effectiveness and genuineness of our individual and collective voices.

Our scholarship is critical, political, and controversial; it is concerned with the processes that comprise law. The best feminist legal scholarship is about law in its broadest form, as a manifestation of power in society, and recognizes no division between law and power. Law is not found only in courts and cases, and legislatures and statutes, but in implementing institutions, such as social work and law enforcement, as well. Law is found in the discourse used in everyday life. Law is evident in the beliefs and assumptions we hold about the world in which we live and in the norms and values we cherish.

Feminist Methodology and Issues of Differences

Not surprisingly, much of feminist legal methodology considers the issue of "differences."[14] This examination is not an easy task. In fact, much of the rather antagonistic interaction among legal feminists has arisen from disagreement about the fundamental question of whether or not there are cognizable differences between men and women.[15] The early, "founding mother" members of a broadly defined legal feminist community would disagree with the exploration of such differences and would deny their existence or significance.[16] More recently, some feminist scholarship has emphasized that there are differences *among* women, and the question arises whether these differences should be considered legally, as well as theoretically, significant.

Focusing on differences is particularly difficult for women trained in the law because any recognition of differences challenges dominant legal equality theory and its accompanying paradigms, such as sameness of treatment. The initial approach of early contemporary legal feminists trying to break the barriers of the profession, therefore, was to develop the existing rhetoric of equality and to seek laws that were gender neutral. Equality in the market and in the home were their articulated goals, and, as a strategy, early feminist theoreticians and lawyers minimized or denied the existence of significant differences between men and women.[17]

Recently, the representation of equality embodied in the "gender neutrality" paradigm has undergone sustained attacks. Gender neutrality as a universal concept has been recognized as an objective that accepts the terms and structures of

14 For a collection of essays organized around the differences theme, *see* 3 WIS. WOMEN'S L.J. (1987), a compilation of papers presented at the 1986 Feminism and Legal Theory Conference held in Madison, Wisconsin.

15 *See* Wendy Williams, *The Equality Crisis: Some Reflections on Culture, Courts, and Feminism,* 7 WOMEN'S RTS. L. REP. 175 (1982).

16 *See* Wendy McElroy, *The Roots of Individualist Feminism in 19th-Century America, in* FREEDOM, FEMINISM, AND THE STATE 3–26 (W. McElroy ed., 1982).

17 Wendy Williams, *The Equality Crisis: Some Reflections on Culture, Courts, and Feminism,* 7 WOMEN'S RTS. L. REP. 175 (1982).

the status quo, the dominant culture. To argue that gender neutrality is or should be the goal of feminist reformist law is to further legitimate the underlying institutions constructed and maintained in the context of patriarchy and dominance as neutral, objective, and value-free.

Strong voices within the feminist legal community are joining in a chorus to celebrate the liberating realization that anything we legitimately can call *"feminist"* legal theory must begin with a conceptual statement about differences because, by its very definition, *feminist* theory must be a gendered theory. Feminist theory is woman centered and is, therefore, gendered by its very nature. It takes as its raw building materials women's experiences. Because women live gendered lives in our culture, any analysis that begins with their experiences necessarily must be a gendered analysis. It cannot be a gender-neutral theory, nor can it have as its goal equality in the traditional, formal legal sense of the word.

Because the differences between men and women have been the source of women's past oppression, to recognize these differences as the basis of feminist theory is to risk being dismissed as naive or being accused of advocating a position that will harm women. Furthermore, advocates of difference recently have faced the possibility of being labeled "essentialists" – those who advocate a belief in an "essential womanhood" that exists outside of language and society, and who are insensitive to race, class, and other differences among women. The "essentialist" label is more significant and, therefore, more difficult to address. I recognize that there are some differences among women that may, in some instances, be more significant than are the gendered life differences between men and women. However, in the aggregate, I believe women's shared or collective gendered experiences, both actual *and* potential, differ significantly from men's experiences in our society. These gendered experiences require adequate reflection and consideration in our legal system. These gendered experiences may be cultural and linguistic constructions, but they define the parameters of women's lives – even if only as constraints to resist. Incorporation of women's gendered life experiences is not accomplished by rules conceived in and constrained by a system that refuses to recognize gender as a relevant perspective, imposing "neutral" conclusions on women's circumstances. Furthermore, the recognition that there are differences among women should not defeat the attempt to "gender" law.

The possibility that women's perspectives differ from men's is relevant because, given their perspective and positions, women often may make different observations, ask different questions, and consider different issues from similarly situated men. A difference in *perspective* often is reflected as a difference in *perception.* Women from different cultures, classes, races, and economic circumstances might argue about conclusions, tactics, and values, but they also understand a common gendered-life reference point that unites them in interest and urgency around certain shared cultural and social experiences. Therefore, legal theory that is uninformed or uninfluenced by these different perspectives and perceptions is incomplete, inequitable, and indefensible.

Differences Between Women and Men

The assertion of a gendered existence is contested in our legal culture.[18] Even when accepted, the premise generates issues concerning how much significance should be attached to such a realization.[19] My exploration of these issues has led me to reach some tentative (and perhaps totally idiosyncratic) conclusions about the types of gender differences that might be significant in legal theory.

I believe that many women experience society in ways significantly different from the ways that men experience society. I believe certain real *or* potential experiences can be described as constituting the basis for a feminist development of the concept of "gendered life." These experiences lead many women to develop a perspective qualitatively different from what is reflected in dominant legal ideology. This is *not* to assert that all women think alike or have identical experiences. My position is based on experiential, not essential differences.

Women's gendered existence is comprised of a variety of experiences – material, psychological, physical, social, and cultural. Some of these experiences may be described as biologically based, while others seem more rooted in culture and custom. The actual or potential experiences of rape, sexual harassment, pornography, and other sexual violence that women may suffer in our culture shape individual experiences. So, too, the potential for reproductive events such as pregnancy, breast feeding, and abortion has an impact on women's constructions of their gendered lives. Further, some gendered experiences, such as aging, are events shared by men. But women often live or experience such events in unique ways. Thus, while both men and women age, the implications of aging from both a social and economic perspective are different for the genders in our culture.[20]

Human beings are the product of their experiences. As organisms, they have little or no independent "essence" distinct from their experiences. Of course, certain physical and chemical components or characteristics of human beings both provoke experiences and act as filters through which such experiences are processed. A person, therefore, is the sum of these physical attributes as acted upon, by, and through his or her social and cultural experiences. What we call knowledge, what we label virtuous, grows out of these experiences. The very questions we ask, along with the answers we fashion, express these experiences. Therefore, if women collectively have different actual and potential experiences from men, they are likely to have different perspectives - different sets of values, beliefs, and concerns as a group.

I am not arguing that *all* women react the same way to or reach identical conclusions about issues in our society, nor do I believe that all women experience any one or more of the gendered experiences. Uniformity in

18 *See* Wendy Williams, *The Equality Crisis: Some Reflections on Culture, Courts, and Feminism,* 7 WOMEN'S RTS. L. REP. 175 (1982).

19 *See* Herma Hill Kay, *Models of Equality,* 1985 U. ILL. L. REV. 39 (1985).

20 *See* PAUL E. ZOPF, AMERICAN WOMEN IN POVERTY 109–11 (1989).

interpretation and experiences is not necessary to the concept of gendered life. Individual experiences may differ from the socially constructed and culturally defined nexus, but they are still affected by them. Unadorned, uninterpreted events are not in and of themselves what one "experiences." Interpretation of events is an extremely significant aspect of this process of individual experiencing. Experiences do not take place in an interpretive vacuum, however, but are part of a social, interactive process. Culture and society provide the media through which experiences are understood. Our twentieth century society has universal, totalizing cultural representations of women and women's experiences. Even those critical of such cultural constructions of essentialist images of women must recognize the force these images hold. None of us completely escapes the dominant images of the society within which we operate. Interpretation of events, the process whereby events are given meaning, is not an autonomistic, individualistic procedure. Social action and interaction, as well as dominant cultural images, significantly contribute to individual interpretations of and reactions to events.

Further, I recognize that individual responses to similar experiences may differ as individual options (economic and otherwise) vary due to external circumstances such as race, sexuality, and social class. Additionally, previous experiences may filter new ones, having in some instances much more significance than gender. To recognize that there may be differences *among* women does not, however, refute the observation that women's actual *and* potential shared experiences are female experiences, inescapably gendered within the larger culture and society.

Differences Among Women

A tendency to question the ability of any group of women to speak for others has begun to emerge in feminist legal theory. Initially, this perspective developed in response to minority women's criticisms that feminism was a "white, middle-class, heterosexual movement."[21] Such criticism has made many feminist theorists reluctant to speak unless they have first disclaimed the notion that they are representing anything other than their individual (and, perhaps, their own class, race, and sexual preference) perspective. Many feel they must rattle off a litany of differences among women at the beginning of any discussion about feminism, society, and law – a distance placed between groups of women filled with assumptions about the nature of "representation" and about the essential and determinative character of race, class, and sexuality in defining an individual or group.

21 For recent critiques of mainstream feminist legal theory for its white, middle-class, heterosexual bias, see ELIZABETH V. SPELMAN, IN ESSENTIAL WOMAN: PROBLEMS OF EXCLUSION IN FEMINIST THOUGHT (1988); *Race and Essentialism in Feminist Legal Theory*, 42 STAN. L. REV. 581 (1990); Marlee Kline, *Race, Racism, and Feminist Legal Theory*, 12 HARV. WOMEN'S L.J. 115 (1989).

While few would dispute that characteristics such as race, class, and sexuality may be significant to one's experiences, it is a mistake to regard these markers of difference as the only relevant ones. Women may have other characteristics that give them a basis for cooperation and empathy. For example, in addition to race, class, and sexual preference, factors such as age, physical characteristics (including "handicaps" *and* "beauty" or lack thereof), religion, marital status, the level of male identification (which is independent of both marital status and sexual preference – what Gerda Lerner has referred to as "the man in our head"[22]), birth order, motherhood, grandmotherhood, intelligence, rural or urban existence, responsiveness to change or ability to accept ambivalence in one's personal life or in society, sources of income (self, spouse, or state), degree of poverty or wealth, and substance dependency, among others, shape how individual women experience the world.

Separating out a few differences as conclusively and exclusively determinative results in analyses that are impoverished reflections of the very complexity of women's gendered lives, which feminists should seek to understand and address. Such separation also results in a privileging that fosters the creation of hierarchies of oppression and claims of exclusive or genuine oppression. These, in turn, lead to a competition among oppressions that serves only the interests of the dominant social group. It is members of this group who are benefited when dominated groups fight among themselves at the margins of powerful institutions, which condescendingly have made room for only a few outsiders.

Privileging any one or two characteristics when so many have the potential to inform and create women's gendered lives is simplistic and will impede an articulation of the problems women share in society. Hierarchies limit participation and exclude voices necessary for the creation of solutions relevant to a broad spectrum of women. It would be interesting to consider how some characteristics or clusters of characteristics may cancel out, compensate for, or compete with others. For example, how do we place people with multiple sources of oppression in relation to others? If a white woman also is a welfare mother, can we consider her legitimately placed with the dominant group in society merely because she shares their skin color? I would argue clearly not, but where, then, does she fit among the oppressed? Can she really be considered *always* more privileged simply because of her race in a ranking of oppressions? A hierarchy of oppression that always places race at the top would consider her so. I believe oppression to be much more complex. Exclusion leads to conflict and competition. This disunity impedes the aggregation of power necessary for women of all groups to push back the barriers excluding most of us and our experiences.

22 From conversations between Gerda Lerner and the author. For a general discussion of male hegemony over that which is defined socially as "universal truth," see GERDA LERNER, THE CREATION OF PATRIARCHY 217–29 (1986).

The competition should not be with each other in the margins of society but with the powerful, dominant main structures whose visions and versions of reality are reflected in society's institutions. The task, then, for feminists of all races, classes, characteristics, and orientations, as well as for men who seek significant change in our social and cultural institutions, is to find common ground and work together. We must learn about and be sensitive to the many differences among us. Those differences, however, must not divide us to the point where we fight only among ourselves, each internal group urging its unifying source or sources of oppression as the only "true" oppression and seeking to silence others. The task should be to bring the many manifestations of women's gendered lives into consideration, not to argue that only one version of gendered existence is entitled to be heard or addressed.

Conclusion

Feminist concerns are, and must continue to be, the subject of discourses located outside of law. Law as a dominant rhetorical system has established concepts that limit and contain feminist criticisms. Feminist theory must develop free of the restraints imposed by legal concepts of equality and neutrality, or it will be defined by them. Law is too crude an instrument to be employed for the development of a theory anchored in an appreciation of differences. Law can and should be the *object* of feminist inquiry, but to position law and law reform as the *objective* of such theorizing is to risk having incompletely developed feminist innovations distorted and appropriated by the institutionalized and intractable dictates of law.

In developing feminist legal theory outside of the constraints of law, we will be free to confront the inevitable tensions that occur in undertaking any theoretical exploration, such as those that arise in any consideration of differences. Both politically and theoretically, feminists should explore the differences between women and men to expose the exclusion of women's experience in law and to reveal the underlying power imbalance this exclusion represents. At the same time, focusing on the differences among women, while of theoretical significance, can and will be used politically to continue and justify exclusion. Feminism as a political, pragmatic methodology must be able to live with this type of tension which, given the current political arena, cannot be avoided. There are different urgencies in considering differences that are dependent upon the contexts in which feminists must operate. Theory that arises from the circumstances in which women find themselves is destined to contain paradoxes.

Chapter 3

Equality Discourse and Economic Decisions Made at Divorce (1991)

Fineman[1] provides a detailed criticism of the formal equality approach to property distribution rules at divorce. She advocates centering reform on need rather than contribution, an early glimpse into her later focus on the family as the site of dependency management. In criticizing the adoption of a "symbolic" approach to reform rather than an "instrumental" approach, she documents the material harms perpetuated by the ideal of formal equality.

This essay assesses reform legislation dealing with the economic aspects of divorce. Reform was largely the product of feminists' efforts to impose a rule-equality or same-treatment model on property distribution decisions in order to rectify perceived inequities perpetuated against women under prior law. While the economic position of women in our society provides the basis for persuasive arguments that, in general, "unequal" treatment in fashioning rules to govern the economic aspects of divorce is essential in assuring equitable results for most women, liberal legal feminists rejected this model in favor of sameness of treatment.[2] To understand why a rule-equality approach is inappropriate, we must consider three related factors: women's unequal social and economic position in society, the ways in which marriage and family decisions are affected by these and other economic and social circumstances, and the impact of divorce on women with dependent children.

1 This essay is used with permission of The University of Chicago Press, from The Illusion of Equality: The Rhetoric and Reality of Divorce Reform, Martha Fineman, 2nd Edition, 1994; permission conveyed through Copyright Clearance Center, Inc.

2 *See, e.g.,* Kathy Ferguson, Self, Society and Womankind: The dialectic of Liberation 4–5 (1980); Alison Jaggar, *Political Philosophies of Women's Liberation, in* feminism and philosophy 6–9 (Mary Vetterling-Braggin, Frederick Elliston & Jane English, eds., 1977). According to Ferguson, the moderate (liberal) feminists are "[b] est represented by National Organization for Women (N.O.W.) and Women's Equal Action League (W.E.A.L.), and various professional women's groups." The moderates have been defined as "women's rights" advocates who are primarily concerned with bringing women into the mainstream of American life "through reform" in contrast to the more radical "liberationists," whose efforts are directed toward revolutionary social change.

DOI: 10.4324/9781003405627-5

Economic inequalities persist in our society in spite of decades of attempted reforms.[3] The rules governing economics at divorce perpetuate and contribute to this persistence of inequality. In the first instance, women are disadvantaged in the market. They earn less than their male counterparts and, even if freed from the pink-collar ghetto, do not advance as quickly and as far as men. In addition, cultural images and socially constructed expectations compel women to assume unequal responsibilities within the family.[4] Choices during marriage as to who assumes primary care of children, for example, often result in wives shouldering disproportionate burdens.[5] Furthermore, at divorce women

3 "Between 1890 and 1930 the female/male wage ratio in the United States jumped from about .45 to .60 and then remained at about that level for half a century. After 1979 women's wages began to rise relative to men's, but even in the mid-1980s the average American woman earned only two-thirds as much as the average man for each hour of work. This wage gap is the most obvious; and the most important evidence of economic inequality...." VICTOR FUCHS, WOMEN'S QUEST FOR ECONOMIC EQUALITY 49 (1988).

4 "Women are much more likely to work at a paid job now than they were a generation ago, but the proportion of employed women who work part time has shown no tendency to decline... Which women work part time? Not surprisingly, it is those who are married and those who have a small child at home.... The presence of a young child substantially increases the demand for work in the home, making it more difficult to pursue full time employment ... . Part time work often provides a compromise solution. Statistical analysis of working women shows that even after controlling for age, education, and similar factors, the presence of a young child in creases a woman's probability of working part time by about ten percentage points." VICTOR FUCHS, WOMEN'S QUEST FOR ECONOMIC EQUALITY 44–45 (1988).

5 In his analysis of women's economic position in society, economist Victor Fuchs describes the "costs" associated with children as follows: "Having children entails numerous costs-expenditures for goods and services, time lost from paid work, and so on. In addition to these well-known, obvious costs, there is another that falls particularly on women in the form of *lower wages*. This happens for several reasons. First, many women leave the labor market during pregnancy, at childbirth, or when their children are young. These child-related interruptions are damaging to subsequent earnings because three out of four births occur to women before the age of 30 – the same time that men are gaining the training and experience that lead to higher earnings later in life. Second, even when mothers stay in the labor force, responsibility for children frequently constrains their choice of job: they accept lower wages in exchange for shorter or more flexible hours, location near home, limited out-of-town travel, and the like. Third, women who devote a great deal of time and energy to child care and associated housework are often less able to devote maximum effort to market work. For instance, when a young child is present, women are more likely than men to be absent from work, even at equal levels of education and wages. According to Reskin and Hartmann, 'The care of children ... still appears to be largely women's responsibility, and this responsibility undoubtedly conflicts with their entrance into and advancement in a number of occupations that routinely require overtime, job-related travel, or inflexible or irregular hours.' "Perhaps most important of all, because most young women expect to be mothers, they (and their parents) are less likely than men to invest in wage-enhancing human capital while in school and in their first job or two after leaving school. In the past

typically assume an unequal, more burdensome share of the post-divorce responsibilities for nurture and care of children.[6] This is true even in cases of "joint custody," where mothers typically do the bulk of the day-to-day care.[7] The fables we have created around "modern" fatherhood and our newly coined and much-applied legal label, joint custody, obscure the fact that unequal maternal sacrifices are assumed, even mandated, by social and cultural factors in addition to the history of a particular family.[8]

this has been reflected in choice of major, in uncertainty about pursuing graduate school training, and in a reluctance to experience the long hours and other rigors characteristic of apprenticeships in medicine, law, business, and other financially rewarding occupations. The difference between women and men in this respect is narrowing, partly because the barriers of prejudice are weakening, but also because more women are planning to remain childless and those who do want to become mothers expect to have fewer children and to spend less time with them. VICTOR FUCHS, *Id.* at 60–61 (emphasis in original; citations omitted).

6 In this regard, Fuchs comments as follows: "Under correct conditions in the United States, socialization for the roles of wife and mother can frustrate women's quest for economic equality in at least two ways. First, it affects the choices women make in school and in the labor market, choices that limit their lifetime earning power. Not infrequently, women who have sacrificed market skills and ambitions in favor of home responsibilities find themselves at a severe economic disadvantage later in life as a result of divorce. Second, even when individual women resist socialization, they are likely to encounter difficulties in the labor market simply because they are women and are often evaluated and treated according to gender norms." VICTOR FUCHS, *Id*, at 43.

7 As Fuchs observes: "Residential custody patterns for children of divorced parents are also an indication of women's demand for children. A study of divorces in two California counties between September 1984 and March 1985 revealed that in three-quarters of the families there was joint *legal* custody, but in only 20 percent of the cases was *residential* custody joint between mother and father. In the other 80 percent of cases, the mother was fourteen times as likely as the father to have custody. The authors write, 'To our surprise we are *not* seeing an increase in father custody. What about men? Don't they also desire children and care about their welfare? Of course many do, some more so than the average woman. Each sex has its own distribution of preferences, and these distributions overlap. Although many men care a great deal, *on average* their desire and their caring do not seem to be as strong as women's. Hundreds of thousands of children born to unwed mothers never see their fathers or even know who they are. Many divorced fathers see their children rarely and contribute little or nothing to their support. Maternal abandonment of children is a relatively rare phenomenon, but paternal abandonment is not. When parents divorce and remarry, continuing contact between children and their mothers seems to be more important than contact with their biological fathers. In their study of custodial arrangements following divorce, Maccoby and Mnookin find that the noncustodial mothers tend to maintain closer contact with their children than do noncustodial fathers." VICTOR FUCHS, *Id.*, at 69–70 (emphasis in original; citations omitted).

8 Consider the following: "Discrimination against women undoubtedly persists, not only in the labor market but in most economic and social institutions. But the biggest source of women's economic disadvantage – namely, their greater desire for and concern about children – is more fundamental, though it is impossible to say how much results from 'nature' and how much result from 'nurture.' Women's stronger commitment to parenting can be inferred not only from statistical studies but also from a wide variety of other sources, ranging from literary works to the clinical

Societal Factors Affecting Our Perceptions of Marriage and Divorce

Attacks during this century on the legitimacy of the patriarchal family have gradually eroded the historic notion that the husband is responsible for the financial well-being of his family. The decline of this perception of patriarchal obligation has been accompanied by the transformation of the rules governing the economic aspects of divorce.[9] An earlier, status based model of marriage, under which a husband's obligations to support his wife and children at least theoretically survived divorce and could be discharged through alimony or property division, has been replaced by an egalitarian or equality model.[10] We

experience of psychotherapists. Motherhood and fatherhood are not symmetrical, are not simply opposite sides of the same coin. Both are strongly influenced by socialization – but in the case of fathers, socialization is practically the whole story. Motherhood is different. Women make a huge investment in pregnancy, child-bearing, and nursing – an investment that is crucial to the perpetuation of the species. The father's investment, in terms of time and energy, is usually much smaller ...." VICTOR FUCHS, *Id.*, at 140–41.

9 *See* L. WEITZMAN, THE DIVORCE REVOLUTION: THE UNINTENDED SOCIAL AND ECONOMIC CONSEQUENCES FOR WOMEN AND CHILDREN IN AMERICA (1985).

10 *See* Judith Younger, *Marital Regimes: A Story of Compromise and Demoralization, Together with Criticism and Suggestions for Reform,* 67 CORNELL. REV. 45, 89, n. 328 (1981). Doris Freed & Henry Foster, *Marital Property Reform in New York: Partnership of Co-Equals?,* 8 FAM. L.Q. 176 (1974), supported the notion of marriage as a "partnership of co-equals with division of labor that entitles each to a one-half interest in the family assets ... such a system reflects the contemporary understanding of marriage, and the reasonable expectations of the parties" *See* SEX DISCRIMINATION AND THE LAW: CAUSES AND REMEDIES (Barbara Allen Babcock, et al. eds., 1975) for a distinction between commercial and marital partnership. Walter Weyrauch, *Metamorphoses of Marriage,* 13 FAM. L.Q. 415, 418–24, 435 (1980) asserted that the incidents of marriage are governed increasingly by notions of equality of spouses, with spouses viewed as persons entering a voluntary association with equal rights, duties, and contributions. He noted that small-business case law aided the evolution of the partnership concept of marriage. Underlying this conception, however, is a fundamental assumption of freedom of will that is not always born out in reality, as noted by Weyrauch. There are problems, also, with how one views children if marriage is a contract. There seem to be conflicting views: they are seen as chattels, assets, or products of the marriage, or as persons who are consumers of marriage and entitled to protection. An additional problem, not mentioned by those advocating the partnership concept, is that expectations which may be reasonable at the time of marriage or during a functioning marriage may appear substantially unreasonable at the time of divorce, when ongoing benefits of support and mutual cooperation are terminated. The partnership model has long been urged as a way of limiting judicial discretion. In criticizing judicial discretion, one author commented that the "greatest evil is not so bad when certain." Harriet Spiller Daggett, *Divisions of Property Upon Dissolution of Marriage,* 6 LAW AND CONTEMP. PROBS. 225, 229 (1939). Daggett recommended the concept of partnership based on community-property principles and mandatory equal division. She also believed that community-property states were far ahead of common-law property states. With an economic partnership it would make "no difference whether one

now view the economic obligations associated with marriage and divorce as shared responsibilities.

The way that we as a society perceive marriage and the relationship between husband and wife profoundly affects the way that we select, develop, and apply rules governing property distribution at divorce. I assert that this societal perception is most significant and shapes the way that all actors involved in actual divorce proceedings – judges, lawyers, the spouses, as well as legislators – consider the fairness and advisability of various distribution factors. The general social consensus about the nature of marriage and what it entails is the background which frames arguments over the appropriateness of specific rules regulating dissolution.

In this area, controversy has spurred many changes. One source of the controversy about property distribution rules is, I believe, the existence of two competing and, perhaps incompatible and unrealistic, political visions of contemporary marriage. The first is the more modern view that marriage as an institution has been transformed so as to be consistent with formalistic notions of equality between the sexes.[11] The second is the more traditional policy stance that the family is the appropriate, perhaps solitary, institution to resolve problems of dependency or need that inevitably arise in the context of families.[12]

contributes more energy to the task with better material results than the other; nor does it matter if one makes no contribution at all." *Id.* at 223.

11 *See* DOUGLAS RAE, EQUALITIES (1981). The notion of sexual equality is simplistic and formalistic insofar as it means that individuals paired as one man against one woman must be treated the same. *See also* Peter Westen, *The Empty Idea of Equality,* 95 HARV. L REV. 537 (1982).

12 Questions of dependency and need, and how to cope with them, have plagued American society since its inception. Definitions of dependency have changed as the institutions designated to deal with dependency have changed. Until the twentieth century, the problem of need and dependency was dealt with almost exclusively by the family, by private charity, and by state and local governments. W. ANDREW ACHENBAUM, OLD AGE IN THE NEW LAND: THE AMERICAN EXPERIENCE SINCE 1790, 131–41 (1979). The conflict between public and private solutions to perceived need surfaced in the Mother's Assistance movement in the early twentieth century. Illinois passed the Funds to Parents Act in 1911, which provided poor but competent parents with funds to support their children at home. Within two years, 20 states provided cash relief to widows with children. JUNE AXINN AND HERMAN LEVIN, SOCIAL WELFARE: A HISTORY OF THE AMERICAN RESPONSE TO NEED, 131–35, 144–60 (1975). When Aid to Dependent Children was made part of the Social Security Act in 1935, the primary goal was to support dependent children at home with their mothers. This policy was reversed in 1967 when Congress established the Work Incentive Program and increased appropriations for day-care centers. This new program required that the employability of mothers as well as fathers be assessed. At the same time, proposals were being made to pay wages to mothers who decided against entering the labor market in order to care for their children. *Id.* at 280–85. One difficulty with the concept of need is expressed in David J. Rothman, *The State as Parent: Social Policy in the Progressive Era, in* DOING GOOD: THE LIMITS OF BENEVOLENCE 69, 83 (1978): "Progressives were far more attentive to the 'needs' of disadvantaged groups than to their

The choice and application of various distribution rules by legislators, attorneys, and judges, whether in the context of the legislative process, in formal adjudication, or in negotiation, are influenced by these societal factors. These legal actors must develop and apply rules in a legal system in which the longstanding recognition of dependency and need on the part of mothers and children within families is increasingly offset by the desire for symbolically compelling presentations of gender equality and independence.[13]

Marriage is no longer realistically presented as a lifelong commitment with well-defined gender-based roles establishing an interdependency that is easily

'rights.' Needs were real and obvious – the poor were overworked and underpaid, living in unhealthy tenements and working in miserable sweat shops. Rights, on the other hand, were 'so-called' the right of the poor to sleep under the bridge or the laborer to fix his own contract with an all powerful corporation .... This [post-progressive] suspicion of benevolence and anti-institutionalism has encouraged and is reinforced by an acute distrust of discretionary authority." A focus on rights (such as equality) is not, however, an ideal solution: "[T]he expansion of rights solves only part of the problem, for there do remain, like it or not, needs as well, imbalances in economic and social power, in inherited physical constitutions, that demand redress."' *Id.* at 92. Rights discourse has also been criticized as unstable, indeterminate, reified, and politically disutile. Mark Tushnet, *An Essay on Rights,* 62 TUX. L. REV. 1363 (1984). This critique has been contextualized and criticized by Professor Patricia Williams in *Alchemical Notes: Reconstructing Ideals from Deconstructed Rights,* 22 HARV. C.R.-C.L. L. REV. 401 (1987). For a discussion of the changing conception of marriage from status to contract, *see The Course of Change in Family Law,* 5 FAM. L. REP. 4013, 4015 (1979). *See also* M. GLENDON, THE NEW FAMILY AND THE NEW PROPERTY, 101–18 (1981); W. P. Cantwell, *Man + Woman + Property = ?,* PROB. LAW. 9–10 (1980); MARY ANN GLENDON, THE TRANSFORMATION OF FAMILY LAW (1989). *But cf.* Manfred Rehbinder, *Status, Contract and the Welfare State,* 23 STAN. L. REV. 941 (1971). In the common law, *status* came to mean a deviation from full legal capacity. *Id.* at 943. Rehbinder asserted that the importance of contract has now vanished from family law, and the movement in that area is more appropriately described as that from contract to status. The state has reduced the political autonomy of classes to formal legal equality through bureaucratization and monopoly. *Id.* at 945–46.

13 There are objections to language that characterizes women as being in need in many areas other than divorce. There are also objections raised that disguising need in an attempt to give status to nonworking women may hurt some other groups of women. For example, one author objected to the present label for spouse benefits under social security *–dependent benefits* – as "degrading." Robert J. Myers, *Incremental Change in Social Security Needed to Result in Equal and Fair Treatment of Men and* WOMEN, IN A CHALLENGE TO SOCIAL SECURITY: THE CHANGING ROLES OF WOMEN AND MEN IN AMERICAN SOCIETY (Richard V. Burkhauser &Karen C. Holden, eds., 1982) [hereinafter cited as CHALLENGE TO SOCIAL SECURITY]. Compare Edith Fierst's objections in an article in the same volume: "[I am] offended philosophically by [proposals for] homemaker credits and increased child care drop-out years because they increase the rewards of not being employed. Fair play requires that the woman who works and pays taxes should get more for her efforts than the one who does not. Much as I want the homemaker to be secure in old age, I do not want to give her preference over the working woman." Edith U. Fierst. *Discussion, in* Challenge to Social Security, *supra* at 66, 71.

comprehended and reflected in supportive legal rules. Things are more complex today – roles are less defined, and marriage as an institution is in a state of flux. Unfortunately, the laws governing property distribution and other economic aspects of divorce have often become the crude instruments by which we attempt both to implement equality and to address dependency and need. When the law is expected to do incompatible or contradictory things simultaneously, it is no wonder that confusion results.

The Distribution Process

Although the distribution of property is only one of the economic decisions made at divorce, it has a unique procedural posture. It is a final decision, not subject to future modification should circumstances change. This means there are no potential future opportunities to correct errors. Because it is final, it appears more significant. A distribution decision may present an emotional experience for spouses different from decisions about other economic aspects of divorce. Families are more than legalized sexual relations or the repositories for products of those relations. They represent the convergence of a complex set of emotional and material needs which are inevitably frustrated in the divorce process. The distribution decision may psychologically represent to the spouses the final accounting of their contributions to the marriage – a concrete measure of their relative worth. With child support, by contrast, the emotional as well as legal justification is based on the appropriateness of continued obligations of support in the context of an ongoing, even if altered, post-divorce relationship. With children, future support obligations are based on need and premised on the assertion that divorce does not sever the responsibilities or the rights associated with parenthood.

Regarding maintenance (née, alimony), in recent years the existence of a prior marital relationship has come to be considered insufficient justification for a continuing obligation. New theories or premises have been offered to justify the award of something labeled *maintenance* in some cases, but these new rationales suggest a different type of maintenance from the common-law expectation that a husband was obligated to support his wife even after termination of their marriage. Maintenance today is designed as a gender-neutral, temporary, and remedial measure that further blurs the line between property distribution and support. Maintenance has started to look more and more like property distribution in that, if awarded, it is likely to be limited and based on modern perspectives of contribution to either the marriage or the career of the other spouse, or awarded in lieu of property.

Property Distribution Rules

While property distribution may in fact reflect concern about a spouse's future needs, such concern is increasingly considered inappropriate as the image of marriage becomes more that of partnership than of dependency. Need may be implicit in some of the factors utilized for division, but typically the stated rules explicitly reflect notions of *entitlement* based on earnings or, more recently, on marital contributions whether economic or homemaking.[14]

Maintenance and property division are explicitly linked together in the Act. Section 307(a) Alternative A requires a court to consider "whether apportionment is in lieu of or in addition to maintenance." Maintenance awards are limited to a narrow category of circumstances. The court may grant such awards only if it finds that the spouse seeking maintenance (1) lacks sufficient property to provide for her needs, and (2) is unable to support herself through appropriate employment or is the custodian of a child whose circumstances make it appropriate that the custodian not be required to seek employment outside the home. Id. at Sec. 308(a), 9A U.L.A. 347. The commissioner's comments on the section of the Act governing maintenance explicitly state that the provisions of that section and of the section governing disposition of property have the "dual intention" of "encourag[ing] the court to provide for the financial needs of the spouses by property disposition rather than by an award of maintenance." The comment continues: "only if the available property is insufficient for the purpose and if the spouse who seeks maintenance is unable to secure employment appropriate to his [sic] skills and interests or is occupied with child care may an award of maintenance be ordered." Id. at § 308, Commissioners' Comment, 9A U.L.A. 161.

Factors Relevant to Property Distribution at Divorce

Currently, a variety of specific distribution factors are typically noted in common law, state statutes, or court opinions in states with general statutory directives. These factors include:

1 The length of the marriage;
2 The property brought to the marriage by each party;
3 The "contribution" of each party to the marriage, often with the explicit admonition that appropriate economic value is to be given to contributions of homemaking and child-care services;
4 The contribution by one party to the education, training, or increased earning power of the other;
5 Whether one of the parties has substantial assets not subject to division by the court;
6 The age and physical and emotional health of the parties;
7 The earning capacity of each party, including educational background, training, employment skills, work experience, and length of absence from the job market;
8 Custodial responsibilities for children;

14 UNIF. MARRIAGE AND DIVORCE Act § 307, Alternative A. 9A U.L.S. 238 (1977).

9 The time and expense necessary to acquire sufficient education or training to enable a party to become self-supporting at a standard of living reasonably comparable to that enjoyed during the marriage.

Increasingly, some consideration is given to the desirability of awarding the family home, or the right to live there for a reasonable period, to the party having custody of any children. In addition, other economic circumstances may be considered. These include vested or unvested pension benefits, future interests, the tax consequences to each party, and the amount and duration of an order granting maintenance payments.

If a written agreement was made by the parties before or during the marriage concerning any arrangement for property distribution, such agreements are often presumed binding upon the court unless inequitable. Some statutory systems that enumerate various factors explicitly end with a general catch-all for judicial discretion that allows consideration of such other factors as the court may in each individual case determine to be relevant.

Classification of Distribution Factors

There are at least four potential conceptual categories into which one could place the various factors considered in property distributions: title, fault, need, and contribution. These conceptual categories represent rationales or justifications for allocation decisions and may be ordered according to when they first were utilized. This sequencing has been used to suggest that there has been a progression from the simple, common-law emphasis on title to the more complex understanding of the function and purpose of the distribution system as reflecting the valuing of both monetary and nonmonetary contributions to the marriage.

While there has been a movement away from the strict common-law system based on title to the modern notion of a partnership based on equally valued though different-in-kind contributions to the marriage, I believe there is a serious problem with characterizing the movement from title to partnership and contribution as "progress." Progress implies that we have either outgrown the basis for the old concepts or that our initial perceptions were in error and now must be revised. A progression thesis might, therefore, characterize fault and need as "transitional" concepts – inelegant patches that allowed judges to do justice under a strict title system prior to the enlightened presentation of marriage as partnership.[15]

15 Title is a fairly easy category for people to understand. If the property belongs to one spouse or the other as evidenced in a formal legal document such as a deed, the distribution follows. An extended version of title considers ownership not only as evidenced in legal title but also as a result of the provision of economic assets to secure the property. This system has increasingly been understood to be unfair as clearly favoring the market actor who has economic assets with which to accumulate property and devaluing the non economic activities of homemakers. As a result, most common-law states have moved away from a strict title system, and the

I am not convinced, however, that the circumstances that generated arguments for a distribution system focused on needs that no longer exist. Further, I am concerned that the material circumstances of divorcing women and children are being detrimentally ignored by supplanting a focus on needs with a focus on contribution as the primary distributive concept. The ascendancy of contribution may present a nice, neat instance of conceptual progress to legal academics and law reformers, but for many divorcing spouses, as well as for the practicing professionals to whom they tum for advice, adverse material circumstances and the needs they generate have not been left behind.

While title considerations do not seem to be determinative in modern distribution schemes, need and, to a lesser extent, fault are still viable alternatives to contribution as conceptual frameworks for the creation and implementation of various specific distribution factors.[16] When fault and need were first introduced into consideration, they were welcomed as helping to ameliorate the hardships of the title system. But, in contemporary divorce practice, both have increasingly come under attack because they carry negative symbolic connotations. In the context of "no-fault" divorce reform, for example, continued reference to fault as an explicit allocation category would obviously be problematic.

contemporary way we talk about marriage reflects the societal presumption that homemakers should not be left out merely because they have not made monetary contributions to the accumulation of property.

16 Some sorts of extreme misconduct related to marital breakdown have been found relevant to the distribution issue, even in states which explicitly prohibit consideration of marital misconduct. *See Blickstein v. Blickstein*, 472 N.Y.S.2d 110 (N.Y. App. Div. 1984) (court found fault relevant to equitable distribution in "very rare" situations involving misconduct that "shocks the conscience"); *D'Arc v. D'Arc*, 395 A.2d 1270 (N.J. Super. Ct. Ch. Div. 1978), *aff'd*, 421 A.2d 602 (N.J. Super. Ct. App. Div. 1980) (court found misconduct relevant where the husband had attempted to arrange his wife's murder). *See also Stover v. Stover*, 696 S.W.2d 750 (Ark. 1985) (Arkansas Supreme Court held that the trial court could go beyond the statutory list of factors bearing on equitable distribution to consider fault where the wife had been convicted of conspiracy to murder her husband). The Texas Family Code, which doesn't explicitly address fault but directs the courts to distribute property in a manner that is "just and right, having due regard for the rights of each party;" has been interpreted by the Texas courts to permit consideration of fault. Tex. Fam. Code Ann. Sec. 3.63 (Vernon 1975 & Supp. 1985). The court has deemed evidence of adultery and physical violence by the husband relevant to equitable distribution. *Mogford v. Mogford*, 616 S.W.2d 936 (Tex. Cir. App. 1981). Additionally, a conception of "economic fault" – the deliberate dissipation of marital assets – is emerging as a relevant consideration in the distribution decision in many states where marital fault is explicitly deemed irrelevant. Arizona Law allows the court to consider "abnormal expenditures, destruction, concealment of fraudulent disposition" of marital property. Ariz. Rev. Stat. Ann. Sec 25.318(a) (Supp. 1984). California law includes an analogous provision. Cal. Civ. Code Sec. 4800 (West Supp. 1985). *See also* Blickstein, *supra,* and *Smith v. Smith*, 331 S.E.2d 682 (N.C. 1985) (court determined that only financial misconduct can be taken into account in the division of property).

Further, the concept of *need* presents even more complex conceptual difficulties. As a relevant consideration, however, need is not a consideration as easily moved beyond and left behind as fault. Historically, the courts could respond to the existence of dependency since marriage was viewed as a status relationship. The husband and father was obligated to provide support for the needs of his wife and children, and this obligation did not necessarily cease with divorce and could be extended beyond divorce through awards of alimony, through property division provisions, or through both. However, modern attacks on the legitimacy of the patriarchal family have had an unplanned legal impact: the erosion of the traditional notion that the husband is predominantly and perpetually responsible for the financial well-being of all members of the family. Attempts to cast family structure in more egalitarian terms have assisted in transforming our approach to the rules governing the economic aspects of divorce. The earlier status-based model of marriage has been replaced by an individualistic or equality model under which obligations to spouses ideally end with the marriage, and any ongoing economic obligation that is recognized as appropriate, such as child support or payment of existing marital debts, is considered a shared and equal responsibility.

Limitations on Distribution Discourse

Divorce is typically discussed in terms of the nuclear family. Outsiders to this unit, even though they may be family in a broader anthropological sense, are excluded. Moreover, it is significant that most legal writers discussing the economic allocation questions in divorce emphasize primarily the *adults* in the nuclear family. This tendency to limit the discussion of rights and objectives to those of the spouses reflects an important social dimension and is consistent with the contemporary partnership model of marriage. There are no "junior partners" (children) legally recognized with enforceable rights to share in partnership assets.

Except in extreme cases, the state will not be a significant source of support for the spouse who subsequently assumes responsibility for child-rearing. Unless the family is very poor, the resources for the care of children are extracted from the individual parent or parents. This individualistic approach, coupled with the undeniable fact that more resources are necessary when an adult has to care for children in addition to herself, means that the allocation of private resources at divorce has a profound economic and social impact because it affects the future ability of a custodial parent to care adequately for her children.

I assume that private decisions about child custody at divorce and actual assumed responsibility for children after divorce will typically be gender-related for generations to come. As a result, the wife, the parent statistically more likely to be at a disadvantage in the market, will more likely also be the parent who must adjust career activities to accommodate childrearing. This adjustment will result in potentially immeasurable costs to her career and personal development.

Finally, I assume that alimony awards will continue to be extremely rare and that child-support awards will continue to be systematically low and/or only sporadically enforced.[17] Thus, given the predominant view of the children's future economic well-being as a private or family function, and given that enforcement of support orders might be a problem, a custodial parent cannot comfortably rely on future contributions from her ex-spouse in providing for the children, nor can she rely on any other source of support outside her own efforts.

Dependency has not disappeared, however. I believe that marriage often conceals or masks the poverty of women in this country and that divorce removes this mask. The care of children produces dependency, not only for the children, but also for the primary caretaker. The needs that this dependency generates must be met either by society as a whole or by individuals with legally significant connections to children. Moreover, it must be recognized that this dependency does not end when the child reaches 18 or any other magic age. Children's needs may change with the passage of time, but the caretaker has assumed ongoing responsibilities with present as well as future economic consequences, such as a reduced amount of money in a social security or pension fund or an increased susceptibility to requests for loans once the children are fully grown and supposedly "independent."

The laws governing the economic aspects of divorce should be grounded in the realization that some family relationships tend to last. This is particularly true of the primary caretaking parent and her children. The obligations that such a parent may feel are not legal but moral or emotional ones. A parent who desires to assist a newly "adult" child may not be required to do so by law, but that does not mean that the law should be insensitive to (or unsupportive of) the parent's sensibilities when assessing the most socially useful allocation of property at divorce.[18]

17 In spite of a decade of enforcement reforms, collection of child support remains a problem.

18 Noncustodial fathers may not feel the same sort of connection to "adult" children and may not be as responsive to their needs. *See*, for example, Wallerstein's findings: "[A] father's attitudes and feelings about his children can become blunted by divorce – a finding that took me by surprise and one that is hard to understand. Psychologists, lawyers, and judges used to think that a father's relationship with his children during marriage would, within reasonable limits, predict his attitude toward them after divorce. If he was an attentive, loving, and sensitive father before divorce, those attributes of fathering would continue long after the breakup .... But we are finding otherwise .... [W]e have seen that a father's commitment to his children does not necessarily carry over into the postdivorce years .... [M]any fathers who pay all their child support over the years and maintain close contact with their children draw the line with college. While they can afford it, value education, and have cordial relations with their children, they do not offer even partial support through college The majority [of these men] have college educations. But when I ask about college for their children, they don't want to discuss it." J. WALLERSTEIN & S. BLAKESLEE, SECOND CHANCES: MEN, WOMEN, AND CHILDREN, A DECADE AFTER DIVORCE 158 (1989).

Distribution Discourse

Assessment of the various specific distribution factors listed above reveals that four may be categorized under the concept of *contribution* while the other five fit more neatly within the concept of *need*. The fact that within any system the factors are often combined and exist simultaneously reflects the tension between the two incompatible contemporary images of marriage: the modern egalitarian partnership and the older, status-based, dependency model. These represent polar ends on the spectrum of the way society views marriage and the position of women within it, as well as the major transformation that has occurred in this regard.

The partnership image gives rise to the idea of contribution – each person contributes a different but valuable set of benefits to the good of the whole, and the whole should be divided to reflect these contributions if it is dissolved. Under this view, need has no role to play in a true partnership of equals. In fact, contribution rhetoric is often placed in opposition to another vision of marriage – that of dependency. The dependency image, in contrast to contribution, anticipates that a woman has been "victimized" in marriage. She is viewed as having sacrificed career goals and ambitions for the marriage. At divorce she is dependent, and that dependency will continue. She therefore has economic needs that should be recognized and compensated. In this context need is cast as a negative, something demeaning and to be overcome. Dependency and need are dramatized as products of women's victimization by men and marriage and are not rhetorically associated with the dependency and needs of children.

In our contemporary society, the concept of need must necessarily create *some* ambivalence for those who accept equality as the social and legal ideal. The predominance of the equality model evident in much of the commentary and law reform efforts illustrates that there is a strong preference for the legal presentation of women as equal partners within marriage and as independent, equal economic actors outside of it.

Liberal feminist legal reformers, for example, have adhered for the most part to the ideal of egalitarian marriage in addressing the economic questions in divorce.[19] In some states, the equality norm is formally embodied in provisions which establish an initial presumption that all property of the spouses is to be equally divided upon divorce. This rule-equality presumption is consistent with the organizing concept of marriage as an equal partnership. While need is not forgotten, the partnership model is urged because of its symbolic significance in reflecting the preferred or correct vision of women and also, secondarily, because it addresses need. Through ideological fiat, the dependent woman is considered to be benefited in being brought "up" to partnership status and made an "equal."

19 *See* Martha Albertson Fineman, *Implementing Equality: Ideology, Contradiction and Social Change: A Study of Rhetoric and Results in the Regulation of the Consequences of Divorce,* 1983 WIS. L. REV. 789 (1983).

That factors based on both the dependency and partnership models of marriage exist simultaneously within any distribution system does not suggest that the application of these factors will necessarily reflect an explicit, principled balancing process. Rather, it seems that within the context of any distribution task, there may be unavoidable concessions to dependency within a preferred framework that focuses on contribution and equality.

If one rejects the comprehensiveness of either or both of the conflicting images of marriage that the stereotypes of woman as equal and woman as dependent represent, one must confront the reality that many women whose mixed circumstances may require remedial rules are neglected. The stereotypes of dependency and partnership are polar opposites. Thus no single, typical result can be fairly reconciled with the goal of doing justice to both. A woman who operates in both the marriage and the market as an "equal" might be better off under the old common-law system, where she keeps her separate property, and her ex husband is liable only for child support. The true dependent, by contrast, might by her very circumstances have been able to claim all of the property and still be found in need of continued support for herself. In either case, it would seem that what is desirable in the way of reform is the creation of a range of acceptable economic outcomes which could accommodate a variety of differences among women in various circumstances. The focus on the stereotypes of dependency and equality and the futile attempt to reconcile them tend to narrow rather than expand the definition of acceptable results.

Equality and the Contribution Concept

The ideal of equality between spouses is at the center of our current views of marriage and therefore exerts a powerful and symbolic influence on our process of fashioning rules to govern distribution of marital assets. Marriage is considered a union, a partnership of equals. This view mandates that, if the partnership ends, the accumulated assets should be divided in a manner consistent with the model under which they were acquired. The norm or standard against which rules that regulate the economic aspects of dissolution are measured will be that of equality.

This approach of using equality as the organizational concept in assessing appropriate rules for property division creates dilemmas. In its simplest form, equality demands sameness of treatment, and differentiation in any sphere may be considered a concession of inferiority or "unequalness."[20]

20 Westen, *supra* note 11, at 572–82. *See also* D. RAE, *supra* note 11. In 1979, Karen Seal argued that given inequality in the market, feminists in California could have predicted that equal division would have an adverse impact on women. She concluded that the "belief in equality is so fundamental, however, that arguing for more than equal division of assets or income for women could be interpreted as discrimination against men." K. Seal, *A Decade of No-Fault Divorce,* 1 FAM. ADVOC. 10, 14 (Spring 1979).

The ramifications of symbolic adherence to equality may be significant. Contribution is an equalizing concept, while need demands an acknowledgment and evaluation of differences. As such, a commitment to equality initially encourages its proponents to minimize or deny differences between the individuals for whose demands they have become proponents and the individuals they perceive to be in superior positions. Thus, the reformers could conclude that the rule-equality model satisfied their desire for fair treatment of women at divorce, but only by minimizing, rhetorically and conceptually, any differences between the needs of men and women after divorce occurs. Given the contrary statistical evidence on the issue of need, of which the reformers must have been aware, one must question how they could fail to make need the central theme of the reform.

Further, the idea that contribution in the form of household duties should be recognized did not resolve all the potential problems. In fact, the concept of contribution, while conforming to reformers' concern for the extreme circumstances of the stereotypical victimized housewife, may have permitted them to ignore some of the harder questions because it facilitated the perception that equal treatment was the ideal solution. For example, what was to be the standard for division in cases where a spouse made dual contributions by both working and caring for the home and children.

The point is that full-time housewives are an economically elite group – just as women who have careers in which they can earn enough to pay other women to care for their houses and children while they pursue their own interests are privileged. Many women cannot choose to stay at home and do domestic work full-time. They must work at low-paying, often unfulfilling jobs to earn money for meeting family needs and, in addition, must perform the tasks of raising children and maintaining a home.

Under the rhetoric of contribution, these women should be compensated for making a double contribution to the marriage, for fulfilling both market and family duties. Because the victimized housewife was the focus of reform, however, contribution was a concept employed only to reach the result of equality. Its implications were not thought through and coherently applied to circumstances such as these. Thus, unfortunately, these women will probably have to settle for an equal division. In addition, even if the image of the victimized housewife presented the easiest case for understanding the need for reform, it does not explain why the solution to her problems was seen as the imposition of the rule-equality model based on her contribution to the marriage – why her projected circumstances, her future needs, did not demand more than an equal division.

It may be that the reformers did have access to more complete information and therefore should have understood that sameness of treatment would not be appropriate for all women, but chose the symbolically compatible rule-equality model as their organizing concept because their sights were focused on the broader equality concerns of the feminist movement.[21] Any arguments that did not explicitly incorporate the rule-equality concept would undermine that goal.

It also may be that the imagery of women as victims had too powerful an influence on the reformers. The women who successfully initiated the reform movement by using the horror stories may themselves have felt locked in by the stories once the reform momentum was generated. This may have led them to exaggerate the divorced housewife's lack of property claims and to ignore the patterns by which the courts indeed protected these women.

Some evidence suggests that liberal feminist reformers put the equality model at the center of their organizing efforts for reasons that may be characterized as symbolic. In dividing a finite bundle of goods between two contenders, equality means that each receives one-half. On a symbolic level, this measure expresses more than just a method of division. It assumes that each individual's rights or entitlements are equal as well.

The reformers believed that equal property rights would put women in a better economic position after divorce than they would have been in under prior law. More generally, they believed that the representation of marriage as a partnership, with which the idea of equal property rights was so closely associated, would reduce sex-role stereotypes in marriage and would allow each partner to decide on the type and timing of the contributions she or he would make to the family unit. Thus, equal property rights were linked to a broader concept of equal value and freedom of choice in marriage roles.

Equality as an organizing concept is also evident in other divorce-law provisions. Just as the decisions concerning divisions of assets are to be made with a presumption of equality between the spouses, so are those concerning marital "liabilities." Economic responsibility for children is to be shared, with both parents responsible for the children's future support.

Future support for the spouses is to be primarily their individual responsibilities, unless certain well-defined circumstances indicating need justify one spouse receiving some temporary, limited support from the other to re-educate or rehabilitate herself for the job market. The equality conceptualization of

21 Weitzman detailed that in the first year after their divorces under the equal-division rules, men in California experienced a 42 percent increase in their standard of living, as measured by income in relation to needs. Divorced women, by contrast, experienced a 73 percent decline. Lenore Weitzman, *The Economics of Divorce: Social and Economic Consequences of Property, Alimony and Child Support Awards*, 28 U.C.L.A. L. REV. 1181 (1981). Earlier studies had also shown this pattern, even if the reported differentiations in positions were not exactly the same as the Weitzman findings. *See* Seal, *supra* note 20. In addition, in 1976 researchers found that while there was a 19 percent decline in a typical husband's income in real money terms, his economic position actually improved by 17 percent when assessed in terms of his needs after divorce. Women's positions, however, showed a decline in income relative to needs of 29 percent. S. Hoffman & J. Holmes, *Husbands, Wives, and Divorce, in* FIVE THOUSAND AMERICAN FAMILIES-PATTERNS OF ECONOMIC PROGRESS, 27–31 (1976). The Hoffman and Holmes study was available prior to the passage of the Wisconsin reform legislation.

marriage inherently places tremendous significance and primary focus on the symbolic nature of the "partnership" relationship between men and women, with the concept of contribution supplying the distribution standard.[22]

The Discarded Discourse

As noted earlier, at the time of divorce reform, there were two concepts in addition to fault that permitted judges to ignore title in dividing property equitably. Using the concept of need, for example, a judge could award the bulk of the marital property to a dependent wife who would not be able to support herself adequately after divorce. Using the concept of contribution, a judge could award the wife a share of her husband's property based on the notion that her services in the home had assisted him in accumulating the property.

Only the contribution concept, however, was compatible with the reformers' overriding commitment to equality. To fit need within the context of equality, as they defined and employed the term, would have been impossible. Need is a concept that might be said to characterize women as unequal. To admit that women might have more need for the accumulated assets than their husbands may have been understood as conceding that they were not as capable of caring for themselves.

Contribution, by contrast, could be rehabilitated within the equality model by assuming that a non-wage-earning spouse supplied a sufficient amount of effort and labor to the marriage to establish her "right" to property and other assets acquired by her wage-earning spouse. Title, therefore, the traditional

22 As noted in an unpublished article in 1982: "In some cases, an equal division might not fairly reflect the contributions of the parties. In *Kobylack v. Kobylack,* the parties had a marriage of ten years, in which both had maintained careers as if they were not married and had treated their marriage as a partnership. The court determined that the division of the two major marital assets, the residence and the automobile, should be in accordance with the parties' economic contributions to the partnership. Thus, because the court did not want either party to retain a 'monetary advantage merely by the virtue of having been married,' the court based its decision on purely economic considerations. The court determined that the husband's financial contributions to the partnership were one-and-a-half times that of the wife and made a division of the marital property in accordance with that rationale. On the other hand, a purely equitable distribution often might result in an equal division. For example, in *Jolis v. Jolis*, 111 Misc.2d 965,446 N.Y.S.2d 138 (sup. Ct. 1981), after 41 years of marriage and an affluent lifestyle, the parties had acquired marital assets that included cash, securities, a farm, a New York City co-op, and a Paris studio co-op. The court determined that the marital property should be divided equally, emphasizing the wife's abandonment of a promising career as a singer to be a companion and social asset to her husband, the wife's lack of future income and loss of inheritance rights, and the husband's comfortable financial status." Note, *The North Carolina Act for Equitable Distribution of Marital Property,* 18 WAKE-FOREST L. REV. (1982) 735, 752 n.121. For such women, the equality model is a form of property reallocation or asset-sharing based on other women's social or cultural disadvantages and not on their own circumstances.

common-law basis for determining allocation of assets at divorce, could and should be disregarded, because she was an actual contributor to their acquisition.

The logical ramifications of symbolic adherence to equality may be significant. A commitment to equality initially encourages its proponents to minimize or deny differences between the individuals they perceive to be in superior positions and those who are in socially subordinate positions. Contribution is an equalizing concept, while need demands an acknowledgment and evaluation of differences.

Overreliance on symbolic concerns may create several difficulties, however. The contribution concept may impede the development of instrumental rules that directly address practical problems. For example, arguing that housework and childcare are equal to monetary contributions and are therefore entitled to equal recognition when property is divided can be viewed as one way of dealing with need in the overall context of the equality concept. The need concept is disguised but not abandoned. This is only satisfactory, however, if the conceptual limitation on the contribution notion (one-half, or an equal share) results in decisions which satisfy need in an overwhelming majority of cases. If it cannot, the equality solution is inadequate for the problem of need. In fact, need cannot be alleviated by equal divisions so long as other factors between men and women remain unequal.

The concept of need is often the unstated argument that underlies all the arguments in the area of property division. Because it is disguised, though, the solutions which are proposed necessarily fail to deal effectively with the problem of need. To emerge from a divorce in a position that even begins to put them on an economic par with their ex husbands, many women need to receive *more* in property division than the strict equality concept applied to a narrower and more traditionally appropriate definition of marital property will allow. The triumph of the rule-equality concept in this area has been by the sacrifice of equity.

Since sharing responsibility is often translated into assuming equal responsibility, the result is unrealistic, even cruel, given the practical situation of many women.[23] The problem is not that the idea of sharing financial responsibility between husband and wife is inherently unreasonable or unfair, but rather that sharing expectations must be tempered by reference to evidence indicating that equality in the financial circumstances of men and women does not exist. *Shared* responsibility, therefore, should not be equated with *equal* responsibility.[24]

23 *See* Seal, *supra* note 20, at 10. The author's analysis of court records in San Diego revealed that California's rule-equality reform has had an adverse effect on wives. Under the former system, the home and furniture typically were allocated to the wife. After the reform, the home and other assets usually were divided, and the wife was ordered to pay a share of the family debts. Seal also concluded that the actual value of child-support awards tended to be less under the equality mode. The combination of the wife's loss of assets with her increased responsibility for family debts often meant that she had less disposable income and that she would end up contributing more than half to support the children. *Id.* at 13–15.

24 The difficult questions of why one spouse (typically the husband) should absorb an unequal share of the family financial responsibilities or any responsibility for the future financial well-being of his ex-wife deserve more comprehensive treatment

Simplistic, rule-equality changes in divorce laws premised on an unrealized egalitarian marriage ideal will tend to further impoverish women and their children. Under such laws, divorced women are to assume sole economic responsibility for themselves and joint economic responsibility for their children. Theoretically, this requirement is fair because divorced women will assume this responsibility under the same terms and conditions as their ex-spouses. Equal treatment in divorce, however, can only be fair if spouses have access to equal resources and have equivalent needs. Realistically, many women do not have such economic advantages. In addition, they continue to care for children.

than is possible here. The difficulties caused by serial monogamy and ongoing support for prior spouses have been noted. *See* M. GLENDON, THE NEW FAMILY AND THE NEW PROPERTY 87 (1981). Fewer conceptual difficulties are presented, however, if decision making is based on the theory of ongoing responsibility for children. If it is possible to make a distribution of property (i.e., a one-time allocation) which will not seriously impair a man's assumption of new family responsibilities while at the same time allowing his ex-wife and children a better chance for a reasonable economic future, it would seem fair to do so. This result could be achieved if laws focused on specific circumstances such as custody awards in determining appropriate property divisions.

Chapter 4

The Individualization of the Family

Child Advocacy (1991)[1]

Increased gender neutrality in divorce reform necessitated the appointment of independent child advocates, tasked with determining the best interest of the child. Here Fineman argues that this advocacy harms families by conceptually separating parents from children and framing all children of divorce as victims. Further, the purported neutrality of such advocates dangerously obscures the political and social biases that inform child custody decisions.

There are two critical problems with the idea of child advocacy that I want to explore. The first problem is with the creation and acceptance of the child as an independent client separable from his or her parent and in need of advocacy services at divorce. Even were the need for such advocacy clear, however, there is a second problem concerning the process of articulating and defining the child's best interest. The very fact that the client is also a child raises questions about the feasibility of accomplishing this difficult task.

The Focus of Advocacy

For purposes of this discussion, the significance of the continued use of the best-interest test, post-maternal-preference and post-fault, is found in its theoretical separation of the child from the family. When the maternal preference was viable, the child was conceptually aligned with the mother, and (absent compelling evidence) it was presumed that she acted in her child's interest. The designation of the "innocent" (not at fault) spouse could be viewed as functioning in the same way as an allocation device. Removing these "easy" indicators necessitated a focus on the child alone, as an independent individual with interests that might differ from those of both of his or her parents. It is this development that clearly created the need for a child advocate distinct from those who represent the parents or family.

1 This essay is used with permission of The University of Chicago Press, from The Illusion of Equality: The Rhetoric and Reality of Divorce Reform, Martha Fineman, 2nd Edition, 1994; permission conveyed through Copyright Clearance Center, Inc.

DOI: 10.4324/9781003405627-6

The child is now viewed as a free-floating entity and as the focus of the custody proceeding. As in all assertions of "rights" in the United States, with its constitutional tradition, the language used in advancing arguments for child advocacy is symbolically powerful and compelling. This is particularly true because the term *child* is highly sentimentalized in our culture. For example, in an early Family Court "Bill of Rights for Children in Divorce Actions" the first right listed is that of the child "to be treated as an interested and affected person and not as a pawn, possession or chattel of either or both parents." The justification for child advocacy is set forth in the form of a right attached to the child: "the right to recognition that children involved in a divorce are always disadvantaged parties and that the law must take affirmative steps to protect their welfare, including the appointment of a guardian *ad litem* to protect their interests."[2] Note that this Bill of Rights emphasizes children's need for, and right to, protection from their parents. This protection is to be implemented through a legal advocate. It argues that the right of the child to advocacy is one to which the state must respond. Intervention is not only desirable but inevitable. The entire argument is built upon the unquestioned assertion that children are being used as "pawns" or are viewed as "property" by their parents.[3]

Implications of the Paradigm

There are two questions we should ask. The first is whether or not it is accurate or helps discussion of the issues to cast children as victims of divorce. The second question to consider is, even if children are victimized by divorce, does this necessitate the establishment of separate, independent legal advocacy?

The first question gives rise to additional ones. For example, if it is true that parents during the divorce process are typically so self-absorbed as to use their children as pawns, isn't it appropriate to require child advocates in all divorces where there are children? After all, pawns are not only sacrificed in games that end up in court but are equally at risk in negotiated or non-contested cases.

Further, and more importantly, if it is true that a large number of parents can comfortably be presumed to have a tendency to sacrifice their children's well-being in this way, isn't the real conclusion we should reach that there are many people out there who are unfit parents, unable to separate out their own needs and act in their children's best interest? Could they ever be trusted to do so? Can a parent who views his or her children as property or treats them as

2 Robert W. Hansen, *The Role and Rights of Children in Divorce Actions*, 6 J. FAM. L. 1, 5 (1966).

3 Historically, children were the property of their fathers, who upon divorce received custody under the legal doctrine of paterfamilias. *See* JAMES SCHOULER, A TREATISE ON THE LAW OF DOMESTIC RELATIONS 61, 333 (1870). Such ownership entailed a corresponding duty to support the children, a duty which today is fulfilled through child-support payments without the father having actual physical custody of the children. *See* WILLIAM BLACKSTONE, COMMENTARIES 435–38 (rev. ed. 1966).

pawns be expected to convert and be nonexploitive with the granting of a divorce decree and a custody award?

The second question about the ability of child advocacy to remedy victimization also raises additional considerations focused on what ideological or political purpose such advocacy actually serves. The typical characterization of the problem places great faith in professionals and assumes that, at best, parents involved in the vast majority of custody cases become temporarily incapable of acting in both their own and their children's interests. I am not sure we should be satisfied by unadorned assertions of wanton parental self-absorption and blatant sacrifice of children's interest, no matter the degree of professional assurance or the force with which such assertions are made.

The net result of the uncritical acceptance of the child-as-victim construct is state-sponsored substitution of informal, nonlegal, professional decision making for that of parents or that of the courts. The significant input into the custody decision-making process is no longer from parents but from professionals, inaccurately designated as "neutral" or "disinterested" and legitimated by the notion that they alone are capable of acting in the best interest of the children. For example, on the role of behavioral scientists in custody disputes, one commentator has stated:

> [A]n analysis of the criteria inherent to the recently enacted [custody] statutes reveal *[sic]* a strong reliance upon factors that can best be evaluated by behavioral science. Among other factors, assessments must be made of the parent's intelligence, morality, knowledge of child development, personality, child-rearing attitudes, emotional ties with the child, and a host of other factors that are of a social and/or psychological nature.
>
> The behavioral scientist has essentially been given a societal mandate for involvement and must be prepared to function appropriately in child custody determinations.[4]

Furthermore, the locus for the decision making is no longer the judge but these same professionals. I am far from convinced that this development benefits children and have serious doubts as to whether it is even desirable. There is a belief among professionals associated with custody disputes that representation is the only way to protect the child(ren) of a divorce: "The most important single safeguard which could be utilized to assure the psychological best interest of the child, in a custody action, would be to provide counsel to represent him."[5]

The acceptance of children as victims, which is evidenced by the rhetoric surrounding discussions of divorce and is manifest in the interpretation of the

4 Robert H. Woody, *Behavioral Science Criteria in Child Custody Determinations*, 3 J. MARRIAGE & FAM. COUNSELING 11 (1977).

5 Andrew S. Watson, *The Children of Armageddon: Problems of Custody Following Divorce*, 21 SYRACUSE L. REV. 55, 66 (1969).

best-interest test, is the ideological basis upon which the arguments for increased state involvement implemented through extrajudicial actors have been constructed. A battery of experts who are presumed to act in the best interest of children are added to the process. As a result, both the questions and the solutions concerning any individual child are developed *independent of parental decisions or initiative.* The description and characterization of the problems facing the child, the important judgments which must be made, and the solutions which are suggested are all in the hands of the professionals. The rationale for this is that the divorcing parents can no longer be trusted to act on behalf of their children. Child-advocacy proponents believe that if a child's future cannot be entrusted to his or her parents, then a child advocate is essential. To these proponents, the fact that the parents are enmeshed in an adversarial contest is sufficient to deem them incapable of acting in their children's best interest. They are assumed to be concerned only with their own self-serving ends. As Rosenberg, Kleinman, and Brantley stated:

> In addition to the universal and unconscious distortions and misunderstandings of relationships by each individual, in custody evaluations everyone is consciously distorting and misinterpreting. The situation precludes total honesty. Each parent is trying to present him- or herself as the best, the other as the worst, and will often censor or distort information to achieve that goal.[6]

Construction of the Child-Client's "Best Interest"

Related to the observation that the terms of the substantive legal test for custody have created a climate in which we easily accept the necessity of child advocacy is the question of how a child's best interest is to be ascertained. When the child is perceived as separate or independent – a client in need of separate counsel – there must be some way in which to assess what the content or goal of the representation should be. How does the child's advocate in the divorce proceeding determine what is in the child's best interest and act to advocate that interest?

If the advocate is a member of the helping professions, the assumption is that he or she possesses the skills to make the best-interest determination. Normally, however, these professionals are not advocates within the context of particular cases but are viewed as expert, neutral witnesses. Thus, professional assessments are considered evidence to assist in the determination of best interest, yet another actor is necessary to perform the advocacy role in the adversary context – to represent the child. In most instances this advocate is a lawyer.

The presence of an attorney as the child advocate creates problems that transcend (while they also complicate) those associated with the involvement of

6 Elinor Rosenberg, Judith Kleinman, & Thomas L. Brantley, *Custody Evaluations: Helping the Family Reorganize*, 63 SOC. CASEWORK 203, 205 (1982).

mental health professionals who perform custody evaluations. This is particularly true because of role confusion between these professions,[7] coupled with uncertainty as to who and what is represented.

The Function of the Legal Advocate

Even if one accepts the idea of a need for independent child advocacy, a critical problem is connected to the perceived need for legal representation, or an adversarial "champion."[8] Once we establish a need, we must consider the problem of the appropriate function of the independent child's advocate.[9] This creates a dilemma because the role of the advocate is dependent upon the acceptance of and belief in the characterization or creation of the child-client as the potential victim of his or her parents. If this is a true characterization, then the parents cannot be trusted to provide objective or neutral information about the child and his or her interests. All information from them is suspect. The parents going through a divorce are portrayed as using their child(ren) for purely instrumental reasons in the divorce proceedings:

> It is tempting to believe that in a case where two parents are contesting the right to custody of a child, each one is arguing for the child's best interests as he or she perceives them. Unfortunately, the motivations behind the custody demands of the parents are often ambivalent. Mothers may seek custody of children though antipathetic to them, in order to exert influence over their former spouses who seek visitation arrangements. Fathers may seek custody as a bargaining tool to lower the mother's child support and alimony demands, or may fail to seek custody, despite their fitness, because of the realization that mothers obtain custody in most cases. Finally, many parents seek custody as a vindication of their innocence in the break-up rather than to provide the best home for the child.[10]

7 In recent years there has been considerable interpenetration of the legal profession and the helping professions. The members of the helping professions are now, in many respects, far more central to custody determinations than lawyers, while the lawyers are moving more towards the growth area of mediation.

8 *See* Martin Guggenheim, *The Right to be Represented but not Heard: Reflections on Legal Representation for Children*, 59 N.Y.U. L. REV. 76, 100–9 (1984) (making a distinction between the advocate as Champion and the advocate as Investigator).

9 One commentator has pointed out that "an equally crucial issue is posed by the question of the role that the attorney should play – is he guardian ad litem in the traditional sense, or is he an advocate?" Robert E. Shepherd, *Solomon's Sword: Adjudication of Child Custody Questions*, 8 U. RICH. L. REV. 151, 169 (1974).

10 James Kenneth Genden, *Separate Legal Representation for Children: Protecting the Rights and Interests of Minors in Judicial Proceedings*, 2 HARV. C.R.-C.L. L. REV. 565, 573 (1976) (citations omitted).

Thus, ascertaining the child's interests involves the advocate in constructing the child's best interest – that which is to be represented or advocated in the divorce proceeding. The significant question is, How is this interest created independently of parental input?

Since the modern conceptualization of the process has already eliminated parents as sources of this best-interest determination, and the desire for gender neutrality has made social and informal empirical observations about mothers and nurturing suspect, we are left with three potential sources of determination. First, and easiest to dispose of quickly, is the suggestion that we look to the child to ascertain what solution should be advocated. The legal advocate could ask the child which parent he or she prefers and then simply advocate whatever result the child indicates. This is roughly how an attorney would act in representing a competent adult client. However, many children are unable, or unwilling, to express a preference between competing potential custodial parents. Further, some research indicates that it may even be harmful for older, competent children to choose between parents at divorce. Thus, the children's-choice approach is not considered a viable option, at least for children under the age of 14 or 15.[11]

The vast majority of legal child advocates do not adhere to such a narrow view of their responsibility. They do not conceptualize the role of the child advocate as that of an advocate for the child *per se* but as that of an advocate for the child's best interest. This is a distinction of considerable importance. Instead of merely representing the child's preference, such an approach demands that the child's legal advocate undertake the task of assessing or evaluating what is in the child's best interest independently of, though it may consider them, the child's wishes as to his or her custody.

The Advocate and Ascertaining Best Interest

How, then, can the legal advocate make an evaluation of what is in a child's best interest? In practical terms, the requirement of independent advocacy means that there are two nonparental contenders for the role of primacy determiner of the best interest of the child at divorce. There is a need not only for the advocacy but also for the construction or creation of what is urged as being in the child's interest. The societal signals which would indicate that in most instances this would lead to a maternal preference are to be excluded by the demands of gender neutrality. Structurally, we are thus presented with a choice between two types of professionals who hover around the divorce process: the legal advocate on the one hand and the helping professional on the other.

The legal professional may make the decision, acting first both as an investigator and collector of information, and thereafter as an informed expert who has

11 *See* Guggenheim, *supra* note 8, at 121–26 (arguing that appointing attorneys for children too young to have control over them undermines the legitimate interests of the parents in familial privacy and autonomous decision making).

examined the evidence and reached a conclusion as to what is in the best interest of the child. This choice creates the necessity for the legal advocate to investigate, to collect information from both experts and nonexperts about the child and family, and to make a judgment about what should be the appropriate placement.[12] Thus, the legal advocate acts as an investigator and as an expert within the legal process; in this regard, the role of advocate is one with substantive dimension.

In these circumstances, not only has a client been created for the legal advocate, but the characteristics of that client necessitate that one primary function of the legal advocate is to construct the client's interest in a manner which, to a large extent, is independent of the client's direction. In this instance, where the legal advocate is making an independent assessment of the quality of evidence accumulated, he or she is no better equipped than a judge to make such an assessment and would seem, for that reason alone, to be unnecessary to the process.

In other circumstances, the legal advocate's role may be more limited, and the various mental health professionals, who have increasingly become more significant in the divorce context, will explicitly serve as the arbiters of the child's best interest. In this process, the legal advocate often acts as nothing more than the advocate of the expert helping professional's opinion as to what is in the child's best interest. Thus, in effect, the mental health professional becomes the substituted client, one who speaks for the constructed child-client, and is the vehicle through which the child's best interest is realized.

Experts' conclusions in this area have increasingly centered on imposing the ideal of shared parenting after divorce. In a gender-neutral world seen to require the devaluation of nurturing, these experts have undertaken the task of bringing fathers back into the post-divorce picture. This has resulted in the creation of professional norms which give custody to the "most generous parent" or the parent most willing to share the child with the other parent.[13] A desire for sole custody has been labeled "pathological"[14] and is to be

12 In the words of one writer: "Without a separate advocate, the court may not perceive the existence of the special needs of the child. Even if the court does recognize such needs, so long as other parties have separate advocates to represent their interests, the court will need an advocate to articulate the child's interest and to marshall the supporting facts." James Kenneth Genden, *supra* note 10, at 573.

13 *See, e.g.*, Rosenberg, Kleinman, & Brantley, *supra* note 6, at 207 ("It is clear that the best interests of the child involve much more than the linear relationships between parent and children One major consideration often may be the custodial parent's ability to allow an arrangement for an appropriate continuing relationship with the noncustodial parent as well as significant others."). Some states have enacted these so-called friendly-parent provisions. *See, e.g.*, CAL. CRV. CODE § 4600(6)(1) (West Supp. 1988). For a discussion of these statutes, *see* Joanne Schulman & Valerie Pitt, *Second Thoughts on Joint Child Custody: Analysis of Legislation and Its Implications for Women and Children*, 12 GOLDEN GATE U. L. REV. 539, 554–55 (1982).

14 *See, e.g.*, Joan B. Kelly, *Further Observations on Joint Custody*, 16 U.C DAVIS L. REV. 762, 769 (1983) (recognizing some problems of abuse but emphasizing the problem of "emotionally disturbed women who, due to their own pathology, vigorously fight a father's desire to be involved in the children's lives"). *But see* Nancy K. Lemon,

discouraged or punished by legal rules which mandate post divorce cooperation and sharing. The child advocate is part of a larger process whereby professional norms such as these are incorporated and made operative within the context of the legal system, with the child advocate representing the professional ideal.

Political Implications of the Acceptance of the Idea of Child Advocacy

As stated earlier, the crux of the problem is that the evolving best interest standard without its historic referents is so amorphous, undirected, incomprehensible, and indeterminate as to be meaningless without a substantial "extra-judicial implementation team." The only response to a degendered, no-fault divorce system, short of scrapping the best-interest-of-the-child test, is the creation of alternative decision-makers and the referral of all substantive decisions to them. There are problems with this no matter which professional is the source of the best-interest determination. However, as discussed earlier, the problems for a legal advocate are extreme.

The legal advocate functions to give the illusion of neutrality to the decision-making process. This illusion allows the system to limp along without serious reassessment of the political and practical roles played by mental health professionals and others who seek to define the best interest of children through processes and standards which enhance the position and power of their own professions. Custody decision making and the rules that govern it involve more than just making individual decisions regarding placement of children. Submerged in the rules and processes are political and ideological conflicts between "mothers" (or nurturing and caretaking values) and "fathers" (or independence and financial security values); between the legal profession (or advocacy and adversariness as values) and the helping professions (or treatment and therapy as values); between the moralists (who would burden the divorce system so as to impede or discourage divorce and to punish those who seek to divorce) and the secularists (who would seek to implement rules that ensured no one lost too much in deciding to leave a marriage). The illusion and pretense of objectivity and neutrality, of which the legal advocate is but one part, serve the interests of those empowered by the status quo and the bias in professional opinion-making.

Joint Custody as a Statutory Presumption: California's New Civil Code Sections 4600 and 4600.5, 11 GOLDEN GATE U.L. REV. 485, 527–31 (1981) (suggesting that the stereotype of the manipulative and vindictive mother opposing joint custody is overstated). The therapist is viewed as having a potentially powerful role in correcting pathological behavior. *See* David Abelsohn, *Dealing with the Abdication Dynamic in the Post-Divorce Family: A Context for Adolescent Crises*, 22 FAM. PROCESS 359, 365 (1983) (stating that "[t]he therapist delivers this basic message to the mother – you lose, you do not win, if you succeed in keeping your children from their father").

Chapter 5

The Illusion of Equality (1991)[1]

In the conclusion to her book, *The Illusion of Equality*, Fineman succinctly exposes how rhetoric can shape law in obfuscated ways, masking true inequality. She ends with a call to reform our ideals of equality; a call that has informed subsequent decades of critical legal thought.

Confined by images of equality, liberal feminists historically have used two compelling images in their attempts to gain access to powerful social institutions. These images initially appear to be complementary. The first image is a negative one: the image of woman as the victim of existing institutions. This image has been useful in convincing large numbers of both women and sympathetic men that women have indeed been oppressed in this society, and that women need and deserve laws removing this oppression from their social, legal, and political experiences. The second image is a positive one: the image of equal treatment. Equality has emerged as a potent ideal with which to rectify the victimization of women in society, and to that extent it complements the image of woman as victim. Equality rhetoric can be used both as an organizational tool and as the basis for proposing specific formal changes in the laws.

Because of its practical political uses, it is hardly surprising that the victim/equality imagery has sometimes been overdrawn in liberal feminist arguments. In the context of marriage and divorce reform, however, these exaggerations have had unfortunate consequences. The divorce-reform process discussed here is an example of a situation where an interest group with societal concerns that encompass specific legislative problems, but also extend far beyond them, directly articulated reform goals in legal abstractions in an attempt to implement these broader concerns. This group, because of its composition, was viewed as uniquely legitimate within the political process; it represented the interests of women and was therefore seen as the appropriate purveyor of solutions to the problems that were being addressed.

1 This essay is used with permission of The University of Chicago Press, from The Illusion of Equality: The Rhetoric and Reality of Divorce Reform, Martha Fineman, 2nd Edition, 1994; permission conveyed through Copyright Clearance Center, Inc.

DOI: 10.4324/9781003405627-7

The liberal feminists used the ideology of equality both to attack the existing rules, demonstrating the need for reform, and to supply the theoretical underpinnings that shaped the formal content of the reform rules. The liberal feminist equality ideology gave the reform rules legitimacy as it simultaneously removed legitimacy from the rules that were to be replaced. Actions subsequently taken by legal institutions will have the appearance of neutrality and fairness insofar as they are consistent with the reformed rules.[2] Because of the legitimacy conferred by the prevailing ideology during the crucial political process, the substantive rules are viewed both as unbiased and as actually operating to confer equality before the law. The individuals, groups, and interests that were perceived as disadvantaged under the old rules are now viewed as having been vindicated through the process of reform. The formal bias in the system, as represented by the old rules, has been removed, and the once-disadvantaged can no longer complain about results, because the system now treats them neutrally and equally under the law.

However, if one rejects the comprehensiveness of the "equal" and "victim" stereotypes of women and marriage, one must confront the fact that there are many women whose circumstances have not been addressed by equality legislation and who will not benefit from the reforms. In addition, once children are included in the equation, it becomes even clearer that equality just doesn't add up to needed reform. The changes, however, have been potent and powerful on a symbolic level, and this has operated to frustrate more instrumental concerns and resulted in the generation of reforms that cause great damage to women and children.

The rhetoric of equality is too easily appropriated and utilized to gain support for antifeminist measures. Equality rhetoric is a rhetoric that belongs both to no one, and to everyone. For this reason alone, it would seem time to abandon equality.

2 Richard O. Lempert, *Grievances and Legitimacy: The Beginnings and End of Dispute Settlement*, 15 LAW & SOC. REV. 707 (1980–81), noted this relationship between legal action and legitimacy in producing prima facie neutral decision making. He suggested that neutrality is questioned, however, when the ideological underpinnings of the law or rule are open to attack. If a rule is attacked successfully, it can no longer be viewed as neutral and so must be discarded for a "legitimate" (ideologically supported) rule, so that neutral legal action is again perceived as possible.

Part II

The Sexual Family

Teemu Ruskola

Martha Fineman's early work presents a powerful critique of the limits of formal gender equality in family law, especially with respect to distributive justice upon divorce. In her landmark book *The Neutered Mother, the Sexual Family and Other Twentieth Century Tragedies,* published in 1995, she extends her analysis further. She works beyond a painstaking examination of the inability of formal equality to address gender bias within a legal arrangement that is socially and economically fundamentally gendered – not essentially or necessarily so, as she is careful to point out, but as a matter of historical, political, and social fact. In her subsequent work, she turns from an investigation of marriage and its internal logic to analyzing the structural position of the family unit vis-à-vis the political and economic institutions within which it is situated. The implications of this examination are nothing short of revolutionary, not only for family law but for the structural relationship among the family, the market, and the state. This is critical theory at its most expansive.

At the heart of *The Neutered Mother* is Fineman's critique of what she calls "the sexual family." In the course of the twentieth century, liberal feminist critiques of gender inequality succeeded in dismantling the Blackstonian vision of family in which a woman's legal personality was literally absorbed into that of her husband, turning her into little more than his legal shadow, or *femme couvert* in the parlance of the common law. Liberal feminism replaced this hierarchical construct with a new, egalitarian view of marriage as a contractual relationship between two individuals, a man and a woman. The Blackstonian family was a patriarchal system for the exploitation of labor, including the productive labor of both the wife and children and the wife's reproductive labor. In contrast, the new contractual relationship envisions a democratic arrangement for mutual satisfaction, which in turn provides the foundation for the modern nuclear family, or what Fineman calls the sexual family. Fineman's critique of this arrangement refers to liberal feminism's misguided commitment to privileging a sexual partnership among spouses, in the updated gender-neutral parlance of twentieth-century family law.

But Fineman's critique is not just that in the gendered world in which we live, formal equality is not capable of delivering substantive equality, given its

DOI: 10.4324/9781003405627-8

willful blindness to lived experience and social circumstance. Rather, even if it were possible to guarantee real gender equality between spouses, the elimination of a gendered division of labor would still leave unaddressed the problematic nature of the underlying sexual contract itself. For one thing, although Fineman doesn't put it in quite these terms, marriage is in essence a form of state-sponsored discrimination against single people: it delivers material as well as ideological subsidies to women and men who choose to marry. What is more, this (formally) egalitarian view of marriage still privatizes caretaking labor within the family. Regardless of whether that labor is performed by the wife or the husband, taking care of children, aging parents, or other family members remains an uncompensated "labor of love," the costs of which are borne by the family unit. The problem isn't therefore "just" the gendered inequality that defines much of family life, but the privatization and devaluation of the social costs of care that it entails. The family in effect subsidizes the costs of social reproduction, including the reproduction of labor for the market.

As Fineman puts it with disarming understatement, the "only" concrete policy proposal she draws from this critique is the abolition of marriage. Sexual arrangements among consenting adults ought to be of no concern to the state. Eliminating marriage as a legal institution would open the playing field to all manner of voluntary sexual affiliations. Sexual relations among adults would be regulated by contract law, tort law, and criminal law, like other relations. Neither the gender nor the number of one's sexual affiliates would be a matter of state regulation any more – "nothing prohibited, nothing privileged," in Fineman's succinct formulation.[1]

As I have noted elsewhere, Fineman's marriage abolitionism looks even more radical today than it did in 1995.[2] Her primary concern in *The Neutered Matter* is the public devaluation of caretaking labor and the need to restructure the way in which it is organized, but looking back, it is important to recognize that the book intersects also with queer theory. (The relationship between feminism and queer theory is an abiding concern in Fineman's *oeuvre*.[3]) Prefiguring critiques of homonormativity by queer theorists, *The Neutered Mother* warns that even if same-sex marriage were to be legalized – a notion no one at the time could have entertained as a serious possibility – it would only serve to reinforce the status of marriage as both a privileged sexual contract among two adults and a site of uncompensated labor. As unlikely as it seemed at the time, a movement that was launched in the Stonewall era did in fact move away from the utopian search for freedom toward equality. Effectively, the utopian goal of "sexual liberation" transformed into "marriage equality." Same-sex marriage is

1 MARTHA ALBERTSON FINEMAN, THE NEUTERED MOTHER, THE SEXUAL FAMILY AND OTHER TWENTIETH CENTURY TRAGEDIES 229–30 (1995).

2 Teemu Ruskola, *Notes on The Neutered Mother, Or Toward a Queer Socialist Matriarchy*, 67 EMORY L.J. 1165 (2018).

3 FEMINIST AND QUEER LEGAL THEORY: INTIMATE ENCOUNTER, UNCOMFORTABLE CONVERSATIONS (Martha Albertson Fineman et al. eds., 2009).

unquestionably an important legal achievement, precisely because of the numerous vitally important material privileges it affords to couples who qualify, but it is equally clear that it only reaffirms rather than challenges the sexual contract at its foundation. Stated differently, Martha Fineman is, and was already in 1995, in many ways far queerer than LGBTQ politics is today.

What, then would a post-marriage world look like? After jettisoning (the fiction of) an egalitarian sexual partnership, she in effect replaces it with a new vertically structured relationship – not the Blackstonian patriarchy but a new one rooted in care, or what she calls "dependency." Although autonomy may be a worthwhile goal if and when it can be realized, too often it is only a cruel myth. Rather than hiding behind an ideological façade of aspirational equality, Fineman starts from the recognition that intimate relations are often, even paradigmatically, those of a caretaker and a dependent. Her call for the abolition of marriage is therefore emphatically not a call for the abolition of family but for a reorientation of our vision. Instead of basing family on a contract between two adults, Fineman wants to reconstruct it around the dyad between Mother and Child, replacing the horizontal ideology of the sexual contract with the recognition of relations of dependence and care. Significantly, Fineman observes that the existential fact of dependency, or what she calls the "inevitable dependency" associated with childhood, illness, and old age, gives rise also to what she calls "derivative dependency": those who take care of dependents have to depend on others. It is this recognition of derivative dependency that grounds her call for societal compensation for caring of dependents.

While the uncompensated labor of mothers – whether single or married – is perhaps the most egregious example of derivative dependency, it is important to realize that Fineman's emphasis on Mother and Child is ultimately metaphorical rather than literal. That is to say, "Mother" refers to anyone caring for dependents. Mothers, therefore, include people of all genders, or as Fineman states, men, too, "can and should be Mothers": "if men are interested in acquiring legal rights of access to children (or other dependents), they *must* be Mothers, in the stereotypical nurturing sense of that term—that is, engaged in caretaking."[4] The term Child similarly denotes any kind of dependent, whether an infant, a sexual affiliate, a cousin, a friend, or indeed any person who relies on others' care. The reason for this choice is Fineman's belief that only the protean Mother-Child metaphor is one strong enough to be able to stand up to the sexual family and to resist its gravitational pull.

It bears noting that Fineman is fully aware that marriage is not likely to be abolished anytime soon. Methodologically, she characterizes her work explicitly as "utopian theory." On the one hand, she is fully and fiercely committed to seeing the world as it exists in fact – hence her insistence on the harm caused by gender-neutral laws in a world where gendered hierarchies continue to abound.

4 Fineman, *supra* note 1, at 234–345 (emphasis in original).

On the other hand, she also insists that in order to see a way forward, we must be capable of reconsidering our most fundamental assumptions:

> Sometimes re-visioning, even if utopian, is valuable simply because it forces us to look at old relationships in new lights and thereby understand some things about how we perceive the natural or normal, as well as how we create the deviant.[5]

Fineman's critique of the sexual family accomplishes that goal brilliantly.

5 *Id*. at 232.

Chapter 6

The End of Family Law? Intimacy in the Twenty-First Century (1994)[1]

Fineman delivered this keynote address at Drake University's Constitutional Law Symposium, shortly before publication of *The Neutered Mother, the Sexual Family and Other Twentieth Century Tragedies*. She previews the book's revolutionary call for complete transformation in our conceptualization of family and intimacy and a "radical reform" of family law. She presents a vision of society organized around nurturing and caretaking that remains a worthy goal for the twenty-first century.

Although I titled my talk, "The End of Family Law," part of what I'm going to speak about is the end of "the family," that being the nuclear family. My concern has been with the single mother as an object of my research. In that research I'm haunted by two statistics: one is the divorce rate, which has remained fairly stable, with and accompanied by a mother-custody norm (which of course creates single mothers); the other is the increase in never-married mothers across all classes and races, but particularly middle-class and professional women choosing to become single mothers – not to marry but to become mothers without marriage. It occurs to me that what we need is a new paradigm in thinking about the family in order to accommodate or deal with these single mothers.

A family, of course, is constructed in law as it is in social institutions. In fact, property, contract, and family law have been called by Mary Ann Glendon the "three pillars of the civil law." However, the family differs from the other pillars in that it is an area of associational relations and intimate expectations. "Special" rules have been formulated to regulate families. These rules are related to the assumption that individuals interacting in the context of family law do not interact with the same independence and distance as strangers dealing with property and contract issues. In fact, the family – the nuclear family – is considered so "special" that the state is a necessary partner to the formation and dissolution of the foundational relationship – marriage – and is thereafter actively involved in determining the contractual terms and property consequences of the family.

1 This essay originally appeared in: Martha Fineman, *The End of Family Law? Intimacy in the Twenty-First Century*, 5 DRAKE L. REV. 23 (1994).

DOI: 10.4324/9781003405627-9

The family is an "assumed" institution – basic, inevitable and always in the background in theoretical or jurisprudential musings.

Family law orders the interactions of individuals, creates rights and obligations, interests and expectations, entitlements and options as does the law of either contract or property, but it does so within the context of assumptions about the family as an institution and its place within society. Once established, the family traditionally has held a favored place and privileged position within that society, entitled to "privacy" and protection from state intervention and regulation. Again, this is the nuclear family.

Historically, the American family has been our most explicitly gendered institution. It was gendered in its operations and expectations as well as in the values that it represents. The family has been justified and valorized as an institution for its perceived role in reproducing and transmitting norms of social behavior to all its members, but most particularly to the young. Concurrently (and complementarily) the legal roles of Husband-Father, Wife-Mother, and Child-Adult are formulated in the context of the relationship between State and the contrived institution of the "official" family. Dependency is "naturally" assigned to the family and, since it is not anticipated in the ideology that either the market or the State will contribute or assist in the necessary caretaking, it must be allocated within the family institution.

Within some segments of society, traditional family and behavioral norms have been challenged by word and deed during the last several decades. Yet, it appears our deeply held beliefs about family and our personal expectations for it as a functional institution seem fundamentally unaltered. Real change seems elusive, in part because of the gendered nature of the American family, which is not only structural but also ideological.

Gender was certainly the basis for the initial contemporary attacks on the family. For over 25 years the American family has been the object of so-called "second-wave feminist criticism" and attack. The family considered in this discourse was sometimes revealed as a potentially violent and dangerous social institution, marred by long-standing power imbalances and the specter of gender domination. Paradoxically the family was also recast as potentially the most fulfilling site of intimacy – the case that allowed the construction of a complete life if it was based on principles of equality and sharing.

These recent feminist critiques of the family have had some significant impact in regard to law reform. No longer is domestic violence invisible and ignored. Laws explicitly forbid child abuse, marital rape, and other domestic violence historically considered "normal." In addition, and affecting all families, the veil of privacy has been partly pulled aside, revealing the hierarchical nature of the family and its conceptual core of common law inequality. In response to feminist agitation (and after much time and effort) the language of the law of marriage and divorce has changed.

On a rhetorical level family law issues may no longer be resolved according to gendered assumptions. The legal allocation of tasks and responsibilities associated with families has ceased to be formally allocated in law on the basis of gender with the husband as the "head" of the household with obligations to support a wife and children over whom he exercised control and who correspondingly owed him obedience and, and on the wife's part, other sexual and domestic services.

The law has adopted a gender-neutral ideal. Our linguistic model is now one of an egalitarian family, based on the marital "partnership" of husband and wife. Gone from our formal, official discourse is the hierarchical organization of the common law marriage described so graphically by Blackstone under the doctrines of "unity" and "merger."

Female subservience is no longer assumed nor is our inherent incompetence for the business and market world seriously asserted and used as a basis for exclusion. Wives and mothers are equally responsible for the economic well-being of their families and no longer presumed by virtue of their sex to be the preferred parent in custody disputes.

However, rhetorical changes often do not reflect "real" changes (and seldom compel them). In considering the empirical data on the operation of the family, for example, the inescapable conclusion – rhetoric aside – is that gender divisions persist. Women continue to bear what I call the "burdens of intimacy" – the "costs" of "inevitable dependency" – in our society.

As a definitional note, "burden" is *not* the same as "oppression." I use the term to clearly signify that there are costs associated with what women typically do in regard to caretaking in our society. These labors may provide "joy," but they are also burdensome and have material costs and consequences. Not to recognize them as "burdens," is to ignore the costs and to continue to make women's labor invisible, condoning that it is also uncompensated.

A second definitional point is that dependency is "inevitable" in that it flows from the status and situation of being a child and often accompanies aging, illness, or disability. In this sense dependency will always be with us (and always has been with us). Furthermore, caretakers are dependent too – a derivative dependency derived from their roles as caretakers and the need for resources they generate to fulfill those roles.

To point out that the costs of caretaking associated with these dependencies continue in our society to be allocated to women should not be misunderstood to be an argument about essentialism. The allocation is accomplished and reinforced by the culture and our ideology of the family as a functioning institution. Nonetheless, to label something as a social construct does not mean it will be easy to change.

In spite of the introduction of a radical alternative and well-articulated equality model, the unequal, gendered expectations and distribution of the burdens of dependency have not shifted. There are no obvious answers as to why these burdens continue predominantly to be borne by women, but it is clear any inquiry cannot be limited or confined to the language of law or the traces and fragments of legislative history that remain in the wake of reform.

To understand the failure to effectively implement equality in terms of the shared responsibility of dependencies, one must look beyond law and formal mandates and try to understand something about the process of reform and the tenacity of the still potent traditional ideology of the family in American culture.

In part, the failure of changes based upon an equality ideal in the family arena has to do with the nature of the initial attacks on the family. By and large, it was the liberal legal feminist calls for equality within the larger society that prompted a reconsideration of the institution of the family. This began in earnest during the 1960s and 1970s, but has left relatively undisturbed the core concept of what constituted a "family." The feminist concept of the "new" family continued to reflect an idealized image of the family core as a couple.

The family was defined as an entity, built around and arising from the sexual affiliation of two adults. This organization of the family, of course, was historically exemplified by the heterosexual, formally married couple, a unit considered so basic it is referred to as the "foundation" of the American family. This heterosexual unit continues to be considered as presumptively appropriate and it has ongoing viability as the core family connection. At worst, heterosexual marriage is viewed to be merely in need of some updating and structural revisions.

In contemporary questioning of the institution of marriage it is often argued that other sexual affiliations, such as non-marital cohabitation or same-sex relationships, are deserving of the same privileges afforded to that, most basic, building block of society. These arguments, far from challenging the privileged status of marriage, reinforce it by inscribing onto it the attributes of normalcy, desirability, and privilege.

Furthermore, we seem caught in an "equality trap" in discussions about the traditional family. Specific suggestions for reform focus on the need for a reorganization of existing gendered roles within the confines of the traditionally populated family unit. Fathers would be expected to share more in the domestic tasks as modern mothers spend more time and energy in market endeavors. The marital partners simply would rework the parameters of their relationship which, nonetheless, would continue to serve as the anchor defining and giving content to other family associations. The privileged status afforded marriage would remain even if there was some role shifting.

This type of approach to family reform is evident in the changes made in law during the past several decades – the fashioning of the "egalitarian family" from the structure of its old common law hulk. The grand aspirations about equality are manifested in the terms we now use to discuss family relationship – "partnership" substituted for "marriage"; "shared parenting" substituted for "mothering and fathering"; "interdependency" and "contribution" substituted for "need" and "obligatory domestic labor."

The equality direction of early feminist reform had severe limitations, both practical and theoretical. Reformers naively assumed that sharing could and would happen. With the egalitarian aspiration ensconced in law, women would be freed to develop their careers, men unconstrained in choosing nurturing over other endeavors.

Furthermore, the reform vision was a particularly narrow one, considering only some family actors in its reconstituted vision. The roles of husband and wife were restructured in regard to childcare and vaguely described household domestic tasks, but little thought seems to have been given to the demands on domestic time and labor represented by the less attractive specters of caring for the elderly, the ill, or the disabled. The egalitarian family was structured around sexual affiliation – the assumed inevitability of heterosexual pairing and its association with reproductive destiny were expressed in family form.

On a most basic level the reforms unrealistically continued the notion of husband and wife as a couple forming the basic family core, the unit of social and political concern. It did so in a society in which the divorce rate approached 50 percent and never-married motherhood was on the rise.

Perhaps it is understandable given the dominance in the discussion about inequality between the sexes in the "public sphere" that the interaction between male and female in the family was symbolically and practically the central focus of the reformers' concern. The identified problems of male dominance and control drew the reformist energy toward hammering out the relationship between male and female prototypes, even when the nurture or care of others was the ostensible topic of inquiry. However, to recognize that there were reasons why heterosexuality was so central to feminist thinking does not mean that we can't criticize a focus on sexual affiliation as a limiting paradigm and family theory built upon it as inadequate.

However, in attempting to analyze the resilience of traditional family behavior in the face of forceful legal articulations of idealized egalitarian role assignments, we must look beyond the failure of a radical vision or the excessive naivety of feminist reformers to the public role of the private family. While the egalitarian family they envisioned may have had radical potential, the societal context in which it was launched ensured it would offer little hope for more than symbolic, rhetorical changes. We must consider the structural position of the family – the role it plays within the larger society which influences us even today in our reform efforts.

In this assessment, we move away from preoccupation with the roles of individuals within the family and concentrate on the institution of the family in regard to its role within the state – its interaction with the state. It is important to remember that the family is first and foremost a social institution. As such it is defined and given social content and definition by systems of belief or knowledge more significant than law, and with coercive potential far exceeding that of law. In this regard, the family as an institution embedded in social practice and understanding should also be understood to be resistant to redefinition.

Furthermore, individual understandings about family are shaped by societal forces and manifest them. So, while one may "choose" to live outside of the conventional norms, one does not escape them totally and the challenge is apt to be slight. No one is exempt from the implications of the culture in which they live – it influences our actions, our aspirations, our politics, and what we can see as possibilities.

Within the variety of extra-legal cultural and social systems that shape our beliefs about families there are certain core concepts or "meta-narratives" that predominate and affect law, shape and influence reform. There are two related meta-narratives about the family that are of most significance in considering the possibility of radical reformation and restructuring of the family. The first is that of the natural nature of the family – the belief that the family has a "natural" form.

This natural family form – husband, wife and child [the nuclear family] – is built around a foundational sexual affiliation which is ultimately reinforced by reproductive biology. The social construct follows the biological imperative. This natural family is postulated as predating the state. It also is expressly viewed as a complement to the state, essential for the very existence of the state. Feminist legal reformers replicated this social model of the family when they focused on male/female relationships.

The second meta-narrative is that of the private family – a unit entitled to protection and assistance from the state. This privacy has historically been conferred on the appropriately functioning family unit as a "reward" for fulfilling our societal and political expectation that the family is the natural repository for inevitable dependency. The private family is the social institution that will raise the children, care for the ill, the needy, the dependent. It ideally will be a self-contained and self-sufficient unit in accomplishing those tasks – located within the larger society, complementing the state which protects it, but not demanding public resources to do so. The idea of private family is the way the ordering of responsibility for inevitable dependency between public state and natural family is accomplished. Dependency is ideologically allocated away from the state to the private grouping.

In this regard the notion of the private family has important ideological and political currency. Its existence as an ideological construct masks and hides dependency and allows our official and public rhetoric to be spun out in terms of ideals of capitalistic individualism, independence, self-sufficiency, and autonomy. And it is significant that the ideals of self-sufficiency and autonomy operate on two levels –they become the bases of an ideal family as well as an ideal individual within our culture. Note here, of course, that a caretaker is exactly the opposite of independent and autonomous, therefore not within the construct of the ideal individual.

These two meta-narratives –that of the natural family and that of the private family – are related. They are composed of interdependent assumptions that reinforce one another on an ideological level. They perversely interact in that the societal tasks assigned in the narrative of the private family inevitably assume the role differentiated configuration of the natural family.

Privatizing dependency, in fact, mandates that "successful" natural families, as entities, will uphold the burdens of caring for dependency. To do so, the burdens or costs must be allocated and this allocation is gendered. In other words, the way we perceive the family as a social institution facilitates the continuation of gendered role divisions and frustrates the egalitarian ideal.

In order to illuminate the previous abstractions it is interesting to consider the circumstances where the social idea of the independent, natural, private family fails. There are two contemporary situations currently labeled as "problems" that call into question the continued viability of the caretaking capacities of the private-natural family. The first problem is in the tension generated by the wide acceptance among elites of the notion of the egalitarian family. The second problem is the sense of crisis surrounding the increase in the number of women from all classes and races becoming single mothers as a result of either our high divorce rate or because they never married in the first place.

The very existence of these "problems" and our inability to respond to them within the confines of our family ideology are strong evidence for assertions about the failure of the nuclear family paradigm. They illustrate that the private-natural family is no longer viable as the sole, or even primary, institutional response to dependency.

First when the egalitarian family as an articulated ideal is imposed on existing couple-based family units, it generates tensions in so far as one of the goals to be attained by the partners is equal career or market proficiency. Equality in ambition in non-family matters leaves the two-parent family an institution with potentially *no* available caretakers.

Second, the never-married or divorced single mother case presents a version of the same dilemma. Not having a designated "partner," if she devotes her time to market work to support her child she will not be available as a caretaker. However, if she fulfills her assigned obligations in bearing the burdens of dependency, she is single and there is no wage earner to support her, so she will starve or go begging to the state. In either case, her family has not privately dealt with its dependencies.

Both these situations reveal to me the inherent flaws in the concept of the private family. The tasks assigned to the private family – its societal role as the private repository of inevitable dependency – necessitate a certain form of role differentiation and division and that form seems destined to be gendered and unequal. It will assume the traditional natural form almost inevitably.

Of course, the rhetorical resolution for the potential dilemma of no caretaker in the egalitarian coupled family has been to "share" care giving. But rhetoric aside, empirical information indicates sharing is not what is happening. The figures are overwhelming – not much has changed in terms of who does domestic labor, and this is true even when both partners are employed.

In instances where it is necessary that one career be temporarily put aside, there are strong economic incentives that guide the choice. Equality fictions in the family may abound, but the reality of continuing market inequalities which result in women earning lower wages than their spouses typically dictates that the woman is the one "selected" when there is a need for a family member to accommodate caretaking by sacrificing market time, wages, and career opportunities.

In addition to this gross economic structuring of choice, centuries of social and cultural conditioning operate to shape the ways women understand the nature and scope of their "choices" in defining their own family role. Family failures in regard to children, evidenced in even minor deviations from an unattainable ideal, are most likely to be placed at a mother's feet. It is mothers in the workplace who elicit fears of generations of children abandoned to neglect and the horrors of day-care regimentation and potential abuses.

The social assignment of dependency is even more pronounced (and less challenged) when it comes to care for the elderly or ill. It is daughters to whom elderly parents look for expected accommodations.

In the case of single mothers, whether divorced or never married, the inadequacies of the private family are not capable of resolution by pretenses toward equality within the natural or nuclear unit. These families are stigmatized in response. Single mother families are consistently referred to as "deviant" and "pathological," their very existence the occasion for crime, the cause of poverty and societal decline.

The very nature of reforms in this area shows the strength of the natural and private family concepts in tandem. The reform objective for both types of single-mother families is to reconstitute the natural family in some form – to bring the male [back] in so that dependency can be properly privatized. In fact, it is striking that the figure of the male continues to be so central to our rhetoric about single mothers.

Paternity proceedings and child support enforcement are seen as the solutions to poverty. Both divorce and welfare reforms are attempts to reconfigure the natural family, bringing the father into the picture through the traditional economic connection reminiscent of his position in the hierarchical family as head of the household.

In the construction of the problems presented by and the solutions offered to both the never-married mother and the divorced mother, it is the physical absence of a man that is cast as the cause of the problem. And its solution – his metaphysical presence in the form of support and the opportunity for discipline and control will "complete" the family in some mystical way. He is the social policy offered for resolving the problems of poverty and despair. Patriarchy is reasserted, although modified to meet new social realities.

My response to the meta-narratives of the natural and the private family is not only to point out that we must consider them failures, but to call for some radical re-visioning of the problems and potential solutions to guide our reforms when thinking about what will happen in the next century. I want to reconceptualize the family narratives with a few basic principles in mind. For example, I think we must abandon pretenses toward achieving equality through family law reform. The egalitarian family myth remains largely unassisted by other ideological and structural changes in the larger society and is belied by the statistics reflecting the ways people live.

We should begin to explicitly think of family policy as a form of state regulation in terms of making decisions about what should be protected and what should be encouraged through social and economic subsidies. Furthermore, family policy must be secular, not based on one religious model. It should reference the functional aspirations we have for families in our society and be supportive of those aspirations. In this regard, I argue for a dependency-based rather than our traditional sexually-based family model around which to build policy. In this way, we would have to focus on the restructuring of the relationship between the state and the family, consider the position of the family within the state.

My concrete suggestions consistent with these principles are not extensive in number at this time (although they may be viewed as radical in scope). First, I think we should abolish marriage as a legal category and with it any privilege based on sexual affiliation. There would be no special rules governing the relationships between husband and wife as there are now in family law. Instead, the consequences of interactions would be governed by the same sets of rules that regulate other interactions in our society – specifically those of contract and property as well as tort and criminal law. The illusive equality between adults in sexual and all other areas would thus be asserted and assumed, a result which is symbolically pleasing to many.

Furthermore, sexual interactions would be of no concern to the state since there would no longer be a state preferred model of family intimacy to protect and support. All adult sexual relationships would be permitted – nothing prohibited – nothing privileged.

I also feel that abolition of marriage is necessary. If the institution of marriage remains, it will continue to be paradigmatic. Its existence will define other relationships as deviant and will determine the standard against which people will want to measure their own non-marital relationships.

In response to potential questions about the fate of the "weak" members of society – those in need of protection, I would give new content to the "family" configuration entitled to special, preferred treatment. The new family line would be drawn around dependency. Specifically, I envision a redistribution or reallocation of social and economic subsidies now given to the natural family allowing it to function "independently" within society. Family and welfare law would be reconceived so as to support caretaking as the family intimacy norm.

This re-envisioning reflects current empirical and social reality as to evolving family form. Instead of being a society where our ideals and our ideology (the private-natural family) are out of sync with the real lives of many of our citizens, we would become a society that recognized and accepted the inevitability of dependency. We would face, value, and therefore, subsidize caretaking and caretakers.

Of course, rethinking on this scale is a quite grandiose objective, requiring massive reconsideration of many assumed roles and institutions on an ideological level as well as a structural level. It is certainly utopian to assume that such an endeavor will be undertaken, or, even if it is, that it would result in a significant shift in the way we as a society order intimacy. We can be sure that change will not occur any time soon (or any time at all).

It is important to note that in using the term utopianism I apply it to the possibility of ideological change. It is not a label appropriate to reference to the single-parent family form at the center of my analysis – that form is a growing reality. My argument is that our ideology of the family should conform to these new families and confront and accommodate the need for change they represent. But change is hard and if it's to occur at all we need a powerful imagery with which to propel and project the possibility of change. Abandoning myself to ideological utopianism, I have concluded that there is only one cultural metaphor powerful enough to combat the private-natural family with sexual affiliation at its center.

I selected what to me was the most vivid and shared countervailing image of connection in order to set out the lines for a redefinition of intimacy – the Mother/Child unit. This is the prototypical nurturing unit, a fitting substitute for the Husband/Wife unit – the sexual family affiliation – as the new core or basic family paradigm. Our new, "special," family-law rules would focus on the needs of this unit. Mother/Child would provide the structural and ideological basis for the transfer of societal subsidies (both material and ideological) away from the sexual family to nurturing units.

I have chosen not to make my alternative vision gender neutral, using terms such as "caretaker" and "dependent." Historically and in terms of its cultural cache, "mothering" is both a gendered concept and, partly for that reason, is qualitatively different than terms currently (incorrectly) substituted for it, such as "caretaker." I realize that affirmatively introducing Mother into a feminist debate will be considered by many to be too dangerous, but I believe it is essential.

Motherhood has unrealized power – power to challenge the hold of sexuality on our thinking about intimacy which is why men have tried for so long to control its meaning. Mother/Child is a metaphor for a specific ethical position or practice for the exercise of social and emotional responsibility. The strength of the image is in its redistributive potential, grounded on empirical evidence ("reality") about the need for and the assumption of caretaking.

Two additional theoretical caveats are necessary. First, I believe that men can and should be mothers. In fact, if men are interested in acquiring legal rights to access to children (or other dependents), I argue they must be mothers in the stereotypical nurturing sense of that term. Second, the "child" in my dyad stands for all forms of inevitable dependency – the dependency of the ill, the elderly, etc.

Mother and child would combat the grip on our collective imaginations of the private, natural family with its centrality of sexual affiliation. This unit, graced as the new family norm, would provide the structural and ideological unit to which societal subsidies (material and ideological) would be transferred –our special family law rules, no longer oriented around protecting sexual families would bolster nurturing units. This is my vision for the twenty-first century.

Chapter 7

A Claim for Justice (1995)[1]

In this conclusion of *The Neutered Mother, the Sexual Family and Other Twentieth Century Tragedies*, Fineman discusses how conceptions of power and justice operate to reinforce the traditional social and legal definitions of the family. She urges us to consider a more just approach to family law.

On an ideological level, our understandings of justice are inseparable from our concepts of appropriateness or naturalness when discussing the family. Our appreciation of the implications of grand theoretical concepts, such as justice, is dependent upon our understanding of the effects and influences of power. Our societal sense of what constitutes justice for families as social entities, as well as our conclusions about what is just when conflicts must be resolved within families, are formulated in the context of existing, historically legitimated relations of power. Our definition and acceptance of the family as a legal and, perhaps to a somewhat lesser extent, social institution, and the acceptance of assigned roles to individual family members reflect the contemporary (and temporal) resolution of struggles of power and dominance.

Conversely, our experience of power is filtered through our perception of justice. Justice is the societal conclusion legitimating and condoning what might otherwise be viewed as inappropriate coercive maintenance of certain traditional family forms and expressions of individual power within families. Society's sense of justice allows the state to condemn alternatives to the preferred family arrangement as "deviant" and to subject them to exercises of state power that would not typically be condoned if directed toward traditional entities. The process of securing and maintaining state norms in regard to families reveals an interesting interaction between appeals to dominant cultural and social stereotypes and the process of law making and reform.

To be a "just" society, we must treat "all" families with respect and concern at the same time that we realize that the traditional family is not a panacea for

1 This essay is used with permission of Taylor & Francis Group LLC, from The Neutered Mother, The Sexual Family, and Other Twentieth Century Tragedies, Martha Albertson Fineman, 1995; permission conveyed through Copyright Clearance Center, Inc.

DOI: 10.4324/9781003405627-10

the problems society faces. Our approach to the question of inevitable and derivative dependencies is crucial to the project of societal definition. The family can no longer be an assumed institution in policy discussions, but must be an explicitly self-conscious, constantly reconsidered configuration that reflects both existing reality and collective responsibility.

Part III

Dependency

Michael Thomson

As this skillfully curated collection demonstrates, a constant within the four decades of Martha Albertson Fineman's academic practice has been a concern to radically rewrite how the state and other actors understand and respond to human life and experience. From the earliest work represented here – challenging orthodoxies around gender equality – to her ground-breaking work on vulnerability, Fineman has challenged how the individual is imagined in legal (and other) discourses and practices. Within an overarching desire to make law more responsive to human lived experience, she has challenged America's ossified "founding myths," attending instead to what these obscure or erase. Key to this has been a career-long focus on dependency. In this, Fineman has sought to naturalize dependency, "a universal and inevitable" part of being human.[1] She has sought not only to destigmatize dependency – it "is neither contingent, nor deviant"[2] – but also to embrace it for its generative effects. In a volume that addresses Fineman's work to date, it is unsurprising, therefore, that dependency is the concept addressed at its very center.

The place of dependency as a "golden thread" running through her conceptual and political innovation began with early work on key family-law reform questions of the 1980s and 1990s. Here, Fineman challenged the liberal feminist discourse of formal equality, focusing a spotlight on the economic dependency arising from the socio-economic factors that limited women's participation in the marketplace.[3] This work addresses the stigmatizing of dependency and the way in which this delegitimizes the lived experience and material needs of most women. Foreshadowing a method repeated in the decades to come, Fineman argued that our conceptual and regulatory tools should draw on lived experience rather than abstract concepts or ideals. In her work on

1 Martha Albertson Fineman, *Cracking the Foundational Myths: Independence, Autonomy, and Self-Sufficiency*, 8 AM. U. J. GENDER SOC. POL'Y & L. 13, 16, 18 (2000).
2 Martha Albertson Fineman, *Reasoning from the Body: Universal Vulnerability and Social Justice, in* A JURISPRUDENCE OF THE BODY 17, 27 (C. Dietz, M. Travis, & M. Thomson eds., 2020).
3 MARTHA FINEMAN, THE ILLUSION OF EQUALITY: THE RHETORIC AND REALITY OF DIVORCE REFORM (1991).

DOI: 10.4324/9781003405627-12

dependency and vulnerability, she also demonstrates how attention to such experience – and what it means to be human – can mean doing the hard work of taking words and concepts from which we've been alienated and recuperating them in the struggle for greater social justice.

The attention to dependency continued to be honed in her engagement with the gravitational effects of the nuclear family within family law and policy. In *The Neutered Mother*, Fineman argued against the primacy afforded two individual adults, and an alternative centering of the Mother/Child dyad.[4] In elevating this relationship of care and dependency in a radical and provocative reconceptualization of family law, Fineman highlights how dependency is an inevitable element of the human condition and a necessary part of social organization. Nevertheless, the state has been inattentive to this, still engaging in fantasies of independence and self-sufficiency. As she writes, "[j]ustice requires constant mediation between articulated historic values and current realities."[5]

As dependency surfaced more directly within her work, so did the need to fully set out how we might understand and respond to this universal human experience. In this work, Fineman argues for recognition of dependency as an inevitable and universal part of human embodied existence. However, dependency was not only a singular ontological fact, it was also derivative as caretakers were necessarily dependent on others for economic support. Fineman argues that this dual model of inevitable and derivative forms of dependence should structure governmental action. This would recognize the social debt to caretakers for the necessary public role they fulfil in social reproduction, acknowledging that care is "fundamentally society preserving."[6] As much necessary care work takes place in the private family, this should become the focus for state responsibility and subsidy.

As already noted, dependency may be characterized as one of the "golden threads" that runs through Fineman's work and its egalitarian imperative. It ties early work on gender equality in law to later political theory that challenges the reification of personal autonomy and reimagines the architecture of state responsibility. Across this work, a significant focus is the "fictive figure"[7] of the liberal legal subject; that "autonomous, independent being along the lines of Lockean lore."[8] Shaped when our current world and lives were unimaginable, this "limited and disingenuous vision of legal subjectivity"[9] has inhabited and

4 MARTHA ALBERTSON FINEMAN, THE NEUTERED MOTHER, THE SEXUAL FAMILY AND OTHER TWENTIETH CENTURY TRAGEDIES (1995).

5 Fineman, *supra* note 1, at 16.

6 Fineman, *supra* note 1, at 19, 20.

7 Sam Lewis & Michael Thomson, *Social Bodies & Social Justice*, 15 INT. J. LAW CONTEXT 344 (2019).

8 Martha Albertson Fineman, *Injury in the Unresponsive State, in* INJURY AND INJUSTICE: THE CULTURAL POLITICS OF HARM AND REDRESS 50, 57 (A. Bloom, D. Engel, & M. McCann eds., 2018).

9 Fineman, *supra* note 2, at 33.

impaired the governing imaginaries of law and politics for over 200 years.[10] This figure has helped to erase care and caretaking as essential social activities, and contributed to the unintelligibility of certain corporealities, embodied ways of being, and harms.[11] It underpins the rhetoric of personal responsibility that denies our dependency and the legitimacy of reliance on the institutions of the state.[12] Fineman's most recent work has, of course, focused on the vulnerable subject as a "more inclusive and realistic legal subject." This alternative figure foregrounds the fact that "injury and injustice ... inevitably arise when the state remains unresponsive to human vulnerability and dependency."[13] It is perhaps her most compelling challenge to the "ideological placebos of independence, autonomy and self-sufficiency."[14]

The vulnerable subject is built on the twin pillars of our ontological or embodied vulnerability and our embeddedness in institutions and relationships. Vulnerability is "a universal, inevitable, enduring aspect of the human condition."[15] This universal experience of vulnerability has driven us to build social institutions to help mitigate our vulnerability and build resilience. This includes health, educational, and social welfare institutions. Importantly, we are dependent on these social institutions, which then drives the logic of the approach: "a vulnerability approach is primarily focused on exploring the differences and dependencies that arise from the fact that we are embedded within society and its institutions."[16] Thus, Fineman articulates a framework in which the state is "tasked with a responsibility to establish and monitor social institutions and relationships that facilitate the acquisition of individual and social resilience." This is essential as our positions within this complex network of relationships "profoundly affect our destinies and fortunes, structuring individual options and creating or impeding opportunities."[17] This focus on our dependency on formal and informal institutions and relationships has led Fineman's model of vulnerability to be characterized as "vulnerability as dependency."[18]

Within and across Fineman's work, "simplified pejorative notions"[19] of dependence are challenged and its essential and generative forces embraced. Thus, Fineman has attended to inevitable and derivative forms of dependency

10 Fineman, *supra* note 8, at 57.
11 Michael Thomson, *Health Inequalities: Law and the Pain of Others*, SOCIAL & LEGAL STUDIES (2022).
12 MARTHA ALBERTSON FINEMAN, THE AUTONOMY MYTH: A THEORY OF DEPENDENCY (2004).
13 Martha Albertson Fineman, *Vulnerability and Inevitable Inequality*, 4 OSLO LAW REVIEW 133, 149 (2017).
14 Fineman, *supra* note 12, at 6.
15 Martha Albertson Fineman, *The Vulnerable Subject: Anchoring Equality in the Human Condition*, 20 YALE J.L & FEMINISM 1, 8 (2008).
16 Martha Albertson Fineman, *Vulnerability, Resilience, and LGBT Youth*, 23 TEMP. POL. & CIV. RTS. L. REV. 307, 318 (2014).
17 Fineman, *supra* note 13, at 134, 145.
18 HANK TEN HAVE, VULNERABILITY: CHALLENGING BIOETHICS 101 (2016).
19 Fineman, supra note 1, at 17.

as a way of revaluing care and caretaking. She has also centered the fact that dependency has led us to come together and build social institutions that respond to this inevitable human experience. In both instances, attention to dependency has been central to persuasive accounts of how a state might be more responsive to human lived experience and need. In this, dependency has underpinned the work of one of the most influential legal scholars of our era.

Chapter 8

A Dystopian Fantasy (2000)[1]

Here, Fineman engages in a rhetorical exercise intended to reveal the shortcomings and fallacies of America's foundational "myths" of autonomy, independence, and self-sufficiency. Through an imaginary world in which America is a true meritocracy, she illuminates the inequality and privilege that constrain opportunity and invites us to imagine a more just society.

I want to offer a dystopian fantasy in which I imagine what changes would have to be made in order to really foster our self-proclaimed national ideals of independence, autonomy, and self-sufficiency. I contend that if we seriously want a world in which each individual is assumed to stand alone, to rise or fall on his or her individual merit, and be beholden to no one for her or his success, we must shape our policies so as to facilitate that model of society. As it stands now, we give lip service to the ideals in a world where policy and law protect and perpetuate existing and historic inequality, a world where some individuals are subsidized and supported in their "independence," while other individuals are left mired in poverty or burdened by responsibilities not equitably shared.

For example, a society that truly sought independence as an ideal for individuals should institute a 100 percent inheritance tax. It seems obvious that inherited wealth carries with it the potential to corrupt individual initiative. Not only do we risk removing incentive with inheritance, we also distort the meritocracy. People should not be deprived of the opportunity to demonstrate their inherent merit and worth because they are burdened by the wealth of their fathers.

Of course, inherited wealth is not the only distorting factor that interferes with independence and the realization of a true meritocracy. There are also existing and unequal economic and social advantages, and it is unlikely that they will ever be totally eradicated. I struggled with how to address this fact and concluded that a lottery system is the most appropriate and just way to distribute disparate social goods. The lottery would not eliminate differences in social conditions, but advantages and disadvantages would be distributed by

1 This essay originally appeared in: Martha Albertson Fineman, *Cracking the Foundational Myths: Independence, Autonomy, and Self-Sufficiency*, 8 AM. U. J. GENDER SOC. POL'Y & L. 13, 27–29 (2000).

DOI: 10.4324/9781003405627-11

chance. Although this might eventually ensure a much more level playing field, I am willing, for the purposes of this exercise, to concede that social equality is not attainable. If that is so, and we believe that each individual can demonstrate merit and ability independent of the burdens presented by social and economic contexts, we can at least democratize or randomize the process whereby benefits and burdens are disbursed.

For example, if we wanted to put each individual to the test, we might at birth assign each child a social security number along with a list of the professions they might legitimately pursue, appropriately grouped into categories, such as "service worker" or "professional." We could also assign the schools they would be permitted to attend. If an individual was not inclined to be satisfied with her or his lot later in life, she or he would have to find a willing person with whom to bargain or trade in order to alter the luck of the draw. To further equalize contexts, perhaps each child should be compelled to spend time in a number of different neighborhoods during childhood – two or three years in Westchester County would be balanced by equivalent time in Harlem, Alabama, Ohio, and California.

The point of this exercise is not to suggest seriously that this is what anyone would want, but to point out that context does matter. We do not begin our lives in equal circumstances but in unequal contexts. Society's winners and losers become so, in large part, because of benefits and privileges or disadvantages and burdens conferred by family position and unequal distribution of social and economic goods. The approach to a resolution to this type of inequality is not found in simplistic and hypocritical prescriptions, ideological placebos of independence, autonomy, and self-sufficiency.

Chapter 9

Dependency and Social Debt

Cracking the Foundational Myths (2000)[1]

In one of her most cited works, Fineman presents her foundational theories of dependency, collective responsibility, and state responsiveness. She subverts the stigmatization of dependency and subsidy, arguing that we are all dependent and lead subsidized lives. As such, she establishes that the mostly private and invisible work of caretakers in managing this dependency is, in fact, vital to the continuation of society. Dependency and caretaking, Fineman argues, should be the basis of state responsibility and subsidy.

Here, I will bring into view the family, or more explicitly, the dependency hidden within the assumed family. Policy development and social theory considerations should center on assessing the appropriateness of the aspirations and expectations we have for the family. This assessment is crucial to one of the most compelling problems facing society at the end of the Twentieth Century-the increasing inequitable and unequal distribution of societal resources and the corresponding poverty of women and children.

Collective Responsibility

Perhaps the most important task for those concerned with the welfare of poor mothers and their children, as well as other vulnerable members of society, is the articulation of a *theory* of collective responsibility for dependency. The idea of collective responsibility must be developed as a claim of "right" or entitlement to support and accommodation on the part of caretakers. It must be grounded on an appreciation of the value of caretaking labor. A further important concern is to ensure that any *theory* of collective responsibility does not concede the right of collective control over individual intimate decisions, such as whether and when to reproduce or how to form one's family.

The rhetorical and ideological rigidity with which contemporary policy debates have been conducted makes the claim of collective responsibility a

1 This essay originally appeared in: Martha Albertson Fineman, *Cracking the Foundational Myths: Independence, Autonomy, and Self-Sufficiency*, 8 AM. U. J. GENDER SOC. POL'Y & L. 13, 15–27 (2000).

DOI: 10.4324/9781003405627-13

particularly difficult task at the end of the twentieth century. Core components of America's founding myths, such as the sacredness of individual independence, autonomy, and self-sufficiency have been ossified, used as substitutes for analysis, and eclipsed rather than illuminated debate. I do not reject these core concepts. I do, however, insist that we have a responsibility to re-examine them in the context of our present society and the needs and aspirations of people today. We must view these ideals with the complexity they deserve, perhaps redefining them in the process. A commitment to a process of ongoing re-examination of core concepts recognizes that, even if we are absolutely confident (which we are not) that we know the historical meaning, the demands of justice, as well as perceptions of legitimacy, require that our implementation of foundational principles resonate in the current realities of our lives.

Justice requires constant mediation between articulated historic values and current realities. It is not found in abstract pronouncements. Our understanding of independence, autonomy, and self-sufficiency, therefore, should be evolving as societal knowledge, realizations, aspirations, and circumstances change. Unfortunately, the political and governmental institutions that should be facilitating and encouraging debate and reconsideration are currently partisan and polarizing in the methods they use and, thus, are actually impeding understanding and exploration.

Dependency and Social Debt

Historic ideals of independence and self-sufficiency are complementary themes in our political discourse. These aspirational ideals are applied to individuals as well as to families. Their dichotomous terms, dependence and subsidy, are also complementary, viewed as occurring in tandem. Both dependence and subsidy have been successfully used in a simplistic and divisive manner by politicians, social conservatives, and advocates of small government to control and limit contemporary policy discussions.

Dependence is negatively compared with the desirable status of independence – subsidy with the meritorious self-sufficiency. Independence and self-sufficiency are set up as transcendent values, attainable aspirations for all members of society. Simplified pejorative notions of dependence and subsidy are joined, and condemnation or pity are considered appropriate responses for those unable to live up to the ideals, particularly those who are dependent and in need of subsidy.

In fact, dependency is assumed if an individual is the recipient of certain governmental subsidies. Furthermore, the mere label of dependency serves as an argument against governmental social welfare transfers. Policy makers argue that the goal should be independence and favor the termination of subsidy so the individual can learn to be self-sufficient.

It is puzzling, as well as paradoxical, that the term dependency has such negative connotations. Its very existence prompts and justifies mean-spirited and ill-conceived political responses, such as welfare "reform."[2] Far from being pathological, avoidable, and the result of individual failings, dependency is a universal and inevitable part of the human development. It is inherent in the human condition.

All of us were dependent as children, and many of us will be dependent as we age, become ill, or suffer disabilities. In this sense, dependency is "inevitable" and not deserving of condemnation or stigma. Note that the examples I have chosen to illustrate this category of inevitable dependency are biological or physical in nature. Biological dependencies, however, do not exhaust the potential range of situations of dependence. For example, in addition to biological dependence, one may be psychologically or emotionally dependent on others. In fact, these other forms of dependence may even accompany the physiological or biological dependence, which I have labeled inevitable. But economic, psychological, and emotional dependency are not generally understood to be universally experienced. As a result, assertions about their inevitability in each individual's life would be controversial. It is the characteristic of universality (which indisputably accompanies inevitable dependence) that is central to my argument for societal or collective responsibility. In other words, the realization that biological dependency is both inevitable and universal is theoretically important. Upon this foundational realization is built my claim for justice – the demand that society value and accommodate the labor done by the caretakers of inevitable dependents.

I argue that the caretaking work creates a collective or societal debt. Each and every member of society is obligated by this debt. Furthermore, this debt transcends individual circumstances. In other words, we need not be elderly, ill, or children any longer to be held individually responsible. Nor can we satisfy or discharge our collective responsibility within our individual, private families. Merely being financially generous with our own mothers or duly supporting our own wives will not suffice to satisfy our share of the societal debt generally owed to all caretakers.

My argument that the caretaking debt is a collective one is based on the fact that biological dependency is inherent to the human condition, and therefore, of necessity of collective or societal concern. Just as individual dependency needs must be met if an individual is to survive, collective dependency needs must be met if a society is to survive and perpetuate itself. The mandate that the state (collective society) respond to dependency, therefore, is not a matter of altruism

2 One prominent example is the "Personal Responsibility and Work Opportunity Reconciliation Act" of 1996. This legislation, signed by President Clinton, made receipt of welfare benefits contingent upon employment (a "work requirement"), placed lifetime limits on federal funds received, and loosened oversight of state welfare programs. Upon signing the bill, Clinton remarked that it "gives us a chance we haven't had before to break the cycle of dependency that has existed for millions and millions of our fellow citizens." Andrew Glass, *Clinton Signs 'Welfare to Work' Bill, Aug. 22, 1996*, Politico (Aug. 22, 2018), https://www.politico.com/story/2018/08/22/clinton-signs-welfare-to-work-bill-aug-22-1996-790321. (Note added by editor.)

or empathy (which are individual responses often resulting in charity), but one that is primary and essential because such a response is fundamentally society-preserving.

If infants or ill persons are not cared for, nurtured, nourished, and perhaps loved, they will perish. We can say, therefore, that they owe an individual debt to their individual caretakers. But the obligation is not theirs alone – nor is their obligation confined to their own caretakers. A sense of social justice demands a broader sense of obligation. Without aggregate caretaking, there could be no society, so we might say that it is caretaking labor that produces and reproduces society. Caretaking labor provides the citizens, the workers, the voters, the consumers, the students, and others who populate society and its institutions. The uncompensated labor of caretakers is an unrecognized subsidy, not only to the individuals who directly receive it, but more significantly, to the entire society.

Institutions and Dependency

Society preserving tasks, like dependency work, are commonly delegated. The delegation is accomplished through the establishment and maintenance of societal institutions. For example, the armed services are established to attend to the collective need for national defense. But delegation is not the same thing as abandonment. The armed services are structured simultaneously as both the responsibility of only some designated members (volunteers or draftees) and of all members of society (taxpayers and voters).

This dual and complementary responsibility is consistent with our deeply held beliefs about how rights and obligations are accrued and imposed in a just society – collective obligations have both an individual and a collective dimension. Certain members of society may be recruited, volunteer, or even be drafted for service, but they have a right to be compensated for their services from collective resources. They also have a right to the necessary tools to perform their assigned tasks and to guarantees that they will be protected by rules and policies that facilitate their performance. Caretakers should have the same right to have their society-preserving labor supported and facilitated. Provision of the means for their task should be considered the responsibility of the collective society.

Society has not, however, responded this way to caretaking. The most common form of social accommodation for dependency has been its assignment to the institution of the private family. Within that family, dependency has been further delegated as the individual responsibility of the family equivalent of volunteer or draftee – the person in the gendered role of mother (or grandmother or daughter or daughter-in-law or wife or sister). But the resources necessary for caretaking have not been considered to be the responsibility of the collective society. Instead, each individual private family is ideally and ideologically perceived as responsible for its own members and their dependency. A need to call on collective resources, such as welfare assistance, is considered a family as well as an individual failure, deserving of condemnation and stigma.

Derivative Dependency

The assignment of responsibility for the burdens of dependency to the family in the first instance, and within the family to women, operates in an unjust manner because this arrangement has significant negative material consequences for the caretaker. This obvious observation allows me to introduce an additional, but often overlooked, form of dependency into the argument-"derivative dependency." Derivative dependency arises on the part of the person who assumes responsibility for the care of the inevitable dependent person. I refer to this form of dependency as derivative to capture the very simple point that those who care for others are themselves dependent on resources in order to undertake that care. Caretakers have a need for monetary or material resources. They also need recourse to institutional supports and accommodation, a need for structural arrangements that facilitate caretaking.

Currently, neither the economic nor the structural supports for caretaking are adequate. Many caretakers and their dependents find themselves impoverished or severely economically compromised. Some of their economic problems stem from the fact that within families, caretaking work is unpaid and not considered worthy of social subsidies. There are also, however, direct costs associated with caretaking. Caretaking labor interferes with the pursuit and development of wage labor options. Caretaking labor saps energy and efforts from investment in career or market activities, those things that produce economic rewards. There are foregone opportunities and costs associated with caretaking, and even caretakers who work in the paid labor force typically have more tenuous ties to the public sphere because they must also accommodate caretaking demands in the private. These costs are not distributed among all beneficiaries of caretaking (institutional or individual). Unjustly, the major economic and career costs associated with caretaking are typically borne by the caretaker alone.

Further, most institutions in society remain relatively unresponsive to innovations that would lessen the costs of caretaking. Caretaking occurs in a larger context and caretakers often need accommodation in order to fulfill multiple responsibilities. For example, many caretakers also engage in market work.[3] Far from structurally accommodating or facilitating caretaking, however, workplaces operate in modes incompatible with the idea that workers also have obligations for dependency. Workplace expectations compete with the demands of caretaking – we assume that workers are those independent and autonomous individuals who are free to work long and regimented hours.

In discussing the costs and impediments associated with undertaking the tasks of caretaking, it is important to emphasize that, unlike inevitable dependency, derivative dependency is not a universal experience. In fact, many people in our

3 *See* Julie Novkov, *A Deconstruction of Motherhood and a Reconstruction of Parenthood*, 19 N.Y.U. REV. L. & SOC. CHANGE 155, 165–66 (1991) (discussing the roles of working mothers).

society totally escape the burdens and costs that arise from assuming a caretaking role, perhaps even freed for other pursuits by the caretaking labor of others. The status of derivative dependency is structured by and through existing societal institutions, culturally and socially assigned according to a script rooted in ideologies, particularly those of capitalism and patriarchy. These scripts function at an unconscious (and therefore, unexamined) level, and channel our beliefs and feelings about what is considered natural and what are appropriate institutional arrangements. When individuals act according to these scripts, consistent with prevailing ideology and institutional arrangements, we say they have chosen their path from the available options. The construction of this notion of individual choice allows us to avoid general responsibility for the inequity and justify the maintenance of the status quo. We ignore the fact that individual choice occurs within the constraints of social conditions. These constraints include ideology, history, and tradition, all of which funnel decisions into prescribed channels and often operate in a practical and symbolic manner to limit options.

As it now stands in this society, derivative dependents are expected to get both economic and structural resources within the family. The market is unresponsive and uninvolved, and the state is perceived as a last resort for financial resources, the refuge of the failed family. A caretaker who must resort to governmental assistance may do so only if she can demonstrate that she is needy in a highly stigmatized process.

Subsidy

In popular and political discourse, the idea of "subsidy" is viewed as an equally negative companion to dependence, the opposite of the ideal of self-sufficiency. But a subsidy is nothing more than the process of allocating collective resources to some persons or endeavors rather than other persons or endeavors because a social judgment is made that they are in some way "entitled" or the subsidy is justified. Entitlement to subsidy is asserted through a variety of justifications, such as the status of the persons receiving the subsidy, their past contributions to the social good, or their needs. Often, subsidy is justified because of the position the subsidized persons hold or the potential value of the endeavor they have undertaken to the larger society.

Typically, subsidy is thought of as the provision of monetary or economic assistance. But subsidy can also be delivered through the organization of social structures and norms that create and enforce expectations. Taking this observation into account, along with the earlier discussion of inevitable and derivative dependency, it seems obvious that we must conclude that subsidy is also universal. We all exist in context, in social and cultural institutions, such as families, which facilitate, support, and subsidize us and our endeavors.

In complex modern societies no one is self-sufficient, either economically or socially. We all live subsidized lives. Sometimes the benefits we receive are public and financial, such as in governmental direct transfer programs to certain individuals like farmers or sugar growers.[4] Public subsidies can also be indirect, such as the benefits given in tax policy.[5] Private economic subsidy systems work in the forms of foundations, religions, and charities. But a subsidy can also be non-monetary, such as the subsidy provided by the uncompensated labor of others in caring for us and our dependency needs.

It seems clear that all of us receive one or the other or both types of subsidy throughout our lives. The interesting question in our subsidy-shaped society, therefore, has to be why only some subsidies are differentiated and stigmatized while others are hidden. In substantial part, subsidies are hidden when they are not called subsidy (or welfare, or the dole), but termed "investments," "incentives," or "earned" when they are supplied by government, and called "gifts," "charity," or the product of familial "love" when they are contributions of caretaking labor.

A More Responsive State

In order to rethink how we might constitute a just system for handling dependency, our society must move beyond simplistic catch words and engage in a nationwide debate. What types of mechanisms can generate and sustain such a series of discussions? Shaped by the successes of early feminist consciousness-raising techniques, which proved powerful in challenging entrenched ideas and assumptions about gender roles, I advocate for a national consciousness raising process. We need a forum for vigorous debate. The forum must not only be public in the sense that it will be created and supported by government, but also public in the sense that it will be participatory and beyond governmental control, inclusive, and not politically partisan in composition.

It is important that the forum be a public responsibility (as antiquated and quaint as that idea seems at this point in our national history). In recent decades, it has become apparent that the role of the state has been overtaken by the presumed inevitability of market forces. As more and more is conceded to privatization, we are rapidly losing any sense of public responsibility. Even public education is in danger of falling victim to the privatizing siege. Missing from our discourse is strong support for an active or responsive state of the kind I am trying to imagine – the public as a mediating force against private, obscured excesses and exploitation.

Although it was less successful than it might have been, President Clinton's initiative on race offers some ideas for how the government might fulfill its public responsibility to generate discussion on important national issues. A

4 *See* Kenneth A. Cook, *The Cash Cropper* (visited July 11, 1999) http://www.ewg.org/ pub/home/reports/Croppers/Chapter_l.html (calculating billions of dollars of Federal payments made through the United States Department of Agriculture (USDA) subsidy programs, including farm programs, conservation programs, and disaster programs).

5 *See* Daniel S. Goldberg, *Tax Subsidies: One-Time vs. Periodic, An Economic Analysis of the Tax Policy Alternatives*, 49 TAX L. REV. 305, 306–7 (1994) (discussing the elements of tax subsidies).

commission was created, made responsible for developing, encouraging, and publicizing public discussions on racial problems, as well as issuing a report on the "state of the nation" in regard to race. While the report suggested some ongoing initiatives that might be helpful, one tremendous benefit of the exercise was that it put people face to face in high school gyms and public halls across the country and encouraged them to talk about race.[6]

Reflecting on this process, I could not help but think that perhaps welfare reform would have taken a very different form if the President had employed the same mechanism in regard to the need and direction for reform. I imagine that we could have generated a series of thoughtful, factually informed, and depoliticized national discussions about the nature and implications of dependency in all its complexity to counter the inaccurate and ideologically driven sloganeering that passed for political debate. We may have even begun as a nation to realize that the real measure of any welfare reform should be whether it positively improved the welfare of all our children. We might have even reached a consensus that there is a collective as well as an individual, parental responsibility for children. The point might have been made that, in today's world, independence and self-sufficiency require a minimal amount of social resources (structural and monetary), and the amount required increases when one has responsibility for the care of others. Dependency on resources and/or on caretakers is not a unique position in which to find oneself; it is a universal, and therefore, unifying experience.

All of this might not have happened, of course. But at a minimum, important questions that need to be resolved and discussed in a very public forum would have been raised:

1 How should the need for caretaking resources be satisfied so that caretakers can act independently, make decisions, and fulfill societal expectations in ways that best respond to their individual circumstances?
2 Should caretakers be primarily dependent on the family in this regard?
3 Given the tenuous status of marriage in this society (where the divorce rate hovers near 50 percent[7] and women are expected to be wage earners, as well as wives and mothers) how can we continue to have a traditional model of the family served up by politicians as the solution to poverty?
4 Shouldn't the richest country in the history of the world have a family policy that goes beyond marriage as the solution for dependency?

6 *See One America: The President's Initiative on Race*, One America on the Move (visited July 11, 1999) https://clinton.presidentiallibraries.us/items/show/88820 (listing the Clinton Administration's efforts to establish national fora for addressing concerns relating to race).

7 *See generally Marriage, Divorce, and Remarriage in the 1990's*, U.S. BUREAU OF THE CENSUS, CURRENT POPULATION REPORTS, 23–180 (1992) (reporting that younger people in the United States who are marrying for the first time face roughly a 40–50 percent chance of divorcing in their lifetime under current trends).

5 Specifically, doesn't the family as it exists today require substantial assistance from other societal institutions?
6 Is it fair that the market and the state (which are totally dependent on caretaking labor and in no way self-sufficient or independent from caretaking) escape responsibility for dependency and continue to be free-loaders (or free riders) on the backs of caretakers and families?
7 Isn't it time to redistribute some responsibility for dependency, mandating that state and market bear their fair share of the burden?

As a result of such discussion, the very terms of independence and self-sufficiency might well be redefined or reimagined in the public mind. Independence is not the same as being unattached. Independence from subsidy and support is not attainable, nor is it desirable – we want and need the contexts that sustain us. A different understanding of independence is needed and attainable. Independence is gained when an individual has the basic resources that enable her or him to act consistent with the tasks and expectations imposed by society. This form of independence should be every citizen's birthright, but independence in this sense can only be achieved when individual choices are relatively unconstrained by inequalities, particularly those inequalities that arise from poverty. Independence, as well as justice, requires that those who are assigned a vital societal function are also provided with the wherewithal to do those tasks. This is a state or collective responsibility and may not be relegated to potentially exploitative private institutions.

The Active State

In order to move from our current situation to a more just resolution for the dilemma of caretaking and dependency, we will need more than a responsive state. The state will also have to be an active participant in shaping and monitoring other societal institutions. One fundamental task will be monitoring and preventing the exploitation and appropriation of the labor of some citizens through institutional and ideological arrangements. This must be prevented even when the justification for the labor's appropriation and exploitation is that it is used for the good of the majority. Further, it must be prevented even in contexts where social constraints and conventions coerce consent from the laborer.

In this endeavor, the state must use its regulatory and redistributive authority to ensure that those things that are not valued or are undervalued in market or marriage are, nonetheless, publicly and politically recognized as socially productive and given value. Conferral of value requires the transfer of some economic resources from the collective society to caretakers through the establishment of mechanisms that tax those who receive the benefits of caretaking in order to compensate those who do the caretaking. Other societies do this in a variety of ways, such as using tax revenues to provide childcare allowances and universal benefits that assist caretakers, or through a basic income guarantee. Money, however, is not enough. The active state must also structure accommodation of the needs of caretaking into society's institutions.

The fact is that today, some workers must shoulder the burdens assigned to the family, while market institutions are relieved of such responsibility (even free to punish workers who have trouble combining market and domestic labor). The state must ensure that market institutions positively respond to dependency burdens. Workers cannot be assumed independent and unencumbered. Quite often, they are dually responsible for economic and caretaking activities. Restructuring workplaces to reflect that reality would more equitably distribute the burdens for dependency and forge a more just relationship between family and market institutions.

Chapter 10

The New Tokenism (1999)[1]

Here, Fineman discusses the operation of a "new tokenism" in the legal profession; one in which women comprise nearly half of the profession but are constrained by the "inherently masculine" legal institution.

I want to discuss a seeming anomaly: women's presence in law seems to have made little difference to the operation and formation of legal structures and institutions. I also want to elaborate on some hopeful developments associated with feminist explorations and challenges to historic representations about the nature and substance of law itself.

When we look at contemporary legal institutions, obviously women are present in greater numbers than in the past. However, we seem to be either clustered at the bottom or assigned to the margins of the most powerful institutions – the large firm, the judiciary, and the academy. This phenomenon is a result of a "new tokenism." Traditional definitions of tokenism refer to a manner of adaptation whereby societally powerful institutions seem to concede to pressure by outsiders by including one or two "representatives" of that group. The accommodations typically are small, often merely formal concessions, and nothing really changes. The "new" tokenism is a different adaptation mechanism. It operates in the context of a greatly changed population of lawyers to contain and minimize the otherwise potentially radical implications of the inclusion of a previously excluded group with different priorities, problems, and perceptions.

The older understanding of tokenism would be refuted by the sheer numbers – women comprise close to 50 percent of law school classes, are judges, legislators, law firm partners, and so on. Understanding the new tokenism reveals that numbers matter little. The presence of women has not altered the legal culture, nor have structures and institutions changed. Assimilation marks the road to success. But assimilation is accompanied by marginality. Many women, assimilationist or not, find ourselves outside of or marginalized within the most highly valued and economically rewarded institutions. For example, women law graduates are more likely to go into public interest work, small

1 This essay originally appeared in: Martha Albertson Fineman, *The New Tokenism*, 23 VT. L. REV. 289, 290–96 (1998).

DOI: 10.4324/9781003405627-14

firm practice, or government agencies than our male counterparts. Women in the academy are under-represented in all faculty positions, but the under-representation is particularly evident in tenure-track positions. Women are clustered in less prestigious substantive areas and in untenured clinical slots and legal writing appointments.

To point out our marginality is not the same as saying that the presence of women does not matter at all – of course our presence is necessary, but it is not a sufficient impetus for change. Nor do I mean to totally disregard the positive aspects of our presence. Some things have changed for the better. There is much less blatant and overt discrimination in terms of recruitment and salary structure for those who do make it into these institutions. Women are formally welcomed, even courted, in places that previously excluded us. But we cannot underestimate the structural impediments that women still encounter. In order to gain acceptance, we are required to conform to masculine norms and to meet gender loaded expectations. We are required to accept and assimilate to the institutions as they have been constituted by and for our male colleagues.

Formal acceptance, even active recruitment, of women is central to the assertion that the new tokenism is a non-exclusionary process. But the clear concession to be extracted in the bargain for inclusion is the promise that our presence will not disturb the status quo. Our presence is premised on assimilation to and acceptance of the existing culture and norms. However, this bargain creates a dilemma for many women who have or will have difficulty integrating other aspects of their lives with norms fashioned for the stereotypical masculine worker. Women are located in different social and cultural contexts than men and this fact has implications for their functioning in the workplace. Family demands compete for our energy and time in ways that typically are not experienced by men. Paramount competitors for the workplace are the various caretaking roles assigned to women within the family – the gendered roles of wife, mother, daughter, or daughter-in-law.

The unequal and gendered distribution of the burdens of caretaking and family means that women do not compete on a level playing field. Our disadvantages in this regard are cultural and structural, as gendered norms and expectations in the family undermine our possibilities and potential within a profession that is built around an unencumbered individual as the ideal worker. The duality of the demands on women means that our attention is divided. Our choices are explicitly confined or burdened by the dilemmas presented by the need to allocate time and energy between family and profession. A typical man in the legal profession can arrange his life according to professional and social expectations without inherent contradictions between the demands of both. Most women cannot because competing demands and social norms invade the workplace. Furthermore, women's struggles with competing work and family expectations are visible to employers and coworkers. As a result, we may be viewed as more tentatively attached to the workplace and less committed to the profession than unconflicted male counterparts. A perceived difference in attachment coupled with other manifestations of different social and cultural contexts results in women typically having less symbolic capital than men. For a convergence of reasons, we may be valued differently and less positively within institutions.

In addition to competing demands, the very nature and characteristics of the workplace may be inhospitable to women. Richard Collier, a scholar from the United Kingdom, characterized the law firm and law school cultures as distinctly masculine. He contends that these institutions are male-built and male-biased.[2] This is apparent in the way that work is structured. For example, in the firm, long hours are the norm, and long work hours are incompatible with other aspects of life, such as family time and caretaking demands.

Another aspect of this bias has to do with the competitiveness of the firm (and law school). The value of a person is measured in quantifiable terms – wealth accumulated, client dollars appropriated, or hours billed. For many in academia, individual prestige is dependent upon how their school is ranked on hierarchical scales such as those published annually by *US. News and World Report*. Collier contends that tying one's personal worth to such external status-conferring mechanisms is more typically male behavior.

Understanding legal institutions as inherently masculine helps to illuminate why the presence of women in the profession alone is not sufficient to transform those institutions. If the elite legal institutions are too masculine – too harsh, demanding, and competitive, too committed to the rational and abstract at the cost of the empathetic and concrete – some women (and some men) will drop out and find alternative careers in or outside of law. Some will try to stay but be driven out. Others will remain in these institutions where they will either assimilate to the norms or be marginalized. Of course, institutions could change by taking into account non-workplace demands that unequally burden women and accommodating them. Such accommodation seldom occurs in a manner that favors women, however.

Typically, we are expected to be flexible – to strain to subordinate family to profession – while work institutions maintain historic expectations that ignore the presence of competing family and caretaking demands. Comprehensive institutional change seems unlikely. In fact, there is little incentive for institutional change along the lines required for facilitating balancing work and family. There is no shortage of men (and women) willing to make sacrifices in order to devote all their time and energy to the firm. The rewards for such a choice are financial, as well as in increased status and power.

Further, it is interesting that in the instances where we do see some change in the workplace, it often is made to shore up existing patterns and workplace

2 *See* Richard Collier, *Masculinism, Law, and Law Teaching*, 19 INT'L J. OF THE SOC. OF LAW 427 (1991). *See generally* Richard Collier, *Coming Together?: Post-Heterosexuality, Masculine Crisis and the New Men's Movement*, 4 FEMINIST LEGAL STUDIES 3 (1996).

norms. For example, Cravath, Swaine and Moore in New York City instituted a day-care program for the children of their professional employees. The center, which is located in the office building, can care for children when nannies are ill or on school holidays and so forth. The partners are very proud of this innovation. I was disheartened, however. What this means is that you cannot even appeal to the demands of parenting as an excuse not to work long hours. Instead, the employer has anticipated and eliminated an obvious set of problems that might detract caretakers from dedication to the firm.

The lack of real change does not mean that there are no challenges to an unrepentant workplace, however. We are beginning to see the construction of competing networks, "old girl" connections within the profession. As our presence increases, so does the potential influence of these networks. At some point, sheer numbers will matter in at least some situations. Of course, presence and alternatives provoke backlash. We see some indications of "hyper-masculinity" as more and more hours at work are required for advancement and more and more footnotes in more and more articles are demanded for tenure.

In addition, as Margaret Thornton has written, there are also attempts to channel women into stereotypical patterns of behavior that are gendered female and, therefore, nonthreatening. Women who transplant socially gendered roles such as the "body beautiful," the "adoring acolyte," the "mother confessor," the "dutiful daughter," or the "queen bee" to the work world seem to succeed. These behaviors are institutionally rewarded by giving conforming women at least qualified acceptance while punishing or ignoring those who resist the stereotypes.[3]

In spite of the difficulties on the institutional front, one truly hopeful, though not uncontested, development explicitly associated with the presence of women in larger numbers has been the generation of an effective and powerful critique of law and legal institutions. Unlike the historically resistant structures of law, theory is relatively receptive to challenge and transformation, and women now are producers and consumers of an alternative vision of law. Although most robust in academic circles at this point, the success of substantial assaults on law as a "neutral," "objective," and "rational" discipline are encouraging. Feminist scholars have introduced ideas of gender and difference, and bias and perspective that question the hegemony of law. Challenging universality and generality with specific and differentiated perspectives draws our attention to the fact that women are more present in an ideological sense than in earlier eras of legal thought. Feminist methodology makes women central to the legal inquiry, displacing or challenging the male legal subject.

Feminist legal scholars have pointed out that it is not only legal institutions that are male constructs, as law itself was produced by men. This presents a

3 *See* Margaret Thornton, *Discord in the Legal Academy: The Case of the Feminist Scholar,* 3 Australian Feminist L.J. 53–71 (1994).

legitimacy problem. Our legal principles and ideals were created and developed at a time when women were excluded from the law and legal institutions. We were not admitted to many law schools. If we did manage to secure the training, we were often denied admission to the bar. Until this century, women could not vote, and many were excluded from jury service. Historically, laws were made, applied, and implemented by men even when the object of law was distinctly of concern to women. To illustrate this point, I use the example of "motherhood." This is a practice or experience biologically available only to women but given social and legal content within institutions that historically have excluded women. What constitutes "good" or "responsible" mothering has been left to processes largely dominated by men. Therefore, from women's perspectives, motherhood can be understood and experienced as a colonized category. Feminist scholars and activists are working to reclaim such categories, redefining them with women's subjectivities as central.

Some feminist legal scholars have developed a gendered analysis of law. This analysis considers the ways in which our lives, and hence our laws, are affected, even defined, by gendered norms and expectations. I think that this work is particularly threatening to traditional scholarly conventions in law schools. For one thing, it means that men cannot continue to set themselves and each other out as unchallenged experts on all issues.

Conferral, deferral, even deference is demanded when it is conceded that women experience the world in ways different from men. Perhaps this explains why within law schools there are attempts to marginalize feminists and our work. We are ignored when it is possible to do so and attacked if it is not possible to ignore us. Our positions are dismissed or ridiculed (typically without first being read or understood). Our motivation is questioned, we are labeled as biased, or the technique of raising gender as a relevant issue is equated with "male bashing."

Feminist legal scholars have had some notable successes in changing law, however. Sexual harassment laws, criminal laws, particularly in regard to rape, and family law have all been transformed via feminist insights and agitation. Sometimes this success has been dismissed in much the same ways as are the women who authored it. And it is true that our successes are mostly in areas historically labeled of special interest to women or of relatively low status in the profession and the academy.

Furthermore, even the victories have edges. There are indications that some of what initially appeared to be progressive alterations in law may actually be implemented or translated in a manner harmful to women. This has been the charge in family law rules that focus on equality to the detriment of women who are in unequal positions in regard to economic possibilities and responsibility for dependent children.

It is important not to overstate the extent of change. Legal culture, including law school culture, tends to be deeply suspicious of competing visions or alternative ways of perceiving the world. In law classes, students who "know" things outside of the analytical, rational framework find themselves socialized out of trusting intuition. They are taught to be skeptical about emotional responses to events and situations and to criticize and reject such appeals by others.

In academic scholarship, there is controversy about the use of narrative accounts in scholarship. Narrative is suspect because it posits the experience of individual women as relevant, even crucial to the production and processing of knowledge about society, law, and legal institutions. There is a general tendency to reject the use of the particular and personal to challenge the abstract and general principles built up and employed over the centuries in law. For feminists, however, this is a legitimate method of knowledge collection, called "consciousness raising." It spurred analyses, theories, and understandings that undermine the very ways we had previously thought about the world. Yet, narratives are criticized by resistant academic gatekeepers as merely biased or irrelevant accounts of personal history. I am hopeful that as the narratives accumulate they will reveal that many individual stories form patterns. Similarities in stories will support generalizations and shared perceptions will lead to theory. It will be undeniable that narrative can express insights into the way experiences can be and often are gendered in our society and legal system.

I want to end on this hopeful note. Perhaps the way to understand backlash and resistance, indeed the operation of a new tokenism, is that they are responses to feminist successes in the theoretical realm. Perhaps we have mounted a real and effective challenge and there is an attempt to devise methods with which to contain the potentially far-reaching consequences of our presence. In other words, our presence represents not the end, but the beginning of the battle. There is still a lot to do. The challenge for us now is to build on whatever successes we have had and work to make the legal institutions and law reflect, accommodate, and respect our presence as women and as feminists.

Part IV

Autonomy

Martha T. McCluskey

Over several decades, Martha Albertson Fineman has critically examined individual autonomy as a foundational myth that impedes democracy and social justice. This myth remains a flashpoint in discussions of twenty-first century problems like climate change, global pandemics, financial system instability, or new technologies of mass disinformation and hate. The ideal of the self-sufficient individual offers an elusive and dangerous escape from the challenges of collective solutions.

First, the autonomy myth places human freedom outside state and society, so that collective power appears to be a major threat rather than a major resource for human flourishing. Second, although it allows room for government action to correct and compensate barriers to autonomy, the ideal of autonomy casts doubt on that action. As a deviation from the norm, state support for equality must be constrained to preserve individual responsibility and agency.

Liberal theory (both right and left political versions) grounds the legitimacy of government and economy in an ideal of individual independence. Law, in this view, primarily maintains a level playing field for individuals to mutually advance their own values and interests in state and market. This liberal vision casts the family in a complementary role of dependency and duty, traditionally ordered through hierarchies such as gender, sexuality, class, race, and age. Positioned as a private realm outside state and market, the family is charged with reproducing autonomous individuals and cushioning their failures and burdens. In addition to the family, the liberal order has typically relied on military, civil, and criminal institutions to supervise, constrain, and discipline persons deemed incapable or undeserving of autonomy.

The liberal autonomy-dependency binary sets up a morality tale where persons, policies, and institutions identified with state and market autonomy deserve superior authority and support. The domestic sphere of care for dependency can be celebrated as a source of civic and market virtue if it supplements rather than supplants the central role of autonomy. Even on a pedestal, dependency stands as an exceptional condition that may deserve special protection and compensation in the liberal state and market, but that also tends to trigger special scrutiny and restriction.

DOI: 10.4324/9781003405627-15

Rather than rebalancing this binary, Fineman's analysis of autonomy changes its basic assumptions. Drawing on insights from family law and feminist theory, Fineman shifts the focus of liberty and well-being from individualized free choice to the institutional conditions that define and support the available options and their associated risks and powers. In this view, the personal costs of women's family caretaking labor cannot be fully addressed as problems of insufficient autonomy for women or others in the home, market, or reproduction. Instead, Fineman highlights the dependent-caretaker relationship as a crucial societal function intertwined with state and market but denied sufficient institutional authority and support within both.

This shift from individual autonomy to institutional status reveals that the autonomous liberal subject of state and market is in fact the recipient of pervasive subsidy and special legal protection. Fineman builds on feminist scholarship showing that the idea of dependency masks questionable, and changing, judgments about the societal value of certain kinds of persons and activities. Unpaid family and community labor, for example, is a major source of economic productivity and civic quality not formally recognized.[1]

Going further, Fineman notes that state and market institutions identified as spheres of self-reliance in fact depend on extensive subsidies from the unpaid or underpaid labor of private family caretakers. In this view, government support for the diverse needs and capacities associated with dependency constitutes payment of societal debt essential to producing long-term state and market value,[2] not discretionary "redistribution."

Fineman's critique of autonomy should not be understood as an argument for community authority over the individual. In contrast to communitarian or "common good" theories emphasizing individual responsibility for collective well-being, her analysis focuses on increasing state responsibilities for individual well-being. Moreover, Fineman unravels the opposition between individual and community. Individual agency depends on an active state, while the well-being of society depends on institutions that affirm individuals as inherently differently situated and valuable regardless of specific conditions of dependency.

By challenging the liberal ideal of autonomy, Fineman's analysis does not deny the many risks of state power, or the histories and current practices of systemic state and private oppression. Instead, it links those problems to deceptive politics and logics masking unequal institutional privileges and penalties as neutral rules facilitating individual autonomy. The fact that individual capacities and choices are inextricably interwoven with social and political

1 Nancy Folbre, *The Unproductive Housewife: Her Evolution in Nineteenth Century Economic Thought*, 16 SIGNS: JOURNAL OF WOMEN IN CULTURE AND SOCIETY 463 (1991); Nina. Banks, *Black Women in the United States and Unpaid Collective Work: Theorizing the Community as a Site of Production*, 47 REV. BLACK POL. ECON. 343 (2020).

2 Martha Albertson Fineman, *Cracking the Foundational Myths: Independence, Autonomy, and Self-Sufficiency*, 8 AM. U. J. GENDER SOC. POL'Y & L. 13 (2000).

contexts means that there can be no space where individuals are fully independent from others.

Advancing the goals of emancipation and individuality will require engaging, not evading, the value-laden policy questions of which institutional arrangements, in whose interests and at whose expense, deserve collective support and authority.

The norm of individualized independence reinforces systems of subordination by making equality morally and politically suspect. Feminist scholarship highlights the problem that both formal equal treatment and different substantive treatment are inadequate legal responses to gender discrimination. For example, pregnancy will disadvantage workers if equality means ignoring their bodily condition but also if equality means accommodating their needs as special exceptions to standards of workplace productivity. Both approaches to equality reinforce systems skewed to favor some people's interests as the neutral baseline, so that their advantages appear to represent self-made individual merit.

Without changing the baseline autonomy norm, equality will appear to require a zero-sum transfer at best, or a net societal loss at worst. As commonly depicted, providing a bigger slice of the societal pie to the disadvantaged will mean taking away others' slices. The demands of dependent "takers," in this view, risk impeding the superior productivity of "makers," so that everyone is likely to end up worse off.

Fineman's critique provides firmer ground for equality by focusing on the institutions selectively defining and supporting successful "making." Individuals pervasively act through formal and informal relationships with others, not as atomized, self-sufficient individuals insulated from others' actions and interests. This shift in ground highlights opportunities for making a bigger and better "pie" for all through institutional rules and processes that reward fairer sharing and caring for human dependencies.

Recent neoliberal and illiberal politics have further inflamed debates about inequality and injustice by hardening the myth of autonomy. Both promote visions of an increasingly scarce societal "pie" that leaves little for dependency and that also shortchanges many seemingly self-reliant individuals. These ideologies promote an ideal of individual choice that rejects substantive equality measures – like affirmative action, universal student debt relief, or Medicare for all – as fundamentally unfair and harmful to those who succeed or sacrifice "on their own." These ideologies also go further to undermine formally neutral equality rules prohibiting overtly harmful differential treatment. If individualized grit and self-interested ingenuity are the primary solutions to a shrinking and disaster-prone pie, then claims for protection from even egregious unfairness or domination logically count as admissions of failure from those who can't take the heat of a world legitimately geared to favor those who fend for themselves and their chosen allies.

This amplified autonomy myth drives a recent paradigm shift in US constitutional law reducing individual freedom to a fundamental individualized right to exit collective systems of mutual protection.[3] In place of rights to collective protection from harm, this paradigm creates new individualized rights to gain by disadvantaging others. Recent Supreme Court decisions, for example, have expanded individual rights to exit public antidiscrimination protections, creating an individualized right to exclude others that overrides civil rights law. Other examples include new fundamental individualized rights to undermine public gun safety protections, unions, and democratic electoral processes.

At the same time, this paradigm also justifies heightened public and private restrictions of personal freedom (such as militarized policing or bans on abortion). It posits an independent individual whose value and powers are persistently threatened by less deserving or disciplined "others."

Dislodging the myth of autonomy will not in itself lead to a more democratic and caring society. Nor will it resolve many complex questions about how to design and govern institutions to better support dependency in a social context of systemic inequalities and cumulative damage to human and environmental well-being. Nonetheless, Fineman's critique of autonomy expands aspirations for justice. It suggests a path toward a politics and law where equitably providing and receiving others' support is treated as normal and necessary for human flourishing.

3 Robin West, *A Tale of Two Rights*, 94 BOSTON UNIV. L. REV., 893 (2014).

Chapter 11

Equality and Autonomy (2005)[1]

Here, Fineman deftly illustrates the tension between our shallow conceptions of equality and autonomy, proposing a reconceptualization of autonomy that values interdependence and recognizes meaningful achievement of substantive equality as a necessary precursor.

Equality in the Shadow of Autonomy

In the United States, equality rests side by side with other foundational concepts that set out further expectations for the citizen in regard to the state. These other concepts are viewed as establishing the structure for ordering the relationships among diverse societal institutions, such as the family and the market. In fact, these other foundational concepts have had a profound effect on the way in which equality has been understood historically, actually shaping the course and direction of its legal history and limiting the concept's potential scope.

Paramount among these limiting values in this regard are contemporary ideas about individual freedom, which is reduced to the idea of autonomy, with its complementary components of individual independence and self-sufficiency. If the state obligation in regard to equality is processed and shaped by an ideological system in which autonomy, understood as the right to be free from governmental intrusion and regulation, is primary, then it can mean little more than state neutrality.

This suggests a second line of inquiry in which equality is placed in context with other societal aspirations and ideals. How do our contemporary aspirations for equality relate to our pursuit of other values, such as autonomy? How do our definitions of terms such as dependency and self-sufficiency shape our sense of what constitutes equality?

In undertaking such an inquiry it is important to examine how concepts like autonomy are used both rhetorically and ideologically. What does a resort to

1 This essay originally appeared in: Martha Albertson Fineman, *The Social Foundations of Law*, 54 EMORY L.J. 201, 222–28 (2005). It is reprinted with the permission of Emory Law Journal.

DOI: 10.4324/9781003405627-16

the rhetoric of autonomy mask? Whose interests are served when it is invoked? Indeed, what does it mean to those who invoke it as well as to those against whom it is invoked?

In current US free market ideology, absent discrimination or some other distortions of the market, any regulatory action by the state designed to confer more than neutral process in order to help some individuals or groups is susceptible to being interpreted as an intrusion on the autonomy of others. This interpretation results regardless of how desperate and (therefore) unequal the circumstances of those the state is seeking to assist or how privileged and (therefore) unequal the position of those who seek to shield themselves with autonomy's mantle. As part of this rubric of individual rights, our entrepreneurial spirit cannot and should not be contained and restrained — freedom for the individual requires freedom from governmental regulation and control. This belief creates a complicated set of hurdles for reformers to overcome when they seek to argue that there is a need for governmental action to remedy inequity and equalize existing unequal conditions.

The problem with substantive equality in this worldview is that it would require the provision of basic social goods through some system of affirmative action in order to ensure some base-line level of material well-being before any free market competition begins. In the United States, however, any type of state redistribution effort is deemed illegitimate by many as inconsistent with eighteenth-century liberal theory – among the most revered foundational concepts of our society. In this country, we conceptualize the individual as a rights holder, separate from, but potentially in competition with, other rights holders within a neutral state. Rights holders are autonomous human beings, protected in their individuality from encroachment by others. Our particular constitutional ordering also implies that freedom from external rules and regulations generated by the government is inherent in individual autonomy. Autonomy is synonymous with a concept of self-governance and is characterized by self-sufficiency and independence – individual qualities that are seen as prerequisites for individual freedom of will and action.[2]

Notions of individual autonomy have been powerfully employed in shaping policy. In recent years, the myth of individual autonomy has been spun out in very individualistic terms by those invoking such terms as "independence" and "self-sufficiency" to describe the ideal citizen.[3] Independence and self-sufficiency are terms that refer to characteristics that are perceived as both attainable and complementary in our political and civic discourses.

In a very simplistic and severely limiting sense, individual autonomy in contemporary America is linked to economic measures. Independence and self-sufficiency are characteristics of an idealized economic status. Attainment of that economic status, in turn, is a necessary precondition for the conferral

2 MARTHA ALBERTSON FINEMAN, THE AUTONOMY MYTH: A THEORY OF DEPENDENCY, 20 (2004).
3 *Id.* at 22.

or recognition of any other type of independence or autonomy by the system. Only when we are economically self-reliant can we be considered independent. Because we are able to supply the economic resources necessary to meet our needs, we are self-sufficient. In this way, independence and self-sufficiency "buy" for us the right to self-governance and "control" over will and actions. They earn us our autonomy.

Equality, Autonomy, and Meaning

Foundational ideals such as equality and autonomy are in fact abstractions – terms with no independent meaning that can be understood in conflicting and incompatible ways. They can also be understood as symbiotically related, with one necessarily enhancing the attainment of the other. Partly, the scope and nature of these terms shape the task that the government has set itself in implementing them. For example, in setting out its notions of equality, South Africa had to address problems associated with its legacy of apartheid. Northern Ireland also has a history of occupation and exploitation with which to contend, although its national trauma was based on religion.

Autonomy assumes independence and the possibility of choice – that nondiscriminatory access to opportunities exists. But it is not clear exactly what might be tolerated in the way of regulatory effort and action to make access to opportunity "real," to say nothing of making it "equal." For example, a desire to equalize opportunity can be used to justify the institutional creation of an affirmative action program to provide meaningful access for members of historically excluded groups. At the same time, such programs serve as a rallying point for opponents of affirmative action who view them as giving some an unequal advantage.[4]

Supporters of affirmative action would argue for context – that individual autonomy is frustrated, and the whole ideal of equality twisted, if existing systems of privilege and power are such that some are disadvantaged and thus unable to compete on equal footing with those who have not been historically subjugated. In contrast, those resisting affirmative action would argue from a more formalistic position – that "special" treatment is not justified. For these individuals, governmental assistance or support compromises the autonomy and options of others and therefore is a perversion of the principles of equality and autonomy. Government intrusion also undermines the worthy goals of independence and self-sufficiency and signals the end of meritocracy.[5]

Likewise, one may assert that a modern marriage is best understood as a partnership in which two autonomous individuals form a union. It follows that in such an arrangement both parties (or partners) should be treated equally if the marriage should end in divorce. However, there are many different

4 *Id.* at 26–27.
5 *Id.*

interpretations of equal treatment in such contexts as well as plausible, different understandings of autonomy. One could argue that equal treatment means the family assets should be divided in half, and that there should be no ongoing entitlement to the future wages of the primary wage earner — this division would constitute a version of equal treatment at the moment of divorce. On the other hand, particularly if there are children, one could argue that the assets should be divided so that the party who is assuming caretaking responsibilities, usually the mother, is able to maintain a living standard nearly equal to that of the other spouse. Under this theory, one could argue that periodic payments should continue for a substantial period of time to supplement the reduced amount the caretaker will be able to provide in working for pay.[6] It could be said that this would be the only way to treat the caretaker-child unit equally and to ensure their future autonomy.

Both approaches to this problem would be based on the principle of equality and a desire for autonomy; however, the focuses of the approaches are different. Husband and wife in this situation have conflicting and incompatible equality and autonomy interests. Achieving equality and the material conditions necessary for autonomy for caretaker and child comes at the expense of equal treatment of the noncaretaker and entails some compromise of his autonomous ability to decide the nature and extent of his obligations. Depending on which perspective is adopted, there would be very different divisions of marital assets and an imposition of ongoing financial responsibility after divorce.[7]

Rethinking Autonomy

The very terms of autonomy, as exemplified by economic independence and a detached notion of self-sufficiency, might well be redefined or reimagined in the public mind. Independence is not the same as being unattached. Independence from subsidy and support is not attainable, nor is it desirable; we want and need the webs of economic and social relationships that sustain us. Thus, a different understanding of autonomy and what it entails is needed. It is not beyond our current ability to imagine a new concept of autonomy, one that recognizes that the individual lives within a variety of contexts and is dependent upon them.

There are important debates that must occur in political and policy circles about the interrelationship between autonomy and equality. Specifically, we should not define our aspiration for equality in the shadow of autonomy. Rather, we must begin to think of autonomy as possible only in conjunction with the meaningful and widespread attainment of equality. For example, some degree of equalization of resources, so that there is a floor below which no citizen shall fall, would seem to be a prerequisite for the achievement of

6 *Id.*
7 *Id.*

autonomy. Autonomy is only possible when one is in a position to be able to share in society's benefits and burdens. And sharing in benefits and burdens can only occur when individuals have the basic resources that enable them to act in ways that are consistent with the tasks and expectations imposed upon them by the society in which they live.

The expectation that one should achieve this form of autonomy – autonomy supported by a societal commitment to the provision of basic social needs – should be every citizen's birthright. Autonomy in this sense concedes that all individuals have an inherent dependence on society. While some, having benefited from history and circumstances, may have the current means and methods that make it fair to expect them to achieve autonomy, others have been disadvantaged and are thus deserving of some compensatory or supplementary societal support.

In addition, this form of autonomy concedes that the concept only has meaning in situations in which individual choices are not made impossible or constrained by inequalities, particularly those inequalities that arise from poverty. The goal of autonomy must be supported through an understanding of collective responsibility for basic needs.

In a paradigm that privileges an uncomplicated notion of autonomy, equality is inevitably also presented in a narrow and simplistic manner.[8] A simplistic autonomy discourse increasingly dominates American politics. Affirmative action attempts by the state to guarantee equality in more than a formal, procedural sense are considered suspect; some regard this as special treatment, the very opposite of state neutrality that the autonomy-driven version of equality is deemed to demand. But the circumstances of privileged members of society are not deemed special in the same way. It is only explicit governmental attempts to assist those who are disadvantaged that are to be prohibited. The laws and structures that perpetuate wealth and privilege are not considered special treatment even though they benefit only those with special status and economic standing.

The situation in which the state ignores everyone's needs equally should no longer be tolerated. Some robust version of substantive equality is essential in a society that imposes on individuals an expectation that they can attain a degree of self-sufficiency as adults. In order to eventually develop competency to the fullest extent possible, an individual during her or his formative stages of life must have access to basic material and social resources. The assurance of some fundamental level of economic security guaranteed to all caretaking units in which such individuals are nurtured would be foundational in this regard. The state must subsidize caretaking just as it does other socially productive labor. It is the articulation of this aspiration for substantive equality that is the first step in building a politics to demand it.

8 *Id.* at 273.

Chapter 12

Posing the Philosophy for an Active State (2005)[1]

Fineman expands upon her reconceptualization of autonomy by urging progressives to advocate for the creation of a responsive state that ensures that all citizens have the basic material resources needed to make and pursue meaningful choices.

While it would seem obvious to most citizens of other Western countries that the state would be implicated in any discussion of possible solutions to the problem of inequality in society, many progressive Americans are almost as suspicious of governmental action as their conservative counterparts. Perhaps this is why the political will to expand the state's regulatory responsibilities has lagged over the past decades, even as recognition of persistent inequality has grown and notions about justice have evolved.[2]

The state is viewed with much more suspicion in the United States than it is in other Western democracies, and arguments about giving it a more active role are bound to be subjected to scrutiny and skepticism. Contemporary legal and policy discussions, which are part of the process whereby the state is altered, are overwhelmingly concerned with limiting and restricting the state, particularly in regard to the economic areas of policymaking. Those who reject the idea that the government has a basic and explicit role in monitoring and mediating change vigorously resist a more regulatory response to market developments.[3] In regard to the market, the state increasingly is either cast in the role of cheerleader or urged to facilitate, not regulate, economic arenas.[4]

In the United States, such arguments have culminated in a philosophy espoused widely from the center to the right of the political spectrum – by business leaders, politicians, and policymakers who urge an increase in the sphere of influence and power of the market and a weakening of the power of

1 This essay originally appeared in: Martha Albertson Fineman, *The Social Foundations of Law*, 54 EMORY L.J. 201, 228–230 (2005). It is reprinted with the permission of Emory Law Journal.
2 MARTHA ALBERTSON FINEMAN, THE AUTONOMY MYTH: A THEORY OF DEPENDENCY, 269 (2004).
3 *Id.*
4 *See generally Homepage of the Libertarian Party*, www.libertarian.org (visited June 1, 2003).

DOI: 10.4324/9781003405627-17

the federal government. Their shared vision is of a minimalist national sphere, ideally accomplished through the privatization of functions previously performed by the government. When government is necessary, the ideal route is through the devolution of responsibility to the smallest, most local units.[5]

This desired withdrawal of the national level of regulation and responsibility is urged even though the history of the United States shows that local rule on some issues cannot be effective and sometimes results in discrimination and concession to local passion and prejudice. Such withdrawal is urged even though it is clear that there has always been a struggle to get businesses to accept progressive labor practices. Deregulation is urged even though the market has shirked responsibility for the provision of social goods – such as health insurance, family and medical leave, daycare, or a minimum family wage – unless "encouraged" to do so by the state.[6]

To abandon progressive aspirations for the state, given this history of the market's failure to make progressive adjustments without coercion, is to abandon all hope for progressive change. The national government is the only organization with the potential to impose such measures. At a minimum, the state must strive to eliminate major disparities that result from unequal social relations and economic exploitation. A strong and vital state is necessary to even begin to undertake, let alone accomplish, that task.

Instead of fighting for the shrinking and weakening of a national government, progressives should be focusing on articulating appropriate objectives for the state to pursue. Defining the norms and aspirations that should supplement or, in some cases, replace the impoverished concepts provided by economic theory would be the place to start. There must be a change in the discourse of politics – one that will stimulate the creation of an alternative paradigm with which to compete for the prize of state policy. The new direction will displace the monopoly of free market imagery in which there is no collective responsibility, but only an exaggerated sense of individual autonomy.

5 MARTHA ALBERTSON FINEMAN, THE AUTONOMY MYTH: A THEORY OF DEPENDENCY, 270 (2004).
6 *Id.*

Chapter 13

What Place for Family Privacy? (2003)[1]

Here, Fineman explores what remains of the concept of privacy in her reimagining of the family-state relationship. She proposes a new conception of family privacy that focuses on enabling autonomy within the caretaking unit.

Privacies

Most commentators focus on privacy as a matter of federal constitutional doctrine. This strand of privacy jurisprudence is individualistic in nature and has been the basis for some important decisions protecting choices concerning reproduction. This individual or constitutional notion of privacy is certainly necessary to deter impulses toward collective control of sexuality and reproduction.

There has been quite a bit of debate in recent years about the effectiveness, as well as the wisdom, of using privacy to secure individual rights. I am not a constitutional scholar and remain an agnostic on questions such as whether equality or privacy is the most potent concept with which to try to preserve individual reproductive rights or whether sexual privacy is essential for the development of individual personhood.

My interest in the legal or doctrinal idea of privacy is focused on its use in consideration of the institution of the family – privacy in its common law sense. The idea of the entity of the family as something "private" predates, and is analytically separate from, the constitutional idea of individual privacy, although this "new" arena of privacy seems rooted in older notions about family relations. For example, *Griswold v. Connecticut*[2] is often cited as the bedrock case for the development of our constitutional concept of individual privacy regarding reproductive decisions. But the *Griswold* opinions articulating the concept of privacy

1 This essay is used with permission of Columbia University Press, from What Place for Family Privacy?, Martha Albertson Fineman, in Women and the United States Constitution: History, Interpretation, and Practice (Sibyl A. Schwarzenbach and Patricia Smith, Eds.) 2003; permission conveyed through Copyright Clearance Center, Inc.

2 381 U.S. 479 (1965).

DOI: 10.4324/9781003405627-18

are clearly looking beyond the individual, referencing an entity or marital concept of privacy.

The question *Griswold* explicitly presented was whether there was a constitutional right for married couples to use contraception. Justice Douglas's majority opinion may have characterized the right to this type of privacy as located in the famous penumbras, but its presence transcended those shadows.

The privacy interests at issue were deemed "older than the Bill of Rights – older than our political parties, older than our school system." And there was little ambiguity about what was being protected: "marriage is a coming together for better or worse, hopefully enduring, and intimate to the degree of being sacred." Justice Goldberg's concurring opinion reiterated the point that it was marriage that was deserving of protection, stating that the statute at issue dealt "with a particularly important and sensitive area of privacy – that of the marital relation and the marital home."[3]

From the family law perspective, it is *Eisenstadt v. Baird* that is the radical departure – Eisenstadt is the case that takes the idea of entity or marital privacy and expands constitutional protection beyond the common law limitations of the family relationship:

> It is true that in Griswold the right of privacy in question inhered in the marital relationship. Yet the marital couple is not an independent entity with a mind and heart of its own, but an association of two individuals each with a separate intellectual and emotional makeup. If the right of privacy means anything, it is the right of the individual, married or single, to be free from unwarranted governmental intrusion into matters so fundamentally affecting a person as the decision whether to bear or beget a child.[4]

This articulation of the principles in *Griswold* established the individual as the relevant subject. *Eisenstadt* effectively threw a constitutional cloak of privacy over certain individual decisions involving sex and reproduction.

If we were to return to the doctrine of family or marital privacy, we would see that it is distinguishable from the new individual variety in several significant ways. The obvious difference is in the designation of the relevant unit for protection, entity vs. individual. Also important, however, is the historic fact that family privacy operated as a generalized form of protection. What was shielded from state intervention and control were not only specific, weighty intimate decisions such as the decision to beget or bear a child but also mundane day-to-day family interactions.

Despite the Supreme Court's recent activity in bringing some aspects of family privacy into constitutional law, the cases that are most relevant in discerning the characteristics of family privacy are state not federal decisions. The task of the

3 *Id.* at 486, 495.
4 *Eisenstadt v. Baird*, 405 U.S. 438, 453 (1972).

state in family privacy cases is not to pronounce grand principles or figure out how to make family privacy mesh with other constitutional limitations. These cases address expectations and aspirations for families, articulating in the process what might be characterized as an ethic or ideology of family privacy. This ideology is rooted in idealizations but also references the perceived pragmatics of family relationships and the acknowledged limitations of legal (particularly judicial) systems as substitutes for family decision making. The ideology expresses the norm of nonintervention in ongoing families – a principle of state restraint because of the needs of the functioning family.

The facts of *McGuire v. McGuire* illustrate the contours of the common law doctrine of family privacy. Mrs. McGuire had asked the court to intervene and require her husband to provide suitable maintenance and support for her. She did not want a divorce or legal separation, just the enforcement of the terms of the state defined marriage contract, which required husbands to support their wives. Her complaints about her husband's lack of adequate support were rather compelling. For example, in spite of the fact that her husband was a fairly wealthy man, she had not received money to buy clothing for several years. She lived in a house with no indoor bathroom, kitchen sink, or functioning central heating. The Nebraska Supreme Court, while indicating that the husband's behavior was inappropriate, nonetheless held that his marital obligations could not be enforced if Mrs. McGuire chose to remain in her family relationship:

> The living standards of a family are a matter of concern to the household, and not for the courts to determine, even though the husband's attitude toward his wife, according to his wealth and circumstances, leaves little to be said in his behalf. As long as the home is maintained and the parties are living as husband and wife it may be said that the husband is legally supporting his wife and the purpose of the marriage relation is being carried out. Public policy requires such a holding.[5]

Mrs. McGuire's petition for a level of support consistent with the family wealth and income would be granted only if she left the relationship. As long as the marriage lasted, the courts would not intervene even if asked to by one of the partners to the marriage and even if all that was requested was enforcement of state-imposed family obligations.

Of course, children present a more problematic situation. We are less certain that children can protect themselves within the family, or that they can protect themselves *from* the family. The nature of the parent-child relationship has occupied state and federal courts' attention. Parental conduct, be it discipline or decision-making, is generally protected unless it constitutes abuse or neglect of the child. Courts consistently reiterate the common law presumption that

5 *McGuire v. McGuire*, 157 Neb. 226, 59 N.W.2d 336 (1953).

parents act in the best interests of their children. The law's concept of the family rests on the presumption that parents possess what children lack in maturity, experience, and capacity for judgment.[6] Consistent with the search for sources in *Griswold,* the opinions about parent-child relationships also have found rights not in explicit textual provisions but in the history and functioning of the family itself.

Both individual and entity versions of privacy have limitations. For example, family privacy is limited in two important senses. First, there is the historic doctrinal limitation that it applies primarily to family units that conform to ideological conventions about appropriate form and function – to intact nuclear families. Second, in recent decades, the idea of family privacy has been severely criticized by feminists, children's rights proponents, and others concerned by the potential for physical, emotional, or psychological abuse of some family members by others. Family privacy was charged with obscuring and fostering inequality and exploitation.

The Problem with Family Privacy

Somewhat of a dilemma is presented for those of us who view "privacy" as essential to the concept of family while simultaneously conceding the more modern notion that privacy can conceal, even foster, situations dangerous to the individuals who comprise the family unit. The focus on the necessity of privacy for family formation and functioning arises from concern with abuses associated with state intervention and regulation of intimacy. By contrast, those who are attuned to potential abuses within the family remind us that hidden beneath the cloak of privacy are power imbalances, perhaps even incentives for the strong to prey upon or exploit the weak. When we consult the empirical information, it seems both perspectives are warranted. Therefore, the obvious course is found in trying to reconcile both concerns and balance family privacy with protection for family members. Too often, however, advocates discard one (particularly family privacy) for the sake of the other.

In trying to reconcile the need of the family for privacy with the obligation of the state to protect its citizens, we should first resolve the question of family population. How are we going to define the "family" that will be entitled to privacy protection? Existing law defines the family through legal affiliations. Only certain ties are significant for the establishment of the status of family. Some ties are purely legally contrived, such as those in the construct of marriage, while others are considered to be reflective of a more "natural" nature, such as the parent-child bond.

The legally conceived family presumptively is, or has been, a reproductive unit. The primary tie is the heterosexual affiliation of husband and wife, and this gives the family its form. Theirs is a connection considered basic to family and to state,

6 WILLIAM BLACKSTONE, COMMENTARIES 447 (rev. ed. 1966).

therefore historically legally mandated to be permanent, exclusive, and stable. This traditional family was hierarchically organized with well-defined gendered divisions of labor. It is this family that is criticized in much of the feminist jurisprudence of recent years. The feminist critique of privacy and the family begins with the assertion that it obscures private, often labeled "domestic," violence and abuse. For example, Catherine MacKinnon criticized liberal thinkers, along with cases such as *Roe v. Wade,* by characterizing "the ideology of privacy" as "a right of men to be let alone to oppress women one at a time."[7]

MacKinnon understands privacy to be rooted in the concept of seclusion and separation from the protections that might be afforded by the state. Privacy is seen as the source of women's inequality, the location of her domination and subordination.[8] In fact, she asserts that to even complain about inequality in the private arena is inconsistent with the whole idea of privacy. To her, privacy cannot be understood outside of its historic manifestations of female subordination.

Anita Allen begins her discussion of privacy in the same place as MacKinnon – within the confines of the historic nuclear family home. Her major concern is not with violence but with exploitation – the sacrifices compelled by "marriage, motherhood, housekeeping, dependence, and women's own moral ideas of caretaking and belonging." Allen disagrees with MacKinnon, disputing the assertion that privacy poses an inherent threat to women, and argues that women are finally in a position to "expect, experience and exploit real privacy within the home and within heterosexual relationships."[9]

Allen views privacy as having many dimensions, referring to "family life within the home, and to the kinds of intimate personal relationships and activities commonly associated with them."[10]

While recognizing past abuses, Allen sees a use for "real" privacy in providing seclusion and solitude for women, in restricting access to information and preserving confidentiality, and in securing decisional privacy. Allen makes an important argument for retaining the constitutional, individualized notion of privacy and making sure that the conditions for its use and enjoyment are

7 Catherine A. MacKinnon, Roe v. Wade*: A Study in Male Ideology, in* ABORTION AND LEGAL PERSPECTIVES 45, 53 (Jay L. Garfield et al. eds., 1985).

8 *See generally* CATHERINE A. MACKINNON, TOWARD A FEMINIST THEORY OF THE STATE (Cambridge, MA: Harvard University Press, 1989). In an early critique of the liberal ideal, MacKinnon argued that privacy doctrine "is most at home, the place women experience the most force, in the family" (*id.* at 190). For women she asserts, "the measure of the intimacy has been the measure of the oppression" (*id.* at 191). When the law of privacy restricts intrusions into intimacy, it bars changes in control over that intimacy through law. "The existing distribution of power and resources within the private sphere are precisely what the law of privacy exists to protect" (*id.* at 193), the subordination and domination of women.

9 *See* Anita Allen, *Privacy at Home: The Twofold Problem*, in REVISIONING THE POLITICAL: FEMINIST RECONSTRUCTIONS OF TRADITIONAL CONCEPTS IN WESTERN POLITICAL THEORY 194 (Nancy J. Hirschmann et al. eds., 1996).

10 *Id.* at 209, note 1.

afforded to women. However, her analysis does not transcend the individual woman to consider the family.

In fact, both MacKinnon's critique and Allen's defense of privacy assume there is danger in the domestic. The danger is located in the operation and expectations associated with heterosexuality (and subsequent reproduction). Women's interests are to be asserted independent of the family unit-typically against men who with greater or lesser degrees of ill will take advantage of women in families. Allen does bring children into the consideration, but retains an individualized analysis. Children mean caretaking, and caretaking precludes "real" privacy.[11] The object is to have a personal sense of privacy that permits women's resistance to reproduction and caretaking. The notion of privacy in this regard is as a tool to "put an end to the psychological predisposition of women to care themselves into oblivion-a defense to intra family abuse."[12]

A second source of criticism of the idea of family privacy is those who focus on the rights of children. Under this analysis, family privacy protects parental authority.[13] In this area the tendency of privacy critics who see abuses has been to individualize the family, by separating children out for special concern and state protection. Some child advocates focus on physical and psychological abuse of children within families, advocating for intervention in these instances. These seem to me to be easy (problems of definition aside) cases. Privacy should never condone or obscure abuse.

What are of concern, however, are the more sweeping claims of some advocates – those who focus on the very basic question of how children are described and treated in law. The discomfort in this regard seems to be with the hierarchical or unequal nature of the parent-child relationship. The charge often leveled is that the law treats children as though they are the "property"

11 *Id.* at 205. Privacy is both a negative and a positive force. As a negative, it provides for resistance to the imposition of reproduction and caretaking responsibilities that can subvert women's positive liberty interests in private pursuits such as solitude, self-satisfaction, and fulfillment.

12 For a historical account of parental rights *see generally* Barbara Bennett Woodhouse, *Who Owns the Child?: Meyer and Pierce and the Child as Property*, 33 WILLIAM AND MARY L.R. 995 (1992). For a discussion of the modern trend in parental rights *see* Barbara Bennett Woodhouse, *A Public Role in the Private Family: The Parental Rights and Responsibilities Act and the Politics of Child Protection and Education*, 57 OHIO STATE L.R. 393 (1996).

13 In *Hatching the Egg: A Child Centered Perspective on Parents Rights*, 14 CARDOZO L. R. 1747 (1993), Barbara B. Woodhouse first advocated this new approach to the parent-child relationship, terming it the "generist perspective." It is based on the view that the nurturing of the next generation is the touchstone of the family. An adult's relationship with children is one of trusteeship rather than ownership. Adult's "rights" of control and custody yield to the less adversarial notions of obligation to provide nurturing, authority to act on the child's behalf, and standing to participate in the collaborative planning to meet the child's needs. For more on the generist perspective, *see* Barbara Bennett Woodhouse, *Out of Children's Needs, Children's Rights: The Voice Defining the Family*, 8 B.Y.U. L.R. 321 (1994).

of their parents, an inflammatory characterization that does more to obscure than illuminate the issues.

There are a number of suggestions for recasting the relationship between parent and child, substituting concepts such as "stewardship" or "trustee" for the more traditional notion of parental authority, thus leveling out the relationship.[14] These ideals, amorphously appealing on a rhetorical level, seem harmless enough as aspirations. The problems arise when they are implemented into laws that can be used at the relatively unfettered discretion of various state actors to undermine, even usurp, parental decision-making authority.

From the perspective of my project, notions of child advocacy can raise some interesting issues. How might a general and broadly construed norm of child advocacy (advocacy and activism absent abuse or neglect) relate to the concepts of collective responsibility without collective control? Perhaps advocacy may be of benefit to the project. For example, noted child advocate Barbara Woodhouse has urged the idea of stewardship. She uses the child advocates' claim that children must be treated as "people in their own right" to argue for laws and policies that focus on children's welfare.[15]

Woodhouse reaches for more than control over parents. With the objective of children's welfare as the organizing tool, she advocates for a more extensive sense of children's rights, which she terms "needs-based rights." These rights are not associated with children's rights to autonomy or independence but are the basis for a positive claim to basic nurture and protection. This right is not only against parents but mandates community and political responses.

To some extent Woodhouse's concern with basic needs rights reflects my own call for collective responsibility for dependency. However, the identity of the rights holder and the source of the right are different in important ways. My claim is a communal one – entity focused and based on a claim of entitlement or right originating as a result of the societal work performed by caretakers. Woodhouse's model is not a compensatory one but is based on the status of the child as a future citizen. She positions the child as the claimholder and, in doing so, sets up the potential (perhaps inevitably) for collective, child protective supervision over and control of parental stewardship. The family is conceived in terms of individual (therefore potentially competing) interests.

Autonomy for Family Functioning

As indicated earlier, rethinking the family and its relationship to the state requires a corresponding rethinking of other primary institutions and foundational concepts. As part of this process, I suggest that we can and should rethink privacy in such a way as to confer autonomy on caretaking or dependency units. The beneficiary of this privacy is the unit, defined through its functioning not its

14 Woodhouse, *Out of Children's Needs, Children's Rights, supra* note 13, at 321.
15 *Id.*

form. In fact, the caretaking unit could adopt a multitude of possible forms. The unifying idea that creates the "new family" is the significance of the caretaker-dependent relationship.

Autonomy (my version of the "new" privacy to complement the new family) would protect entity decision making, giving the unit the space and authority to self-government, including the right to self-definition. Autonomy does not presuppose that the family would be separate from society. The family would be anchored firmly within society, subsidized and supported by market and state but retaining authority within its parameters. Privacy, just like subsidy, should attach to units performing societally necessary and essential functions, such as caretaking.

This version of a reconceived family, entitled to privacy or autonomy, is responsive to some of the criticism of old forms of family privacy. For example, if the family is defined functionally, focused on the caretaker-dependent relationship, the traditionally problematic interactions of sexual affiliates (formerly designated spouses) are not protected by notions of family privacy. MacKinnon's charge that men will exploit women in an intimate context may still be a problem, but it will no longer be a privacy problem. The fact that privacy is refocused removes from the special or family context the entire range of relationships between sexual affiliates, opening them to public scrutiny.

This opening up of some relationships to scrutiny does not mean that my reconfigured family model is going to escape feminist criticism, however. The criticism is most likely to be that a notion of collective responsibility (and therefore social subsidy) and privacy protection for the caretaking-dependent relationship will permanently enthrall women as dependency laborers. I think such arguments are based, in part, on assumptions about women's false consciousness.

In any case, my objective is not social engineering. I do not consider it my place to persuade women not to undertake caretaking. Rather, my objective is to work to ensure that if they do undertake caretaking, they will not be systemically disadvantaged and rendered economically dependent on men or on highly stigmatized state assistance as a result. I do believe in the possibility of women's agency; although we all operate within societal and cultural constraints, we can determine direction and decide to take one path rather than another. Women should have the ability (subsidy and privacy) to undertake a caretaking role.

The second line of family privacy critiques, those presented by the child advocates, will be more on point for the family I envision. This is true because the exemplar of the caretaker-dependent relationship is the parent-child relationship. One significant aspect of these relationships is that they are of inherent inequality, reflecting the fact that one role is that of child or dependent, while the other is that of parent or caretaker.

To point out that the parent-child relationship is one of dependency is not to make an assertion as to how we should value children. Children (or any other inevitably dependent persons) are equally important or equally valuable but typically not "equals" in the sense that society does not presume that they are equivalent to adults in capability or in their ability to make judgments.

Therefore, it is more appropriate to view the parent-child relationship, not as one of equality (as with sexual affiliates) but as one of responsibility. It is not about individuals but about a relationship. And a relationship defined by responsibility requires privacy or autonomy for the caretaking entity.

It is this distinction between equality and responsibility – individuals and relationship that many child advocates fail to make. In fact, some child advocacy attempts seem like efforts to equalize the relationship between parent and child by adding the leavening (in order to level) force of the advocate (as stand-in for the state). My argument about autonomy for the caretaking unit is an assertion that some relationships should be considered outside of the equality paradigm that so dominates liberal legal scholarship. The reasoning of some in the child advocacy community presents the danger that, under the rubric of protecting the child, we facilitate state intervention and control and potentially undermine the autonomy of caretaking units.

The fact that we can think that some intimate relationships are inherently unequal does not mean that they will inevitably be exploitative and oppressive or that the "less equal" participant will have no voice and no power within the relationship. I explicitly make mention of this fact because it seems that many child advocates assume that exploitation necessarily follows once the inequality of the child is posited.

In the same way, the lack of a legal voice is equated with the lack of an actual voice. Of course, the determination of typical and atypical modes of operation in caretaker-dependent units presents an empirical question. My assumption is that a careful study would show that the relationship between typical caretakers and dependents is dynamic (it is in motion), fluid (easily changing shape), and interactive (the participants act upon each other). The reciprocal interactive nature of the relationship ensures that it will not be fixed. The reciprocity also means that in regard to family decision making the dependent will seldom, if ever, be absent.

Caretakers typically consider dependents' needs; often dependents are an explicit part of the process of decision making; and at times they even control it. Just as the relationship is fluid within daily interaction, it is dynamic over time. While the authority of a parent over a child will decline as the years pass, an adult child's authority over (and responsibility for) an elderly and ill parent may increase. This is not to assert that there will never be "wrong" decisions made by caretakers or even that there will never be outright abuse. On the other hand, no system of child advocacy no matter how interventionist and regulatory, can deliver only optimal, non-abusive caretaking.

It is important in this regard to realize that the debates about child advocacy are, to a large extent, only arguments about legal relationships and how legal authority is distributed. As a practical matter, they are arguments about the relationship between state and family more than attempts to define and regulate intrafamily interactions. By contrast, if we focus, as I urge, on entity autonomy and responsibility, we are at least attempting to understand and respond to how family units function. Legal relationships capture only some things about "real" families, often distorting a family's reality in the process. Legal relationships set up adversariness.

One danger of imposing an equality aspiration on relationships of responsibility is pertinent for the ideas of subsidy and collective responsibility discussed earlier. If we look at the child as the recipient of the subsidy and not the unit (in which the caretaker is the "head"), several issues arise. Foremost is the very real possibility that if the child is seen as the object of social policy and justification for subsidy, some form of quality control will be considered appropriate. Standardization and normative judgments in a diverse and pluralistic society can be problematic and contentious.

If, by contrast, subsidy is perceived as going to the caretaker-dependent entity or unit, it is more likely that autonomy over decision making will follow. Units may make "mistakes," but if it is not abuse or neglect (we can argue about where to draw those lines later), then the unit, as recipient of the subsidy, should decide how it is to be used. This way of looking at what is the appropriate focus for policy also gives value to caretaking labor. The dependent may be the beneficiary, but the labor of the caretaker is what has societal value.

To protect caretaking relationships, the right to privacy must be extended beyond individuals. A concept of individual privacy, particularly in regard to the formation of intimate connections can complement family privacy, but some protection that transcends the interests of individual members of the entity is essential. When a caretaking-dependent unit has formed, family privacy would serve to shield and protect the functioning relationships within it. The protection would dissolve only if the entity grossly fails in the performance of its responsibilities or because the underlying relationship is itself dissolved.

Entity privacy would denote a line of nonintervention drawn around ongoing functioning relationships. This version of privacy can provide a barrier between an entity performing family functions, such as the caretaker/dependent unit, and the potentially overreaching state seeking to impose collective standards or controls. Properly conceived, privacy as a principle of self-government allows the caretaker/dependent unit to flourish, supported and subsidized by the larger society without the imposition of conformity.

Part V

Vulnerability

Aziza Ahmed

Martha Albertson Fineman introduced her groundbreaking theory of vulnerability in a 2008 article, "The Vulnerable Subject: Anchoring Equality in the Human Condition."[1] Fineman continued to develop her idea of vulnerability over the following decade and the idea has circulated through the academy producing a range of scholarship critical of liberal legalism and its inability to appropriately address the problems of our time.

Fineman's vulnerability theory posits that the human condition is one of universal and continuous vulnerability. Viewing the human subject this way allows us to challenge the Anglo-American liberal legal account that treats the individual as autonomous, free, and unrestrained by the structural conditions that shape the person's life. Vulnerability theory begs us to look beyond how the state makes us free and enables autonomy. Rather, it asks the state to take responsibility for establishing and monitoring social institutions and relationships that facilitate individual and social resilience. Vulnerability theory understands institutions broadly: from corporations and administrative agencies to the family.

This idea of the state – robust and supportive – sits in contrast to the idea of the state/individual relationship proffered by liberal legalism. Liberal legalism often understands that we should be free from state interference and that the goal of the state should allow for liberal values of autonomy and choice to flourish.

A careful reader of Fineman's early work would detect the seeds of what would become a new theory of human and institutional vulnerability over decades. In path-breaking work like her 2004 book The *Autonomy Myth*, Fineman took on core principles that govern society and often tempt progressives away from a richer understanding of how vulnerability is produced and sustained. In the *Autonomy Myth*, for example, Fineman takes on the idea that it is desirable for families and individuals to become autonomous. This idea undermines the dependency that individuals and families have on society. This, in turn, undermines the flourishing of the family itself. The family as an institution is dependent on other

1 Martha Albertson Fineman, *The Vulnerable Subject: Anchoring Equality in the Human Condition,* 20 YALE JOURNAL OF LAW AND FEMINISM 1 (2008).

DOI: 10.4324/9781003405627-19

institutions and has an internal system of dynamics reflective of broader social ideologies that shift responsibilities, like caretaking, to specific members of the family, especially women.

Fineman's work on the family serves as an important example of what would become another central tenet in vulnerability theory: that institutions matter. This idea of the institution is key to Fineman's work on vulnerability, which acknowledges that power and privilege are "conferred through the operation of societal institutions and relationships."[2] What are the institutions that matter? Fineman's scholarship has generated numerous works considering the unique vulnerabilities of institutional formations from the family to corporations and governmental agencies.

Social problems of our contemporary moment require, as Fineman argues, social and collective solutions. As she states, "From the moment of birth until we die, we inevitably act, interact, and react in relationships with others and within institutions."[3] By recognizing institutions themselves as vulnerable we can better understand the way people are situated within economic, social, cultural, and institutional relationships that alter the trajectories of their lives. Fineman's vulnerability theory begs the question of how the state should be supporting and building resilience through the various institutions that shape people's lives and how these institutions should be structured to ensure resilience.

Using the case *Parents Involved in Community Schools v. Seattle School District No. 1*, Fineman illustrates how vulnerability theory can be applied. This case considers how Seattle-area schools allowed students to apply to high schools in the city. On occasions when too many students had listed the same school first, race became a tiebreaking factor. The goal was to maintain racial diversity. The case forwarded a strict equality and colorblindness framework suggesting that any racial classification, in this case one which helped preserve racial balance, undermines the social project to stop discriminating on race.

The outcome of *Parents Involved* was a disappointment to racial justice advocates, laying bare the limitations of formal equality, which "concerns differences, but seeks relentlessly to minimize or ignore the implications of such differences ...," undermining our ability to use law to bring about true societal change.[4] Vulnerability theory calls for a shift away from difference and discrimination and toward power and privilege. It asks us to consider how the state *could* be more responsive to individuals regardless of individual characteristics. This would challenge what formal equality has produced: "a passive toleration of inequality and complicity in the conferral of often

2 Martha Albertson Fineman, *Equality and Difference – The Restrained State*, 66 ALA. L. REV. 609, 613 (2014–15).

3 Martha Albertson Fineman, *Vulnerability and Inevitable Inequality*, 4 OSLO LAW REVIEW 133, 145 (2017).

4 *Id.* at 610.

unwarranted privilege on the few."[5] In turn, vulnerability theory allows us to shift toward an emphasis on the role of the state in building resilient citizens who are productive and participate in society. The state should have a role in "ensuring that its institutions do not operate in ways that unduly privilege some and disadvantage others" and forces us to acknowledge that we exist in a community of citizens that relies on institutions.[6]

Fineman's theory allows us to move away from a liberal legalistic approach to society's challenges and toward seeing individuals and institutions as vulnerable. This core idea has been enormously generative for legal scholars. Vulnerability theory has been applied to far-reaching sets of topics including environmental law, social justice, corporate law, and health law. It has generated vast amounts of productive and scholarly debate about how to imagine the role of the state and identity in the context of ameliorating social injustice. Vulnerability theory has redefined the role of critical scholarship by recognizing the importance (and inevitability) of law and situating the vulnerable and socially dependent human as the proper legal subject.

5 *Id.* at 613.
6 *Id.* at 625.

Chapter 14

Vulnerability and Inevitable Inequality (2017)[1]

Fineman first introduced vulnerability theory in her 2008 article, "The Vulnerable Subject: Anchoring Equality in the Human Condition." Here, written several years later, she provides insight into the evolution of her feminist approach to dependency and caretaking to a more universal approach focused on human vulnerability and the privileges and disadvantages that accompany social roles and relationships. She offers a broad explanation of vulnerability theory and its focus on social institutions and state responsibility. Further, she expands upon the limitations of traditional equality theories and proposes vulnerability theory as a framework for thinking about how the law should respond to inherently unequal relationships, like that of parent/child.

My work over the past several decades has grappled with the limitations of equality. This struggle has resulted in the development of a legal paradigm that brings vulnerability and dependency, as well as social institutions and relationships, together into an analysis of state responsibility. This analysis goes well beyond concern with formal equality and impermissible discrimination.

What follows is an account of the development of a theory based on human vulnerability in which the state is theorized as the legitimate governing entity and is tasked with a responsibility to establish and monitor social institutions and relationships that facilitate the acquisition of individual and social resilience. The theory is based on a descriptive account of the human condition as one of universal and continuous vulnerability. The Anglo-American liberal legal imagination often obscures or overlooks this reality. The potential normative implications of the theory are found in the assertion that state policy and law should be responsive to human vulnerability. However, the call for a responsive state does not dictate the form responses should take, only that they reflect the reality of human vulnerability. Thus, this approach to law and policy allows for the adaptation of solutions appropriate to differing legal structures and political cultures.

1 This essay is from Martha Albertson Fineman, *Vulnerability and Inevitable Inequality*, 4 Oslo Law Review 133, 134–35, 139–149 (2017). The article is licensed under the CC BY 4.0 license (https://creativecommons.org/licenses/by/4.0/). © 2017 Martha Albertson Fineman.

DOI: 10.4324/9781003405627-20

Vulnerability theory provides a template with which to refocus critical attention, raising new questions and challenging established assumptions about individual and state responsibility and the role of law, as well as allowing us to address social relationships of inevitable inequality. In this regard, vulnerability theory goes beyond the normative claim for equality, be it formal or substantive in nature, to suggest that we interrogate what may be just and appropriate mechanisms to structure the terms and practices of inequality.

In considering human vulnerability it is significant that, as embodied beings, individual humans find themselves dependent upon, and embedded within, social relationships and institutions throughout the life course. While the institutions and relationships upon which any individual relies will vary over time and in response to changes in embodiment and social contexts, the fact that we require some set of social relationships and institutional structure remains constant. A vulnerability approach argues that the state must be responsive to the realities of human vulnerability and its corollary, social dependency, as well as to situations reflecting inherent or necessary inequality, when it initially establishes or sets up mechanisms to monitor these relationships and institutions.

Understanding human vulnerability suggests that equality, as it tends to be used to measure the treatment of individuals or groups, is a limiting aspiration when it comes to social justice. Equality typically is measured by comparing the circumstances of those individuals considered equals. This approach inevitably generates suspicion of unequal or differential treatment absent past discrimination or present stereotyping, particularly if practiced by the state. Even in its substantive form, assessments of equality focus on specific individuals and operate to consider and compare social positions or injuries at a particular point in time.

An equality model or anti-discrimination mandate is certainly the appropriate response in many instances: one person, one vote, and equal pay for equal work are areas where equality seems clearly suitable. However, equality is less helpful, and may even be an unjust measure, when applied in situations of inescapable or inevitable inequality where differing levels of authority and power are appropriate, such as in defining the legal relationship between parent and child or employer and employee. Such relationships historically have been relegated to the "private" sphere of life, away from state regulation. When explicitly addressed, situations of inevitable inequality are typically handled in law and policy either by imposing a fabricated equivalence between the individuals or by declaring that an equality mandate does not apply because the individuals to be compared are positioned differently. An example of the imposition of fictitious equality, in response to inevitable inequality, is evident in situations involving parties who occupy obviously unequal bargaining positions, like the contract that is fabricated in the employment context. The distinction in the legal treatment of children as compared to adults also exemplifies the differently positioned resolution for unequal legal treatment. In both instances, state responsibility for ensuring equitable treatment for differently positioned individuals is minimized within the overriding framework of equality.

Equality in Context

The advent of the gender-equality movement revealed contradictions and incompatibilities between the structure of the family and the workplace. The demands of the employment market conflicted with the needs of the family, preventing gender-equality from being implemented. It seemed clear that in order to achieve such change, other institutions would have to undergo complementary evolutions, incorporating new family expectations into their operations.

To effect such change, I suggested that inevitable dependency should be the concern of society generally, with responsibility shared across social institutions. This responsibility could be fulfilled through accommodation and support for those who assumed the role of caretaker – the derivatively dependent. We all owe a debt to those who care for inevitable dependents and this debt must be paid through collective means; such a duty could not be discharged simply by being nice to your own mother. Making an analogy to military service, I argued that individual soldiers were assigned the responsibility of defending society, but they were also given the resources necessary to do that job, as well as being compensated economically. Caretakers are also dependent on resources to accomplish their socially important and essential work. Those resources could not be (and were not in all too many cases) supplied by the family. I argued that social responsibility must be more equitably spread across the societal institutions that benefited from care work, with the workplace in particular expanding to accommodate caretakers.

State responsibility should result in regulations designed to ensure such accommodation, as well as the provision of services like childcare centers or subsidies in order to ease the structural and economic burdens that inevitable dependency places on the caretaker and family. These arguments were motivated by an understanding of the family as a social institution that is not isolated but, rather, connected to and co-dependent upon other institutions that needed the future workers, citizens, entrepreneurs, and so on that the family nurtured in its role in reproducing society.

The mainstream academic responses to my arguments about inevitable dependency were predictable. The situation of children was easily overlooked when it came to an assessment of equality and state responsibility. They were not equals. Their inevitable dependency differentiated them from the adults in the family, but it was a disadvantage everyone suffered and would outgrow. Children were the responsibility of the family, and their interests could justly be subsumed within it. As for the ill and elderly, they had the personal responsibility to provide for themselves in old age through insurance and pension plans. If they had not, means-tested social welfare programs existed for those who had failed to live up to their personal responsibility to protect themselves.[2]

2 The classic statement of this argument generally is made by Wendy W. Williams in her article *The Equality Crisis: Some Reflections on Culture, Courts, and Feminism*, 7 WOMEN'S RIGHTS L. REP. 175 (1982). *See also* Peter E. Edelman, *Promoting Family by Promoting Work: The Hole in Martha Fineman's Doughnut*, 85 AM. U. J. GENDER SOC. POL'Y & L. (2000).

I thought that the arguments about derivative dependency would be somewhat harder to deflect, but the prevalence of economic modeling for assessing just about any social institution and relationship facilitated its dismissal. Caretakers were free and equal individuals who had made a "personal choice." It was hardly society's responsibility to subsidize that choice. In the words of one commentator, if one person had a preference for a child, while another preferred a Porsche, why should society treat these choices differently?[3] These were merely individual decisions and neither preference deserved social subsidy. Thus, an emphasis on personal liberty and autonomy was combined with an assertion of equality or impartiality and used to argue against directing law and policy to address existing inequality. Once again, arguments for a collective (or social) ideal of justice were beaten back by reference to the ideal of individual, not institutional, responsibility.

While it was not persuasive to the liberal, individual choice-oriented commentators, the development of the concept of derivative dependency in the family context was a theoretically important step in the evolution of vulnerability theory. It had moved my thinking beyond the individual and individual characteristics, such as gender, to focus on societal structures and the characteristics of social institutions and relationships. The advent of formal equality in family law did not mean that society's institutions of family and work were transformed. Those structures continued to subordinate, but no longer formally on the basis of gender. Structural disadvantage remained intact, a product of a reality in which society either does not place much value on caretaking as a social function and therefore need not accommodate it, or that society (or some segments of it) places so much value on caretaking that it should not be diminished by being quantified or monetized in social policy.

In other words, it is the nature of and significance given to the social task of caretaker that operates to disadvantage the individuals who occupy that role, not the gender of the caretaker. If men become caretakers, they also suffer economically and professionally. The market is structured so as to assume no responsibility for the reproduction of society. When the state concedes it has some responsibility, it is only to serve as a highly stigmatized backup when the family "fails." All caretakers, regardless of sex, will be subordinated by this structure and the ideology of family autonomy, independence, and self-sufficiency that supports it. At that time, I realized that what I had been analyzing as a gender problem was actually a societal problem that extends well beyond a gender equality frame. I

3 The "Porsche Preference" argument states that if someone prefers a child, this preference should not be treated differently than any other choice (like the choice to own a Porsche). Society should not subsidize either preference. For recent advocacy of this idea *see* Greg Mankiw, *Is Community Rating Fair?*, http://gregmankiw.blogspot.com/2013/11/is-community-rating-fair.html accessed August 28, 2017. But also, for a more sophisticated development of this line of reasoning, *see* Mary Ann Case, *How High the Apple Pie – A Few Troubling Questions about Where, Why, and How the Burden of Care for Children Should Be Shifted*, 76 CHI.-KENT L. REV. 1753 (2001).

ultimately understood that what was needed was an approach to social justice that challenged the liberal reliance on individual choice and the construct of the private family.

My current focus extends well beyond the family to include all social and institutional relationships and the justice problems they may reveal in contemporary society. In developing a vulnerability approach to the justice issue, I have been guided by the realization that social problems need social or collective, not just individual, solutions. Developing a collective or social justice approach requires that we understand the nature of those who compose the collective. I thus begin with a descriptive or empirical understanding of what it means to be human. From that foundational premise, I develop a normative, or theoretical, perspective on the just allocation of responsibility for individual and societal well-being. Such responsibility must be shared between the individual and the state and its institutions. At the same time, social problems also require a confrontation with, and response to, situations of inherent or inevitable inequality.

Vulnerability Theory

Reconstructing the Political Subject as the Vulnerable Subject in Law

Although it is often narrowly understood as merely "openness to physical or emotional harm," vulnerability should be recognized as *the* primal human condition. As embodied beings, we are universally and individually constantly susceptible to change in our well-being. Change can be positive or negative – we become ill and are injured or decline, but we also grow in abilities and develop new skills and relationships. The term 'vulnerable', used to connote the continuous susceptibility to change in both our bodily and social well-being that all human beings experience, makes it clear that there is no position of invulnerability – no conclusive way to prevent or avoid change.

For the most part, human vulnerability has been ignored or marginalized in mainstream legal theory or political philosophy. Particularly in contemporary politics increasingly shaped by themes of austerity and purported threats from immigration, we see a growing fixation on personal responsibility, individual autonomy, self-sufficiency, and independence, buoyed by an insistence that only a severely restrained state can be an economically responsible one. When the term vulnerability is used, it is typically (and inaccurately) attributed to only some individuals or groups, who are referred to as "vulnerable populations." It is also used as a basis for comparison: some people are viewed as more or less vulnerable, or as differently or uniquely vulnerable. This perspective ignores the universality and constancy of vulnerability as I use the term and is merely another way of identifying bias, discrimination, and social disadvantage rather than focusing on structural arrangements that affect everyone. In other words, it is another way to present an equal protection argument.

Human vulnerability has social, as well as physical and material consequences. On the most obvious level, our embodiment means that we are innately dependent on the provision of care by others when we are infants and often when we are ill, aged, or disabled. It is human vulnerability that compels the creation of social relationships found in designated social institutions, such as the family, the market, the educational system and so on. The very formation of communities, associations, and even political entities and nation-states are responses to human vulnerability. Social problems emerge when these social institutions and relationships are not functioning well.

Importantly, a vulnerability approach does not begin with discrimination or difference in legal treatment as the primary evil to be addressed. Rather, it begins with the assertion that we need to rethink this conception of the legal subject to make it more reflective of the actual human experience. It requires that we recognize the ways in which power and privilege are conferred through the operation of societal institutions, relationships, and the creation of social identities, sometimes inequitably. Because law should recognize, respond to, and, perhaps, redirect unjustified inequality, the critical issue must be whether the balance of power struck by law was warranted.

Social identities are manifested within institutions and do not manifestly reflect individual characteristics, such as race or sex. However, they do represent the allocation of power and privilege between occupants based on the social function of the institution and their social roles within it. Individuals occupy different social identities as they age and expand their interaction with different social institutions and relationships (from child to teenager to adult – from family to school to workplace). General idealized social identities, such as parent/child, employer/employee, and shareholder/consumer, are formed and operate as functional and ideological constructs, which tend to shape individual options. These linked, complementary social identities also may reflect an intrinsic inequality between their occupants, an inequality that is often not only justifiable, but also necessary.

Idealized identities are human constructions and, as such, they are not static. However, as archetypes they do reflect the historic values and priorities of society and tend to be relatively stable for extended periods of time. Proposed changes in, or widespread deviations from, these idealized identities can provoke social turmoil and backlash. So too, changes in individual status can give rise to insecurity and anger or frustration, as well as a sense of accomplishment or opportunity.

What vulnerability theory offers is a way of thinking about political subjectivity that recognizes and incorporates differences and can attend to situations of inevitable inequality among legal subjects. In this regard, one advantage of vulnerability theory is that it can be applied in situations of inevitable or unresolvable inequality: it does not seek equality, but equity. A vulnerability analysis incorporates a life-course perspective while also reflecting the role of the social institutions and relationships in which our social identities are formed and enforced. It also defines a robust sense of state responsibility for social institutions and relationships.

Taking Account of Differences

The process of analyzing the differences that arise from individual experience within social structures does not begin with the particular characteristics of the individual, but with the nature of social arrangements. The abstract and inevitably contested legal principles often referred to in human rights literature, such as equality, liberty, and dignity, are not the measure for this inquiry, however. Nor does it rely on placing individuals into distinct but comparable categories for purposes of equal protection analysis (male/female, white/black, etc.).

There are two relevant forms of individual difference in a vulnerability approach – those that arise because we are *embodied* beings and those that arise because we are social beings *embedded* in social institutions and relationships. Consideration of these two forms of difference will inevitably draw attention to distinct facets of social organization and activities. These differences also require distinct legal and policy approaches and suggest specific roles for the state to play regarding its responsibility for citizens.

Embodied Differences

Perhaps the most evident of embodied differences are the physical variations exemplified in anti-discrimination laws. These represent the horizontal assessment of difference. These physical differences have a census quality, accessing variations and characteristics that exist in society at a given time. They tend to be constructed as static and are often distinguished doctrinally with terms such as "immutable." While discrimination laws address some of these differences, others, such as age and those associated with physical and mental ability, continue to serve as justification for differential treatment.

In addition to the bodily differences that are manifest across various members of society at any given time, are those differences that evolve within each individual body. These differences reflect the progressive biological and developmental stages within an individual human life. Individual bodies will mature and grow, as well as age and decline. We can think of these differences as occurring along a vertical and temporal dimension of analysis – within the individual over time.

These differences form the basis for classifying groups along developmental lines: as infants, children, or the elderly. The law as it is currently fashioned does allow for differential treatment, or discrimination, based on these developmental differences.

Based on categorical assumptions about capabilities and competence, the law recognizes "special" treatment for some groups based on developmental difference. The law actually creates a modified legal subjectivity (a distinct legal identity) for those not neatly fitting within the ability boundaries defining the contemporary legal subject. As a result, as an individual passes through various developmental stages, their legal identifier changes: from child to adult, but also from adult to elderly or, sometimes, disabled. To the extent that shifting legal subjectivity also ignores or diminishes what is considered to be the appropriate level of state responsibility for individual well-being, this is a problem. For example, the way that the law defines relationships within the family may result in parental privilege eclipsing or obscuring the state's independent responsibility for the well-being of the child. While the institutions and relationships will change, our understanding of state responsibility with regard to human vulnerability must be consistent across the life course. Infancy and childhood should be understood as merely inevitable developmental stages in the life of the vulnerable subject, not as the occasion for the creation of distinct and diminished categories of state responsibility.

Perhaps not surprisingly, it is the vertical dimension of embodied difference that is of primary interest in a vulnerability analysis. The differences we each experience over time show the inevitability of human dependence on others and on society and its institutions.

They also illuminate the inevitable nature of inequality in social relationships. Physical or emotional dependence on others is particularly evident in infancy and childhood, but is also often found with severe illness, disability, and advanced age. This form of dependency I previously referred to as inevitable: it is universally experienced, an inherent characteristic in the human condition.

There are laws and norms that guide the unequal relationship between a caretaker and a dependent infant, for example. Law defines parental responsibility but has also conferred a parallel parental right that can work to keep state surveillance at bay. Currently, there is a great deal of debate about the nature and extent of parental rights and the tension generated when the child is also positioned as a rights-holder.[4] Each state must respond to this tension as it negotiates the balance between parental privilege (rights) and the child's right to protection and provision from the state in its laws. It addresses this tension when it creates laws governing legal relationships such as the marital family or custodial parent. It is also responding when it defines parental responsibilities with regard to mandatory laws addressing children's education, health, and discipline. The concept of family privacy attempts to draw a line between family and state responsibility in favor of the parent.

Embedded Differences

A consideration of the vulnerability that marks each of us, and does so throughout the life course, should make it apparent that, of necessity, human beings are social beings. From the moment of birth until we die, we inevitably act, interact, and react in relationships with others and within institutions.

4 In the US, this conflict is what led many conservative commentators to reject the United Nations Convention on the Rights of the Child. Martha Albertson Fineman & George Shepherd, *Homeschooling: Choosing Parental Rights over Children's Interests*, 46 UNIV. BALTIMORE L.R. 57, 106 (2016).

However, these social interactions necessitated by our shared vulnerability also produce differences among individuals. All infants are dependent on the care provided within an institutional arrangement, often designated as "family." However, there are differences among individual families with regard to the resources and abilities they bring to the social task of providing care.

Institutional differences affecting individual outcomes are also evident in the expanding sets of social relationships found in educational, employment, financial, and other institutions upon which we must rely as we proceed through life. Predictably, every society is composed of individuals differently situated within webs of economic, social, cultural, and institutional relationships that profoundly affect our destinies and fortunes, structuring individual options and creating or impeding opportunities. The initial questions raised in a vulnerability perspective are structural: does the state monitor a given institution in a way that is responsive to human vulnerability? In other words, can the differences in treatment be justified?

Institutions and Resilience

As previously explained, as vulnerable human beings we are all, and always, dependent upon societal structures and institutions, which provide us with the assets or resources that enable us to survive, and even thrive, within society. This institutional focus has the effect of supplementing attention to the individual subject by placing individuals within their social context. Although nothing can completely mitigate our vulnerability, resilience is what provides an individual with the means and ability to recover from harm, setbacks, and the misfortunes that affect our lives.

While a vulnerability analysis begins with a description of universal vulnerability, it is the particularity of the manifestations of vulnerability and the nature of resilience that are of ultimate interest. Resilience is the critical, yet incomplete, solution to our vulnerability. There are at least five different types of resources or assets that societal organizations and institutions can provide: physical, human, social, ecological, or environmental, and existential. Physical resources determine our present quality of life and include such things as housing, food, entertainment, and means of transportation. Physical resources also provide for our future well-being in the form of savings and investments. Human resources contribute to our individual development, allowing participation in the market, and the accumulation of material resources. Human resources are often referred to as 'human capital' and are primarily developed through systems that provide education, training, knowledge, and experience.

Social resources give us a sense of belonging and community and are provided through the relationships we form within various institutions, including the family, social networks, political parties, and labor or trade unions. In recent decades, identity characteristics, such as race, ethnicity, and gender, have constituted powerful networks of affiliation within political and other institutions. By contrast, ecological resources are related to the positions we occupy in relation to the physical, built, or natural environments in which we find ourselves. On the spiritual level, existential resources are provided by systems of belief or aesthetics, such as religion, culture or art, and perhaps even politics. These belief systems can help us to understand our place within the world and allow us to see meaning and beauty in our existence.

There is a link between these various types of resources and state responsibility. Many of the institutions providing resources that give us resilience can only be brought into legal existence through state mechanisms. Importantly, resilience is not something we are born with, but is accumulated over the course of our lifetimes within social structures and institutions over which individuals may have little, if any, control – whether these institutions are classified as public or private, or are called family, market, or state. Resilience is also cumulative. The degree of resilience an individual has is largely dependent on the quality and quantity of resources or assets that she or he has at their disposal or command. A resilient individual can take advantage of opportunities knowing that if they take a risk and the desired outcome fails to transpire, they have the capacity to recover.

While sometimes a lack of resilience can be deemed an individual failing, often it is a function of unequal access to certain societal structures or the result of unequal allocations of privilege and power within those structures. Too often, we take those who are deemed to be failing and segregate them according to some characteristic or another, such as poverty, illness, or age, and then classify them as "more vulnerable" to harm or disadvantage. However, labeling some individuals and herding them into "populations" defined as differently or particularly vulnerable (and therefore somehow inadequate) stigmatizes those individuals. This is so if the purpose of the designation of a vulnerable population is to protect (as it is with children/elderly) or to punish or control (as it is with at-risk youth/single mothers).

In a vulnerability analysis, the basis for distinguishing some individuals from better positioned *but equally* vulnerable individuals in the first instance would revolve around questions of access to sufficient resources, with a deficit indicating they lacked the resilience that is necessary to address human vulnerability. Significantly, the initial emphasis here is on the distribution or allocation of resources and the structures within which they are produced. This suggests that the first question to be considered is whether institutional, not individual, functioning is inadequate. This inquiry shifts the focus to state and social responsibility because it recognizes that a deficit in resources often reflects an institutional or societal failing more than an individual one.

The fact that a vulnerability analysis brings the life course into focus is also important in thinking about resilience. Resilience-conferring institutions operate both simultaneously and sequentially in society. That they are sequential is significant. The failure of one system in this sequence to provide necessary resources, such as the failure to provide an adequate education, affects an individual's future prospects in employment, building adult family relationships, aging and retirement. Given that institutions farther down the line are constructed in ways that are contingent on an individual's successful gathering of necessary resources in earlier systems, it is often impossible to fully recover from, or compensate for, resource deprivation. Someone lacking a solid education typically will have fewer skills and fewer options and opportunities in the workplace, which will make supporting a family more difficult, and also likely mean a more precarious retirement as well as fewer savings to cushion them in the event of accident, injury, or illness.

Moreover, sometimes privileges conferred in one system can compensate for or even cancel out disadvantages encountered in others. A solid, early start with regard to education, such as that provided by Head Start, an effective pre-school program, may trump poverty as a predictor of success later in school.[5] This is particularly likely when coupled with the advantages that a social or relational system can provide, such as a supportive family and cohesive social network.

Society's institutions provide the assets or resources that give us resilience and in so doing actually produce – or fail to produce – social, political, and economic opportunities. Access to these opportunities can confer privilege, while exclusion acts to disadvantage. Thus, individual failure should not be seen as merely the consequence of individual irresponsibility. It also is, perhaps primarily, the failure of society and its institutions.

Conclusion: The Need for a Responsive State

Recognition of the universality of vulnerability is theoretically important to the normative argument for a responsive state. It provides for both the critique and the suggested [re]construction of social and legal arrangements. The political and legal subject of law in the first instance is conceived of as a universal subject, an idealized ordinary being. The conceptualization of this legal subject encompasses everyone in society: people are seen either as "full" legal subjects, conforming to this ideal, or given a modified legal subjectivity based on their deviations from that legal subject. Fundamental principles of democracy require, at least in the abstract, that laws should be applied equally to those who are determined to be similarly situated, which underlies the slogan that we are a nation of laws, not men (*sic*), and that no man (*sic*) is above the law. A vulnerability approach does not dispute this basic principle but argues that the characteristics of the legal subject that are universalized must be based on human vulnerability and, therefore, inclusive across both horizontal and vertical dimensions of difference.

5 Head Start is a federal program advocating school readiness for children from low-income families up to age five by providing nutrition, health, and social services along with education and intellectual development services. *About Head Start Services*, Office of Head Start, https://www.acf.hhs.gov/ohs/about/head-start accessed August 31, 2017.

When this democratic principle of equality was formed, the political subject was a limited or refined one: white, male, property-owning or tax-paying, of a certain age and/or religion, and free. Over the course of the nineteenth and twentieth centuries, certain qualifiers were removed, and political legal subjectivity formally grew to encompass previously excluded groups. However, this modern legal subject has retained certain secondary characteristics that continue to center on the needs and political sensibilities of an eighteenth century male citizen sheltered by institutions such as the patriarchal family and the privileges of a master-servant mentality. The legal subject typically envisioned in policy and political arguments today assumes a distorted and inappropriate equality of position. It valorizes the fully competent, capable individual adult, as well as liberty, self-sufficiency, and autonomy.

This prototype of the legal subject ignores vulnerability and dependency and is a radically individualistic mischaracterization of what it means to be human. It must be confronted and contested. I believe the concept of the vulnerable legal subject has the power to disrupt the logic of individual choice and personal responsibility built on this liberal stereotype, and to facilitate the construction of an effective counter-discourse with which to confront neoliberalism's fixation on personal responsibility and its insistence that only a severely restrained state can be a responsible one.

It does so by articulating a more inclusive and realistic legal subject – one that makes it clear that injury or injustice does inevitably arise when the state remains unresponsive to human vulnerability and dependency. This legal subject, who is both embodied and socially embedded, needs access to resources that will enable them to endure or prosper from change, even harm, throughout institutions and relationships across the life course. A guarantee of equality is not enough for this legal subject. The responsive state must be one that recognizes relationships or positions of inevitable inequality, as well as universal vulnerability and dependency acting as an instrument of social justice in both its law-making and enforcement functions.

Chapter 15

Equality and Difference – The Restrained State (2014)[1]

Here, Fineman deftly illustrates the limitations of an equality-centric approach to state responsibility, which restrains the state from taking affirmative action to achieve justice. She analyzes a case in which a focus on overt discrimination on the basis of identity characteristics rather than generalized harm defeated affirmative school desegregation efforts. She demonstrates that under a formal equality model "the state and its actors and institutions can legally treat individuals poorly, just as long as they treat them the same." As an alternative, she offers vulnerability theory as an analytical lens through which to examine the allocation of power and privilege among social institutions.

Contemporary American law, culture, and political theory restrain the concept of equality as a tool of social justice. Equality in conjunction with a strong emphasis on personal liberty operates as a mandate for curtailing state action, rather than an aspirational measure of the comparative well-being of individuals. As a check on state involvement, our cramped notion of equality limits the state's ability to affirmatively address economic, political, social, and structural inequalities.[2]

As interpreted in modern Supreme Court jurisprudence, the Equal Protection Clause of the US Constitution actually works to restrict the remedial ability of the state. Equality is understood as a mandate for formalized equal treatment; it operates as a nondiscrimination ideal. This ideal minimizes existing structural disadvantages and thus impedes a more substantive approach to equality, which would recognize and accommodate differences and consider outcome as well as treatment. This formal version of equality, while appropriate on some levels and in some contexts, is not sufficiently flexible to address contemporary disparities in political, social, and economic well-being in America.[3] Any distinctions in the

1 This essay originally appeared in: Martha Albertson Fineman, *Equality and Difference – The Restrained State*, 66 ALA. L. REV. 609, 609–14, 625–26 (2014–2015).

2 *See, e.g.*, CAROLINE KNOWLES, FAMILY BOUNDARIES 108–9 (1996) (discussing popular constructions of children, women, and minorities as vulnerable, pathological, and in a perpetual state of victimhood).

3 *See, e.g.*, *Parents Involved in Cmty. Sch. v. Seattle Sch. Dist. No. 1*, 551 U.S. 701, 733–34 (2007) (holding that a student assignment plan that relied on racial

DOI: 10.4324/9781003405627-21

treatment of individuals can raise suspicion about government action, and this is particularly true with distinctions involving personal characteristics that are virtually impossible to constitutionally justify, such as race or gender.[4] At the same time, the emphasis on discrimination or difference in the treatment of protected individuals or groups has been viewed as the primary affront to the principle of equality, rather than the widespread (but nondiscriminatory) exclusion from the benefits of American prosperity and technological advancement experienced by those who stand outside as well as inside these protected identity categories. That generalized harm and deprivation is not seen as constituting a legally remedial form of inequality indicates that an adherence to formal equality has seemingly eclipsed our moral and political aspirations for social justice. In effect, this means that the state and its actors and institutions can legally treat individuals poorly, just as long as they treat them the same.

Equality and Difference

The emphasis on equal treatment found in contemporary American jurisprudence may be desirable and appropriate when the class or nature of the differences between individuals has been deemed not to matter. This is the case when equality mandates one-person-one-vote or equal pay for equal work. However, an ideology of equality which concedes that differences exist, but seeks relentlessly to minimize or ignore the implications of such differences, makes it difficult to use law as a remedy for many situations and circumstances. In turn, this makes the attainment of substantive equality difficult, if not impossible, to achieve. *Parents Involved in Community Schools v. Seattle School District No. 1* is an example of this phenomenon involving voluntary measures undertaken by school districts to desegregate classrooms.

The case involved a series of Seattle-area school districts which had voluntarily incorporated a race-sensitive student assignment plan to determine which public schools certain children could attend. The goal of the plan was to ensure that the racial balance of each school fell within a predetermined range, calculated based on the racial composition of the entire school district as a whole; the school district thus considered each individual student's race when assigning them to a particular school. When some students were not allowed to attend particular schools because of their race, their parents brought suit, contending

classification to allocate slots in oversubscribed high schools could not be used to advance racial equality).

4 Concerning the problems with formal equality and equal protection in American jurisprudence, *see* Catharine A. MacKinnon, *Substantive Equality: A Perspective*, 96 MINN. L. REV. 1, 1–2 (2011) ("The emptiness of U.S. constitutional equal protection doctrine has long been apparent from its lack of reach to its shaky grasp on questions of sex inequality.").

that this race-sensitive allocation to public schools was in violation of the Fourteenth Amendment guarantee of equal protection.[5]

Five of the nine Justices held the assignment plan impermissible based on lack of necessity and due to the absence of a history of intentional discrimination in the districts. Justice Kennedy disagreed with the four more liberal members of the Court that the Constitution *permits* such desegregation efforts, even though it does not *require* them in the absence of prior discrimination.[6] Chief Justice Roberts's concluding sentence clearly illustrated the position of the conservative Justices, perhaps marking the future of equality in cases of racial imbalance: "The way to stop discrimination on the basis of race is to stop discriminating on the basis of race."[7]

The approach taken by the majority in this case shows how a focus on discrimination can inevitably result in a narrowed focus on a moment of injury or legal harm rather than on the historical, systemic, and institutional structures that surround that moment. It was not the existence of racial imbalance or isolation that constitutionally justified a response by the school districts, but rather the finding of harm as occurring either in the past in the form of discrimination, or currently as demonstrated by a compelling need for action or a showing of necessity.[8] The inquiry also focused on individuals and their actions to the exclusion of an institutional and contextual assessment.[9] The inquiry thus remained oriented toward specific acts of past discrimination or proof of current harm, while the extent and nature of general state responsibility to respond to racial imbalance and isolation was left unrecognized and in doubt constitutionally.

Ironically, the plurality opinion in *Parents Involved* also demonstrates how, in many instances, taking contexts and structures into account can reveal that the solution or appropriate response to inequality is *not* the imposition of greater equality through law. Resorting to formal equality in situations marked by existing inequalities of circumstances often serves to reinforce and justify those same inequalities. An approach to equal protection developed in response to blatant discrimination and exclusion now prevents remedial measures designed to address the legacy of that exclusion.

Taking Account of Differences

In my recent work, I have argued for the development of an approach to social justice issues that puts equality aside and brings differences into consideration. The emphasis here is placed not on an abstract and inevitably contested legal principle, such as liberty or dignity, or on an inherently comparative or relative

5 551 U.S. 701, 709–11 (2007).
6 *Id.* at 790.
7 *Id.* at 748 (majority opinion).
8 *Id.* at 720–28.
9 *Id.* at 759.

measure, such as equality, but on the ways in which the universal subject who is to be governed by those principles has been constructed in both political and legal discourses. This approach begins with the recognition of universality or sameness among individuals (the fundamental equality position) but also considers the inevitable differences among them. The universality is found in the vulnerability that marks our existence as embodied and finite beings. The differences arise because there are different stages and manifestations of embodiment, as well as from the fact that we are differently embedded in social relationships and within societal institutions. This conceptual approach is what I have called the "vulnerability paradigm." An approach that considers vulnerability would make forms of societally-produced differences a predominant focus because they provide the foundation for the assertion that we need a responsive state – one with a clear duty to effectively ensure realistic equality of access and opportunity to society's resource-generating institutions for everyone regardless of their individual characteristics. Instead, what equality of treatment has provided is the passive toleration of inequality and complicity in the conferral of often unwarranted privilege on the few.

Importantly, a vulnerability approach does not identify discrimination or difference as the primary evil to be addressed. Rather, it calls attention to the way power and privilege are conferred through the operation of societal institutions and relationships. The identities under question in this regard are those social identities or functions that confer privilege and power. Social identities are manufactured within institutional relationships and prevalent ideologies, not found in the designation of attributes associated with individual characteristics, actions, or affiliations, such as race, sex, religion, or sexual orientation. These social identities and the role of the state in establishing and maintaining them raise substantial questions about our historic commitment to the idea of a singular and coherent legal and political subjectivity. Ultimately, the vulnerability analysis seeks to incorporate a theory of differences in order to articulate a more complex legal and political subject – the "vulnerable subject," as well as to make a claim for a more responsive state.

Concluding Reflections – The Need for a more Responsive State

One of the strengths of a vulnerability analysis is that it does not direct focus only or even primarily upon a moment of harm or injury, but rather takes a life-course perspective. This perspective means that a focus on the typical functioning of societal institutions and their role in building resilience is as fundamental to a robust ethic of equality as is attention to individual behavior and discriminatory motivation. Through the law the state creates and maintains this network of institutions and the social identities contained within them. The relationship between the state and its institutions is one of mutual dependence, and a failure on the part of an institution to operate in an effective manner should immediately prompt state corrective action.

Returning to the situation in *Parents Involved*, the state has an interest in ensuring that each individual is prepared to become a productive and fully participating citizen. It may resort to the educational institutions it legitimates to accomplish that task, but it should not be able to abandon responsibility for the ways in which such institutions operate. Nor should it be prohibited from addressing and responding to the potential for future harm to individuals and/or society through the imposition of responsive policies upon those institutions. The school boards in *Parents Involved* were trying to live up to that responsibility, not because discrimination or harm had or was occurring, but because their members understood the long-term advantages of children participating in a racially equitable and diverse educational experience. Unfortunately, the way that equality is currently understood and implemented in American jurisprudence severely limited the schools' ability to assume responsibility and act to prevent future harm or disadvantage.

In contrast to the narrow approach undertaken in *Parents Involved*, vulnerability theory would encourage governmental actions that are directed toward responsiveness, recognizing not only the state's role in preventing discrimination, but a role in ensuring that its institutions do not operate in ways that unduly privilege some and disadvantage others.

Ensuring that societal institutions, such as those which make up the educational system, provide benefits and resilience-building opportunities to all individuals equitably should be the responsibility of the state. State recognition of inherent human vulnerability and dependency should also define how it approaches its obligations to individual persons, familial units, and the vast interconnected community of citizens that rely on societal institutions. A vulnerability inquiry may also suggest that the state sometimes act in a differential manner to those bound within social identities or past histories that currently operate to their disadvantage. True equity in access and opportunity requires that the state take existing structural differences into account and work toward their neutralization, so that those who have been historically disadvantaged are uplifted to a more level playing field.

My hope is that by taking human vulnerability seriously and placing it at the core of our understanding of state responsibility, we may begin to expand the ways in which we think about regulation and market responsibility. It brings into the discussion not only the possibility of human agency and equality, but also the reality of human need and dependency in the past, present, and future. The realities of our universal, constant, and inescapable vulnerabilities argue for a responsive state that ensures equality of opportunity and meaningful, not merely formal, access for individuals to society's institutions. That might require a recognition and response to difference in varied contexts and circumstances. In *Parents Involved*, this might have meant allowing school districts to direct more educational resources toward those students who are actually disadvantaged and the schools that must educate them, or to support the development of policies that attempt to avoid or prevent disadvantage in the future.

Chapter 16

The "Still Face" of a Compassionately-Challenged Society (2017)

In this essay[1], Fineman engages the metaphor of a "still-faced" mother to argue for a more compassionate state. The powerful image of state as mother and citizens as empathy-starved infants fuels her impassioned plea for a responsive state, highlighting the urgent need for vulnerability theory's reconception of state responsibility.

Recently, while reading an article titled "The Decline of Empathy and the Appeal of Right-Wing Politics," I was struck by the relevance of the lessons gleaned from an experiment with mothers and infants to figuring out how to foster a society that valued and practiced policies of social justice.[2] In the experiment, mother and infant interactions were analyzed in two contrasting situations. First, there were the situations where mothers responded with normal reciprocal mirroring to their infants' facial expressions during play. In contrast, in a second set of situations, the mothers were instructed to continue to play with the infants, but to make their facial expression "flat and neutral" for some, relatively short, period of time before reverting to normal interaction. The researchers observed that when the mothers' faces were neutral and still, the infants became anxious and desperately tried to reconnect with their mothers. Failing to receive a reciprocal interaction (per instructions from the researchers), the infants "showed ever-greater signs of confusion and distress, followed by a turning away from the mother, finally appearing sad and hopeless."' The researchers labeled the experiment an example of the "still face paradigm" and concluded that for human beings (and other mammals) a "caretaker's attunement and engagement is necessary to foster security, self-regulation, and empathy in the developing child."'[3]

1 This essay originally appeared in: Martha Albertson Fineman & Silas W. Allard, *Vulnerability, the Responsive State, and the Role of Religion, in* EXPLORING VULNERABILITY 185, 186–91 (H. Springhart & G. Thomas eds., 2017).

2 M. Bader, *The Decline of Empathy and the Appeal of Right-Wing Politics, What Is He Thinking?* (blog), Psychology Today (Dec. 25, 2016), https://www.psychologytoday.com/us/blog/what-is-he-thinking/201612/the-decline-empathy-and-the-appeal-right-wing-politics.

3 *Id.*

DOI: 10.4324/9781003405627-22

The author reviewing these experiments extrapolated from the studies and deemed the still face paradigm to be a "metaphor" for adult life in contemporary society. This breakdown in empathy and the resulting sense of helplessness that infants experience, he asserted, also describes the "experience of many people as they interact with the most important institutions in their lives, including the government."[4] In other words, the stillness of society's face – or the lack of visible response and recognition to growing inequality and widespread suffering and anxiety – betrayed the "natural" expectations and needs of those governed and led to the infliction of social and individual harm. In the author's opinion, governmental inattentiveness and indifference inflicted widespread "damage to our psyches, causing distress, anger, and hopelessness," as well as status-anxiety and causing trust in others to break down (and, one presumes, in our institutions as well).[5] The author continues with the observation that the "profound corrosive effects of social and economic inequality"[6] exaggerates this phenomenon.

My discipline is law, not psychology, but it begins, as do many other disciplines, with a set of assumptions as to what it means to be human, as well as speculations about the effects and consequences of social interaction and norms on humanity. This research on infants is interesting in that regard because it emphasizes that there is a fundamental and "natural" dependence of human beings, at least initially, on the care and attention of others. We are social beings who are inescapably enmeshed in social relations and institutions, and for that reason, we are also dependent on the rules, norms, and values that shape and define those relations and institutions. Those rules, norms, and values are expressed in various ethical systems within society: religion, philosophy, history, and psychology to name a few.

Unlike many other disciplines, however, law is tasked with the development and implementation of a set of coercive rules applicable to all. This process necessitates creating powerful organizing institutions, which are anchored in the state's legitimate monopoly of power over life, liberty, and property. Through what is termed "the rule of law," a society expresses what it considers to be legitimate and universally applicable standards of behavior reflecting its generally shared values and norms. Those rules or laws govern the relationships with and responsibilities to others that members of society have as individuals. In doing so, these laws also shape and define the institutions within which we inevitably find ourselves enmeshed throughout life, such as the family and the market, as well as institutions such as finance, education, health, and the many other structural arrangements that accommodate and facilitate social and economic interactions.

4 *Id.*
5 *Id.*
6 *Id.*

These rules reflect a societal or social judgment as to what is considered the appropriate allocation of responsibility for both individual and societal well being between the collective (be it a governmental or institutional entity) and the individual. Complex and interlocking systems of rules, norms, and socially defined roles within society's institutions create expectations, entitlements, and aspirations, as well as form the bases for collective judgments and reaction. If these institutions (indeed society) are to endure, the rules upon which they are based must reflect a realistic understanding of the relative individual, institutional, and state capabilities and limitations. Furthermore, to be deemed compassionate these rules must also be shaped by an understanding of the needs and challenges of contemporary society and its terms and mode of operation, not based on perceptions formulated in another, simpler, and more homogeneous era, which are then merely reflexively applied.

Understandings of the Human and the Collective in Contemporary Society

Returning to the "still face paradigm," we might ask: what lessons are inevitably learned by those currently struggling within a society that appears unresponsive to human need and suffering? How should we respond when the state is unresponsive? Contemporary Western societies are typically organized around values of individualism and autonomy and reflect a faith in free market "principles" to provide for the collective welfare. In its extreme form (as in the United States), the state is seen as mostly unnecessary to individual and institutional prosperity and urged to get out of the way. In this type of neoliberal market-oriented society, belief in privatization and efficiency have not only prevailed, but triumphed, over more socially attentive and responsive models of society. What happens to social cohesion and trust when the individual is held to expectations imposed by a regime of "personal responsibility," tempered slightly by some recognition of "individual rights" against state excesses? It is a society built around competition, not compassion.

The primary concern here is the damage that occurs to the social fabric of a society when the failure to thrive is blamed on the individual, and the social institutions and relationships upon which we are all dependent have been drained of the resources they need to provide the minimum component of the constitutionally mandated equality of opportunity and access. The complex global and market-oriented societies that have been created in the past several decades are societies where the means for individual survival, as well as the possibilities for flourishing, are cavalierly assumed to be within an individual's grasp, ideally not requiring any sustained governmental responses.

Rather than accepting this designation of individual responsibility, we should be asking ourselves, and those politicians and policy makers who shape our institutions, a bevy of hard questions; we should be demanding answers that reflect at least some recognition of social responsibility. To start this inquiry, let us ask those politicians obsessed with austerity to imagine what lessons children learn when the books and other materials they are provided in public schools are outdated and incomplete and the equipment required for even a modestly adequate technological education is both worn and sparse? What do these children understand as necessary for a fulfilling life when music and art are missing from the curriculum and physical education is deemed a luxury? How do children understand the value society gives them when the buildings in which they are "educated" are desperately in need of repairs and their local community refuses to generate the resources necessary to address the problem? How do these children understand their society's sense of justice and fairness when, at the same time they are experiencing deprivation, they see a multimillion-dollar sports complex or some other symbol of societal indulgence for the well-off being constructed with the assistance of public resources?

This is not just an exercise to engage from a child's perspective. For everyone, the significant question should be: how do we understand and evaluate "justice" when the state acts (or fails to act) in seeming ignorance of the economic and social contexts in which its citizens find themselves? What lessons are learned by those who are ill, elderly, and disabled when they are abandoned to the whims of for-profit insurance companies or the degradation of a public system that views them as failures and potential cheats? How should we judge a society that allows its most-in-need citizens to suffer or die unattended because state protection is seen as "insulting" and a denial of "agency?" And, what lessons are learned from those dependent and needy family members (particularly children) when the state is cautioned not to interfere in that private family, even to protect some members against the neglectful, harsh, or abusive treatment of others except in extraordinary circumstances? What is the response of those abandoned to their assumed autonomy and liberty in a system that privileges privacy and valorizes profit maximization over a norm of welfare provision?

Even those who seem fully engaged with social institutions should question the allocation of responsibilities and rights those institutions have been constructed to contain. What lessons are there for employees and workers when their collective interests are undermined and fragmented into ineffectiveness by perversely named "right to work" laws? When attacks on unions are validated by governmental officials? Workers are left to grapple with the dictates of an increasingly remote employer in an "at-will" employment system; one where employment is the supposed source of welfare benefits, such as health insurance and retirement or social security. What recourse do they have when the legal system provides them little protection from the employer's obsession with efficiency and profit and instead asserts a perverse and hollow rhetoric of equality of liberty which disregards the existing power inequality within the employment relationship? What is the recourse when the meager rules that protect worker health and safety are vilified by multinational corporations? And the politicians whom they influence argue such protections are an unnecessary interference with free markets and threaten to repeal them?

What recourse is there for all of us when those same corporations attack environmental protections, calling them inefficient and unnecessary restraints on a free market, leaving individuals alone to bear the health and other burdens that result in the name of "growth" and "progress" (but, which actually result in an obscene glut of profits to be held by very few while burdening the rest of us with economic and health consequences for which we will be individually responsible)? Who answers the question of why the Dow Jones Index is considered news worthy of hourly reporting, while the number of children without health insurance or going hungry and the very visible and verifiable consequences of climate change are ignored? Such social harms are reported (if reported at all) by those in positions of power as "aberrations" and "exceptions" to a market system we are assured is functioning efficiently and in the interests of all. The "private" market's routinely generated negative social consequences are either ignored or justified by a government increasingly uncaring and unresponsive to individual circumstances and needs.

The list of social arrangements leading to individual and collective disillusionment with the promises of equality and justice could go on, but the central, overriding question – the question that begs for answers steeped in a sense of social justice and compassion – is: what are the lessons we inevitably all learn from our contemporary political system and its fixation on individualism steeped in an "ethic" confined to personal responsibility and a political rhetoric that extolls the virtues of a restrained state and the primacy of market-based social justice? Such an approach to governance asserts and reifies (against realistic assessments of the human condition) the values and virtues of individual independence and liberty and ignores (and sometimes expressly either exploits or vilifies) the reality of human vulnerability and dependency. Ironically, at the same time as the modern state validates and facilitates the perceived needs, ambitions, and appetites of collective economic entities, such as the corporation and other contractual relationships, it fractures and diminishes the social dimension of collective life, isolating individuals and abandoning them to an empty and unrealizable liberty.

The compelling task in the twenty-first century is to address the seeming abdication of state responsibility to the individual that has emerged in modern societies, which seem much more attuned to the needs of the market. What language and concepts can challenge the relentless rhetoric extolling individual independence and glorifying personal responsibility? How can we articulate a compelling argument for the recognition of a collective responsibility to the individual; one that does not revert to the illusion of a meritocratic and unencumbered market as the means to creation and just allocation of social goods? How do we demand that the state be both responsive and compassionate? How do we demand that the state and its laws responsibly appreciate and respond to the realities and limitations of the human condition and accept the attendant responsibility that, of necessity, confers on the state and the institutions it has created to govern our relationships with each other?

Chapter 17

Injury in the Unresponsive State (2018)[1]

Here Fineman explores the idea of state inaction as constitutional harm. She demonstrates the fallacy of the neoliberal belief in the restrained state, arguing that the state is already active through creation and maintenance of social institutions. As such, the question is not whether the state is active, but in whose interest it is acting. She urges consideration of institutional and state vulnerability to address inequities.

Here I consider the limited ways in which "injury" or harm is understood in American political and legal culture. In particular, I am concerned with the inability of contemporary constitutional or political theory to interpret the failure of collective or state action as constituting harm worthy of recognition and compelling remedial action.[2] Here, I am not focused on laws redressing harm to private individuals and entities caused by other private individuals and entities. These legal harms are defined in areas of private law, such as tort and contract. Nor am I focused on those legal harms addressed by areas of regulatory law, such as criminal or administrative law. Rather, I am interested in the norms and values that inform the principles governing the exercise of action and restraint on the part of the state when it acts as sovereign and in relationship to individuals as political or legal subjects. As reflected in these foundational documents and constitutional jurisprudence of the United States, these principles express a theory or philosophy of what constitutes legitimate state authority.

1 This essay originally appeared in: Martha Albertson Fineman, *Injury in the Unresponsive State, in* Injury and Injustice: The Cultural Politics of Harm and Redress 50, 50–53, 66–72 (A. Bloom, D. Engel, & M. McCann, eds., 2018). © Cambridge University Press 2018. Reproduced with permission of the Licensor through PLSclear.

2 *See, e.g., Town of Castle Rock v. Gonzales*, 545 U.S. 748, 768–9 (2005): "Although the framers ... did not create a system by which police departments are generally held financially accountable for crimes that better policing might have prevented, the people ... are free to craft such a system under state law." *See also DeShaney v. Winnebago Department of Social Services*, 489 U.S. 189, 195 (1989): "But nothing in the language of the Due Process clause itself requires the State to protect the life, liberty, and property of its citizens against invasion by private actors. The clause is phrased as a limitation on the State's power to act, not as a guarantee of certain minimal levels of safety and security."

DOI: 10.4324/9781003405627-23

The idea that constitutional injury or harm can be caused by state *inaction* is not well developed in American political and legal culture. The norms and values informing our ideas of appropriate actions on the part of the state, as well as defining the corresponding entitlements of political or legal subjects, are firmly anchored in the principle of nonintervention or *inaction*. The specter of state or public interference with individual privacy or liberty interests haunts our constitutional order and shapes what we perceive as constituting injury by the state. Restraints on state action are viewed as arising from the terms of the social contract and are often referred to as "negative rights." By contrast, the term "positive rights" is used to refer to affirmative obligations placed on the state (and/or others) to provide rights-holders with needed goods or services.

American constitutional jurisprudence, as it has developed within the framework of negative rights, elevates the ideal of individual liberty over any robust sense of the necessity for collective or substantive equality. The liberty limitations placed on governmental action resonate in the very documents comprising the terms of the American social contract.[3] By contrast, positive rights or entitlements are generally considered legitimately based only on current and specific consensual arrangements, such as those found in public legislation or private contract.

The denial of positive rights means that the state has no constitutional responsibility to guarantee access to basic goods and services. As a result, the constitution, as it is interpreted, thus tolerates (and even condones) state disregard for or abandonment and neglect of basic human needs. Profound inequalities in circumstances, status, and well-being are accepted – even justified – by reference to individual responsibility.[4] Proposed remedial and altruistic responses are deflected with warnings about the addictive

3 A social contract is defined as "[a]n implicit agreement among the members of a society to cooperate for social benefits, for example by sacrificing some individual freedom for state protection" (*Oxford Dictionaries, s.v.* "social contract"). The documents comprising the American social contract – the declaration of Independence, the Bill of Rights, and the Constitution with its federalist structure and enumerated powers – uphold individual liberty at the expense of a more substantive equality. The Bill of Rights enumerates some specific prohibitions or limitations on state action. The Constitution also imposes duties of equal protection and due process, and there are legal remedies for individuals excluded from pre-existing benefits or protections offered under law. Some exclusionary categories or classifications made in laws or practice receive greater scrutiny than others, with race classifications being the most suspect in case law.

4 *See, e.g.*, David Brooks, *Op-Ed., The Cost of Relativism*, N.Y. TIMES (Mar. 10, 2015). Brooks discusses Robert Putnam's (OUR KIDS: THE AMERICAN DREAM IN CRISIS (2015)) research on inequality and the divide between children growing up in college-educated and high-school-educated homes: "the first response to these stats ... should be intense sympathy ... But it's increasingly clear that sympathy is not enough ... there are no basic codes and rules woven into daily life, which people can absorb unconsciously and follow automatically. Reintroducing norms will require, first, a moral vocabulary ... next it will require holding people responsible."

dependency asserted to be inherent even in the highly stigmatized system of welfare currently in place.[5]

State neglect of the needs of those individuals living in poverty or suffering under social, economic, and material disadvantage is not seen as requiring legal or political remedy. Quite the contrary: state inaction is typically viewed as the appropriate manifestation of state restraint in the face of individual liberty or autonomy rights that condemn any move toward the "redistribution" of private wealth or property. "Private" structures, such as the family, market, charity, or the workplace, are designated as the prime mediating institutions to provide for the needs of individuals. Arguably, the state may be seen as having some responsibility in regard to the conduct and operation of those institutions, but at best the state is seen as an incremental and contested residual actor when they fail. This understanding of state inaction as not constituting injury or harm is both validated and compelled by the ways in which, over the course of American political history, the political subject and social contract have been understood as anchored in liberty and autonomy.

When should state inaction in the face of some forms and magnitudes of inequality be considered an injury in and of itself? When should the disregard of impoverishment, disenfranchisement, alienation, and exploitation of substantial numbers of individuals within and through the systems of law and politics rise to the level of "gross negligence" on the part of the state? And when should such neglect be understood as the "social-contractual injury" of the state effectively institutionalizing subordination and inequality? To begin to answer these questions, I offer the "vulnerable subject" as an alternative to the liberal legal subject that has impaired our political and legal imagination for over two centuries.

Vulnerability and the Responsive State

The most important aspect of reimagining undertaken in a vulnerability analysis involves understanding how the social contract should envision state responsibility with regard to both the vulnerable subject and resource-conferring institutions. The first step in a vulnerability analysis is to develop an understanding of the nature of the political subject as vulnerable across the life course; the second step places that complex and comprehensive subject within the social and institutional contexts that shape its prospects and possibilities. The third step locates the contextualized vulnerable subject and its institutional

5 See Nicholas Eberstadt, *American Exceptionalism and the Entitlement State*, 22 NATIONAL AFFAIRS 25–38 (2015). Eberstadt asserts that the trajectory of the current "entitlement state appears to be degrading standards of citizenship" by not only "undermin[ing] … the legitimacy of utilizing stigma and opprobrium to condition the behavior of beneficiaries" and the mental state of the middle class as "hard-working and self-sufficient," but by encouraging the "mass gaming of the welfare system [as] a fact of modern American life."

arrangements within the framework of state power and responsibility. How should our understandings of human vulnerability, the nature of institutions, and the role of institutions in providing resilience inform our politics and law?

We begin with the observation that the state is always at least a residual actor when it comes to societal institutions. The state brings societal institutions into being through law and regulation, as well as defining the nature and consequences of the social relations and roles within them. It also works to protect or privilege certain entities and allocates power between and among constituents, stakeholders, and members of institutions.

Powerful, resource-giving institutions like the family, corporations, schools, and financial institutions are constructs of the state. It is the legitimating authority of law and the regulatory machinery of the state that create marriage, define the family, and mandate the corporate form, for example. The state brings these entities into existence as legitimate institutions. The law both assigns and enforces content and consequences, and by doing this the state asserts that it has a monopoly over legitimate means of coercion. This exercise of power is one way in which the state constitutes not only its institutions, but also itself. State mechanisms also enforce "private" agreements (contracts) and provide security for and structure private property.

These examples of state action in regard to institutional formation and operation make it clear that the choice is not one between an active state on one hand and an inactive state on the other – action is what defines the state. Because societal institutions are so vitally important, both to individuals and to society, their flaws, barriers, gaps, and potential pitfalls must be monitored, and these institutions must be adjusted when they are functioning in ways harmful to individuals and society.

The Already (and Unequally) Responsive State

One way of understanding how the state is active is to look at the ways in which it currently responds to individual vulnerability through its creation and maintenance of institutions. Significantly, those institutions that serve as artificial entities should also be understood as vulnerable, although differently so than are individuals. Institutions may not be injured or die as human beings do, but they can suffer decline or decay, be captured, or controlled by destructive forces, or be susceptible to environmental, political, or economic changes. Interestingly, the state as it has been imagined in contemporary political theory is much more inclined to be directly responsive to institutional, rather than individual, vulnerability. Paradoxically, the relative robustness of state response to institutional vulnerability is justified by reference to the role that institutions have in providing resources to both individuals and the larger community. For example, the vulnerability of corporate or business institutions as job creators and/or economic stimulators to startup or ongoing production or operating costs is routinely evoked to justify subsidies. These subsidies can be quite generous, whether they take the form of tax policies, direct transfers, or investment, or are delivered through facilitating access to the mechanisms of state authority, such as law or utilization infrastructures.

Of course, it is not the state response to market or institutional vulnerability that fuels the calls for restraint by small government adherents. Rather, the demands for a restrained state are in response to the monitoring and regulation of the marketplace, which is viewed as increasing market vulnerability. Critics argue that for economic prosperity and job creation the state must assume a position of benign neglect.[6] Considering the complexity and nature of institutional vulnerability, however, this argument is both unreasonable and disingenuous.

Institutions are not only vulnerable to market and economic uncertainties. They are also vulnerable to manipulation, misbehavior, and corruption. This can result from things like the structure of corporate law demanding that corporations produce hefty profits for shareholders and allowing massive salaries for CEOs, while frustrating access to power on the part of employees and other stakeholders.[7] The vulnerability of the corporation is created by the fact that it is primarily a profit-driven entity, providing a compelling argument for a much more attentive and responsive state: one that exposes, contemplates, and balances the competing vulnerabilities of all the interested parties, including society, that are inherent in institutional arrangements.

This is not an argument that the state should not respond to institutional vulnerability, but a demand that it does so in a balanced and measured fashion that is as attentive to human as it is to institutional vulnerability. Consider how the lack of such a state response contributed to the practices that led to the great recession. The state responded to the increasingly vulnerable position of certain big businesses caused by the failing market during the recession, and the heightened risk of loss was met with loans to the auto industry and bailouts for the financial industry.[8] At the same time, the exposed vulnerability of and heightened risks for individual mortgage holders created in the wake of the same crisis was largely ignored. Their plight was assigned to the realm of individual responsibility, and pleas for governmental aid were deflected with cries of "moral hazard."[9]

6 *See* George Leef, *Op-Ed., Trickle-Down Economics – The Most Destructive Phrase of All Time?*, FORBES (Dec. 6, 2013) (arguing that "[f]ree markets and smaller government means greater opportunities for everyone").

7 *See, e.g.*, Jia Lin Yang, *Maximizing Shareholder Value: The Goal that Changed Corporate America*, WASH. POST (Aug. 26, 2013) (discussing how corporate America's focus on maximizing shareholder value led to "an economy in which companies are increasingly disconnected from the state of the nation, laying off workers in waves, keeping average wages low[,] and threatening to move operations abroad in the face of regulations and taxes").

8 Paul Kiel, *The Bailout: By the Actual Numbers*, PROPUBLICA (Sept. 6, 2012).

9 "'Moral hazard' refers to situations in which economic actors, because they do not bear the full consequences of their actions, maximize their utility at the expense of

In other words, the state played favorites, choosing to respond to vulnerable institutions over vulnerable individuals. This ill-considered and unreflective choice failed to take into account the ways in which corporations, acting in ways consistent with the profit motivation, can exacerbate their own vulnerability, create hazards for society, and dissipate the resilience of others. A truly responsive state would consider all interested parties and their competing vulnerabilities.

Of course, it is important to recognize that the state does make erroneous and biased responses to economic, as well as other, crises. The state is capable of being abusive, over-reaching, and authoritative. Like all human institutions, the state is vulnerable to capture, corruption, and misdirection. State misdirection can come from external forces, as happens when powerful entrenched interests hijack even the most egalitarian impulses for their own purposes. It can also be the product of flaws or weaknesses in the design or operation of state structures and practices. Massive misdirection has attended the current corrupted legislative culture produced by ineffective campaign financing and other reform that provides incentives for repressive tactics, distortions of the truth, and democracy-frustrating partisanship.[10]

To many progressive commentators, the failures of the state are reason enough to move beyond politics, even beyond law. This reaction, while perhaps understandable, is naïve and ultimately reactionary. We need the state; we cannot do without it. Society, like all collective human relations, needs rules, which operate as constraints on individuals for the good of the collective, be that collective in the form of a family, a corporation, an economy, a community, or a state or governmental entity.

Further, it is important to remember that although we may talk about "the state," it is not a monolith. The state is actually a cluster of relationships, entities, and agencies reflecting and shaping public norms and values through law and policy. Those relationships include the relationship between citizen and

others. A common example is an individual with theft insurance not protecting an easily-replaceable item." Kevin A. Kordana, *Tax Increases in Municipal Bankruptcies*, 83 VA. LAW. REV. 1035–108 (1997) (citing Y. Kotowitz, *Moral Hazard, in* THE NEW PALGRAVE: A DICTIONARY OF ECONOMICS 549–51 (John Eatwell, Murray Milgate & Peter Newman, eds., 1987)). During the great recession, "the preoccupation with moral hazard was targeted at homeowners instead of banks, creating overlapping income and asset double-checks to weed out the unworthy." David Dayen, *A Needless Default*, THE AMERICAN PROSPECT LONGFORM (Feb. 8, 2015).

10 *See* Lili Levi, *Plan B for Campaign-Finance Reform: Can the FCC Help Save American Politics After Citizens United?*, 61 CATHOL. UNIV. LAW REV. 97–104 (2011) (exploring the potential long-term impacts of Citizens United in light of data from the 2010 electoral cycle showing increases in private donations, overall advertising expenditures, the number of involved "super PACs," and the use of negative campaigning). *See also* Richard H. Pildes, *Why the Center Does Not Hold: The Causes of Hyperpolarized Democracy in America*, 99 CAL. LAW REV. 10–47 (2011), finding that polarization leads to a lack of effective internal checks and balances during times of unified government and deadlock during times of divided government.

state, as well as between state and institutions. And as a democratic institution, the state is also susceptible to political pressure and collective calls for reform.

To realize a responsive state, individuals must appreciate that we too are part of the state and are inevitably affected by its policies and law. We do not – we cannot – stand outside the state, and we therefore have a responsibility to participate in the formation of its policy and practices. We must be vigilant in ensuring that the state is working effectively and in an egalitarian manner, with values and norms of equality and justice being paramount in defining state actions. State vulnerabilities are present whether the state is constituted as restrained or as responsive. Orienting the state to be responsive to the vulnerable subject would require dedication to a different set of values – more egalitarian and collective in nature – than those that informed the state built on an image of the liberal subject.

Vulnerability's values prefer connection and interdependence rather than autonomy and independence in both political and personal visions. This would require the state to respond to the damage done by privileging liberty over equality, necessitating a look at the existing structures of inequality. Institutions serving to allocate society's resources unequally to the benefit of the few must be monitored and reformed. Politicians will tell us that this is an impossible task, but what they really mean is that it will place them in an uncomfortable position, particularly with those who are currently privileged. Perhaps it is no more than a utopian fantasy, but I believe that organizing around our shared vulnerability provides the foundation for building an inclusive and democratic political coalition – one that can both expose and displace unwarranted privilege and demand that the terms of the social contract require the state to ensure a more level playing field, genuine access and opportunity, and institutions that build resilience.

Chapter 18

Vulnerability and Social Justice (2019)

This chapter[1] explores the origins and evolution of the concept of "social justice." Fineman argues that neoliberalism has transformed our notions of social justice from a broader concern for the welfare of the collective to an individualized concern for market-based justice. She offers vulnerability theory as a framework for redefining social justice.

What, if anything, does the designation of "social" add to the ideal of justice? The phrase "social justice" is a rallying cry in progressive circles, perhaps because justice unmodified seemingly fails to convey the magnitude of the underlying demand for change.[2] However, the meaning of the term is not particularly clear, nor is it used in a consistent manner.[3]

1 This essay originally appeared in: Martha Albertson Fineman, *Vulnerability and Social Justice*, 53 VAL. U. L. REV. 341 (2019). Available at: https://scholar.valpo.edu/vulr/vol53/iss2/2.

2 According to the Report of the Special Rapporteur on extreme poverty and human rights on his mission to the United States, "The United States has the highest rate of income inequality among Western countries." UN Human Rights Council Secretariat, Report of the Special Rapporteur an Extreme Poverty and Human Rights and His Mission to the United States of America, 5, U.N. Doc. A/HRC/38/33/ Add. 1 (May 4, 2018). The report states, "About 40 million live in poverty, 18.5 million in extreme poverty, and 5.3 million live in Third World conditions of absolute poverty. It has the highest youth poverty rate in the Organization for Economic Cooperation and Development (OECD), and the highest infant mortality rates among comparable OECD States." *Id.* 4. Moreover, in the words of the *New York Times*: "769 million people lived on less than $1.90 a day in 2013, and 3.2 million live in the United States, while 3.3 million in other high-income countries." Angus Eaton, *The U.S. Can No Longer Hide from Its Deep Poverty Problem*, N.Y. TIMES (Jan. 24, 2018), https://www.nytimes.com/2018/01/24/opinion/poverty-united-states.html.

3 For example, Bruce Ackerman, in his book *Social Justice and the Liberal State*, does not seem to have a clear definition of social justice, even as the title of his book positions it as a central concept. *See* BRUCE A. ACKERMAN, SOCIAL JUSTICE IN THE LIBERAL STATE (2018). Like many others, he seemingly jumbles together ideas about fair distribution of resources, preferred neutrality of the state, disparate power relations, resort to rationality, and the need for education, among other determinants of justice in expressing its social form. *Id.* The concept of social justice is often used to refer to economic justice for individuals or groups, to talk about environmental issues, or to highlight the need for redistribution of

DOI: 10.4324/9781003405627-24

Here I briefly consider the origins of the term social justice and its evolution beside our understandings of human rights and liberalism, which are two other significant justice categories. After this reflection on the contemporary meaning of social justice, I suggest that vulnerability theory, which seeks to replace the rational man of liberal legal thought with the vulnerable subject, should be used to define the contours of the term. Recognition of fundamental, universal, and perpetual human vulnerability reveals the fallacies inherent in the ideals of autonomy, independence, and individual responsibility that have supplanted an appreciation of the social. I suggest that we need to develop a robust language of state or collective responsibility, one that recognizes that social justice is realized through the legal creation and maintenance of just social institutions and relationships.

A vulnerability approach is not centered on specific individuals or groups or on human and civil rights. It is not a substitute term for weakness or disadvantage, nor is it just another way to indicate impermissible discrimination. Rather, addressing human vulnerability calls into focus what we share as human beings, what we should expect of the laws and the underlying social structures, and relationships that organize society and affect the lives of everyone within society. These institutions and relationships also reflect our values and norms and define the expectations for all individuals in their interactions with each other, as well as define legitimate expectations for the state and those who govern it. While it does not prescribe a specific form of state organization, vulnerability theory does call for a state that is responsive to universal human needs and for the reorganization of many existing structures, which are currently based on a conception of legal order that unduly valorizes individual liberty and choice and ignores the realities of human dependency and vulnerability.

The Transformation of Social Justice

Institutions, Ideas, and the Law

Historically, social justice was thought to have emancipatory potential.[4] The term was used as a rallying cry by progressive thinkers and activists, who understood it to be a call for "the fair and compassionate *distribution* of the fruits of economic growth," particularly for the working class.[5] A 2006 report

resources and opportunity. For a general overview of the term, *see* LORETTA CAPEHEART & DRAGAN MILOVANOVIC, SOCIAL JUSTICE: THEORIES, ISSUES, AND MOVEMENTS (2007).

4 It has also been a contested concept, characterized by specific historical and ideological contexts. *See* W. B. GALLIE, ESSENTIALLY CONTESTED CONCEPTS 56, 167–98 (1955), PhilPapers. For an analysis of the origins of social justice, *see* SAMUEL MOYN, NOT ENOUGH: HUMAN RIGHTS IN AN UNEQUAL WORLD 12 (2018).

5 It was the initial distribution of economic gains associated with increased productivity that concerned early social justice advocates. Thiers was not an argument for redistribution but for just original distribution. *See* UN SECRETARIAT DEPARTMENT OF ECONOMICS AND SOCIAL AFFAIRS, SOCIAL JUSTICE IN AN OPEN WORLD: THE ROLE OF THE UNITED NATIONS 7 (2006) [hereinafter SOCIAL JUSTICE REPORT].

by the UN Department of Economic and Social Affairs ("UN Report"), "Social Justice in an Open World," situates the origins of the term in the advance of industrial and urban capitalism, which was consolidated during the years after the Second World War and the advent of social democracies:

> Unlike justice in the broad sense, social justice is a relatively recent concept, born of the struggles surrounding the industrial revolution and the advent of socialist (and later, in some parts of the world, social democratic and Christian democratic) views on the organization of society.[6]

In the wake of the Industrial Revolution, the expansion of large-scale production and growth of markets as the mode of production and distribution increased the availability of goods and services.[7] While this made our collective lives easier and more comfortable, it also resulted in skewed advantages – with material affluence for some but poverty, exclusion, and deprivation for others.[8] Karl Polanyi[9] referred to this era's social and political dislocations as "The Great Transformation" and described how the extension of market dynamics and logic frayed the social fabric.[10] In the context of such societal disruption, social justice, in the words of the UN Report, was "a revolutionary slogan embodying the ideals of progress and fraternity."[11]

Social Justice Success

In the United States, social justice ideas were eventually implemented at a federal level through strategies such as progressive income tax, antitrust legislation, and workplace regulations.[12] Progressive politics led to policies aimed at

6 *Id.* at 2.

7 *See* HENRY HELLER, THE BIRTH OF CAPITALISM 176 (2011).

8 For a general view of the social problems in the US caused by industrialization, *see* WALTER LIPPMANN, DRIFT AND MASTERY: AN ATTEMPT TO DIAGNOSE THE CURRENT UNREST (Univ. Wis. Press 2015) (1914). For a classic analysis of industrial capitalism effects, *see* KARL MARX & FRIEDRICH ENGELS, THE COMMUNIST MANIFESTO (Pluto Press 2008) (1848).

9 *See generally* KARL POLANYI, THE GREAT TRANSFORMATION 42 (Beacon Press 2001) (1944).

10 He also noted the ways in which key elements of society, such as labor and natural resources, were transformed into commodities to be bought and sold. "The Industrial Revolution was merely the beginning of a revolution as extreme and radical as ever inflamed the minds of sectarians, but the new creed was utterly materialistic and believed that all human problems could be resolved given an unlimited amount of material commodities." *Id.* at 42.

11 SOCIAL JUSTICE REPORT, *supra* note 5, at 12.

12 By the first decades of the twentieth century and under President Wilson's government, the Federal Reserve and Federal Trade Commission were created, and the Clayton Antitrust Act was promoted. There was also a push toward the first graduated federal income tax. *See generally* JACOB S. HACKER & PAUL PIERSON, AMERICAN AMNESIA: HOW THE WAR ON GOVERNMENT LED US TO FORGET WHAT MADE AMERICA PROSPER (2016).

the fair distribution of public goods and services, the development of the idea of citizenship, social rights, and the welfare state, as well as the propulsion of reforms regarding education and employment.[13]

Significantly, the principle that social justice should be accomplished by *social* means was important to the reformers. Franklin Delano Roosevelt's (FDR's) "Second Bill of Rights"[14] was a social justice document in which he outlined a vision of "social citizenship" (a fair deal), and it was governmental authority that was posited as ensuring that everyone would be guaranteed protection from the harshness of the market.[15] Importantly, attainment of a fair deal was not designated to be only, or even primarily, an individual responsibility. An active and progressive state and its public agencies were deemed the legitimate sources for robust and coherent distributive policies.[16] Among the specific entitlements enumerated were the right to: (1) work; (2) decent pay; (3) have a decent home; (4) adequate medical care; and (5) protection from the economic calamities arising from sickness, accident, and unemployment in old age or resulting from economic dislocations.[17]

While FDR's social justice ideals were only partially realized, the basic principle that government should intervene to provide some level of economic and social protection to those who needed it, in the face of economic dislocation and disruption, did become institutionalized during that era.[18] Recognition and acceptance of the need for an active social welfare role for government was

13 *See* J. M. Wedemeyer & Percy Moore, *The American Welfare System*, 54 CAL. L REV. 326 (1966) (showing the implementation of social justice ideas). *See also* KAREN TANI, STATES OF DEPENDENCY: WELFARE, RIGHTS, AND AMERICAN GOVERNANCE, 1935–1972 (2016) (providing an updated and detailed history of welfare programs).

14 For a detailed account of the history of this speech and its relationship with social rights and justice, *see* MOYN, *supra* note 4, at 68–88.

15 In FDR's words: As our Nation has grown in size and stature, however – as our industrial economy expanded – these political rights proved inadequate to assure us equality in the pursuit of happiness. We have come to a clear realization of the fact that true individual freedom cannot exist without economic security and independence. "Necessitous men are not free men." People who are hungry and out of a job are the stuff of which dictatorships are made. In our day these economic truths have become accepted as self-evident. We have accepted, so to speak, a second Bill of Rights under which a new basis of security and prosperity can be established for all regardless of station, race, or creed. President Franklin D. Roosevelt, *State of the Union Message to Congress* (Jan. 11, 1944), www.presidency.ucsb.edu/ws/index.php?pid=16518 [https://perma.cc/E7UK VWM5]. Note that freedom here is perceived as contingent on economic security, not on the mere provision of opportunity. This is very different today.

16 *See* President Roosevelt, *supra* note 15.

17 *See id.*

18 Importantly, social justice was not defined by or limited to what have become the "traditional" protected categories, such as race, gender, or disability. Rather, the category was based on the status of citizenship or on a social identity such as worker or head of household. In that way, it was a more inclusive claim, one not grounded in discrimination.

broadly accepted until the 1970s, when the Reagan era seeded and nurtured widespread suspicions about the evils of "big government."[19]

Today, we again face the kind of widespread inequality and consolidation of wealth that occurred in the wake of the Industrial Revolution.[20] However, there is little evidence that a collectivist approach to social justice would be viable in today's political world, and this is the case on both the conservative and the liberal sides of the political spectrum.[21] In fact, the commitment to a collective or social assessment of justice has been profoundly undermined in our increasingly individualistic society.[22] We are much more likely to have a particular and fragmented – rather than a collective – sense of justice.

Social Justice Decline

As the UN Report noted, the meanings of terms change over time in relation to shifting political, economic, and social circumstances, and indeed the concept of social justice has lost much of its social focus. In recent years there has been a discernible trend in international discourse toward the attenuation not only of the

19 The US developed a "liberal" welfare state model that minimizes de-commodification effects, contains the realm of social rights, and erects an order of stratification that blends relative equality of poverty among state-welfare recipients, market differentiated welfare among the majorities, and a class-political dualism between the two. *See* GOSTA ESPING ANDERSEN, THE THREE WORLDS OF WELFARE CAPITALISM 27 (1990). For a detailed history of the welfare state in the US, see TANI, *supra* note 13, at 26. However, the rhetoric over government changed after the seventies. After Carter had won the presidency promising a government "as good as its people," Reagan ran for president on an anti-government program: "government was the people's antagonist, the limiter of their limitlessness." DANIEL T. RODGERS, THE AGE OF FRACTURE 35 (2012). *See also* William Schneider, *The New Shape of American Politics*, THE ATLANTIC (1987), https://www.theatlantic.com/past/docs/politics/polibig/schnnew.htm[https://perma.cc/UE2M-9AJ7] (describing the decline in the acceptance of a need for an active social welfare in the seventies).

20 In fact, it is now commonplace to state that we are living a new Gilded Age, especially after Piketty's pathbreaking book on inequality. *See, e.g.*, THOMAS PIKETTY, CAPITAL IN THE TWENTY-FIRST CENTURY (2014). *See also* David Singh Grewal, *The Laws of Capitalism*, 128 HARV. L. REV. 626, 632–33 (2014) (comparing the current economic climate to the economic climate during the Industrial Revolution).

21 Part of this was facilitated by the way that social justice movements were organized around group identities in the twentieth century following a series of successful mobilizations for civil rights. *See* Deborah Dinner, *"Beyond Best Practices": Employment – Discrimination Law in the Neoliberal Era*, 92 IND. L.J. 1059, 1060–61 (2017). I first expressed concern about an overreliance on antidiscrimination paradigm in Martha Albertson Fineman, *The Vulnerable Subject: Anchoring Equality in the Human Condition*, 20 YALE J.L. & FEMINISM 1, 2 (2008) (providing that a collectivist approach is not likely to happen).

22 *See, e.g.*, PATRICK J. DENEEN, WHY LIBERALISM FAILED (2018) (offering a compelling critique to liberalism and its foundation in individual self-expression and autonomy).

concept of social justice but also of the related concepts of social development and social policy. The social sphere has in many respects been marginalized.[23]

Social justice is now likely to be associated with specific individuals or groups and concerned with discrimination, exclusion, and economic inequality. In assessing the reasons for the decline of the social, the UN Report specifically pointed to the eroding effects of an individually focused human rights agenda that emphasizes formal equality and celebrates individual liberty and choice.[24]

Interestingly, an individualized understanding of human rights also complicates the idea that the state can undertake positive action to effect something called social, or collective, justice. Instead, justice is now to be found in the protection of the individual from discrimination on the one hand and state overreach and interference on the other. Justice is no longer grounded in the creation of broad social welfare projects, unless they target the poor or disadvantaged or are directed at increasing business and entrepreneurial opportunities deemed likely to unleash economic growth and trickle down to communities.[25] In fact, individual equality and liberty are all too often construed as barriers against state action, with such action seen as interfering with individual choices or autonomy.

Neoliberalism

Neoliberalism, another doctrine forged and polished in the twentieth century, reflects a complementary individualistic reorientation. Neoliberalism is perceived as occupying the opposite pole of the political spectrum from human rights, but it also has propelled the shift to an individual, rather than a collective, conception of justice.[26]

Like its classic form, neoliberalism is a political-economic theory based on the principle that freedom, justice, and societal well-being are best guaranteed by a system that protects private property and freedom of contract and promotes open markets and free trade.[27] However, unlike traditional liberalism, neoliberalism is *not* a system in which the state is restrained in the interest of individual liberty. Instead, the power of the state is unleashed to protect the

23 SOCIAL JUSTICE REPORT, *supra* note 5, at 14.

24 *See id.* at 54.

25 *See* MOYN, *supra* note 4, at 173–211 (elaborating on the relationship between neoliberalism and targeted minimum policies); DAVID HARVEY, A BRIEF HISTORY OF NEOLIBERALISM 64–65 (2007) (discussing the specific form of the neoliberal state). In the case of the individual or group, discrimination or profound disadvantage becomes the rationale for social policy, although the family is still seen as the primary social institution for dependency. For a corporation or business, its constructed role in the economic success for society is the justification for favorable policies and subsidies. Both corporations and businesses act as mediating economic institutions between the state and its citizens.

26 *See* MOYN, *supra* note 4, at 173–211.

27 *See* WENDY BROWN, UNDOING THE DEMOS: NEOLIBERALISM'S STEALTH REVOLUTION 28 (2015).

market, which is envisioned as the necessary and appropriate mechanism for ensuring individual liberty and choice, as well as economic success and the reduction of poverty.[28]

Unlike those for whom neoliberalism may be seen only as part of a conservative legal movement that began in the 1990s,[29] I argue that it is a radical theory in which the market – not progressive social welfare policy – provides the logic for ordering society and distributing its benefits and burdens. In much of neoliberal discourse, the market is positioned as inevitably opposed to, rather than being the beneficiary of the public authority of the state.[30] In actuality, the state plays a very active role in supporting the market and its institutions.[31] This restrained state reasoning also follows the widely accepted public/private distinction that is often drawn in political and public policy rhetoric.[32] Within the private sphere, the market is presumed to operate as the realm of freedom and *laissez-faire,* while the public arena is viewed as a realm in which regulation, hierarchy, and constraint may reluctantly be warranted.[33]

However, the market, while understood to be free, is by no means seen as anarchistic in neoliberal thought. The market is perceived as having a specific, natural order, structured by individual actions undertaken, governed by self-

28 *See* Dieter Plehwe, *The Origins of the Neoliberal Economic Development Discourse, in* THE ROAD FROM MONT PELERIN: THE MAKING OF THE NEOLIBERAL THOUGHT COLLECTIVE 238–40 (Philip Mirowski & Dieter Plehwe eds., 2015) (discussing the neoliberal economic development discourse). In the words of the *Social Justice Report*: "[T]he reasoning of the committed neoliberal is that removing the constraints imposed by Governments and archaic social structures will allow the release of long-suppressed initiative, ambition and productive energies, leading to increased opportunities for work and employment and, ipso facto, a reduction in poverty." SOCIAL JUSTICE REPORT, *supra* note 5, at 69.

29 *See* STEVEN TELES, THE RISE OF THE CONSERVATIVE LEGAL MOVEMENT: THE BATTLE FOR CONTROL OF THE LAW 263 (2008).

30 *See id.* (remarking on the politics surrounding the movement).

31 *See* HARVEY, *supra* note 24, at 64 (referring to the government's role in the market).

32 The private/public distinction is at the foundation of eighteenth-century liberal political theory. *See generally* JOHN LOCKE, TWO TREATISES OF GOVERNMENT 287 (Ian Shapiro ed., Yale Univ. Press 2003) (1689) (discussing the private/public distinction). As I have described previously: [O]ne of the primary ordering mechanisms of the American social contract is the creation of categories such as public and private, into which social institutions, people, and problems are distributed with significant policy implications. In particular, the categories of public and private structure the relationships between the state and the market on the one hand (the public category) and the state and the family on the other (the private category). Martha Albertson Fineman, *The Social Foundations of Law*, 54 EMORY L.J. 206–07 (2005). For a history of the distinction and its connection to legal thought, *see* Morton J. Horowitz, *The History of the Private/Public Distinction*, 130 U. PA. L. REV.142–43 (1982). As Horowitz explains, "The hostility to statutes expressed by nineteenth-century judges and legal thinkers reflected the view that state regulation of private relations was a dangerous and unnatural public intrusion into a system based on private rights." *Id.* at 1426.

33 *See* F.A. HAYEK, THE CONSTITUTION OF LIBERTY 4 (Univ. Chi. Press 2011) (1960) (explaining government involvement in a free society).

interest, and disciplined by the mandates of a system of market competition.[34] In the words of perhaps its most influential proponent, Milton Friedman, "[N] eoliberalism proposes that it is *competition* that will lead the way."[35] Note, however, that even Friedman conceded that there must be an active role for the state: "The state would police the system, [and] establish conditions favorable to competition ...."[36] The distinction between state and market functions that he draws here is interesting. The state is to serve as the handmaiden of the market, enshrining a market driven – not a *socially* driven – sense of justice, which is also relentlessly oriented toward the individual.[37]

To neoliberals, the separate consideration of social justice often is considered suspect, undertaken to interfere with the free market, and therefore harmful and unnecessary.[38] In the blunt words of another of neoliberalism's ideological architects, Friedrich Hayek, the term social is redundant in explaining justice "in a society of free men whose members are allowed to use their own knowledge for their own purposes."[39] Justice is what a free society produces through the market and open competition.[40] He also indicated that the "greatest service" he could render would be to "make the speakers and writers among them thoroughly ashamed ever again to employ the term '*social* justice'."[41] For Hayek, the term was a mirage and represented "the gravest threat to most other values of a free civilization."[42]

While Hayek was not successful in banishing the term, perhaps he would not object to the way social justice is currently understood, which I suggest is mostly in ways that are consistent with neoliberal objectives. To be fair, Hayek himself was not totally unsympathetic to what he might deem society's losers. He even explicitly endorsed government action in providing some minimal level of welfare, particularly if it was geared toward making people fit for labor:

> [T]here is no reason why in a society which has reached the general level of wealth which ours has attained the first kind of security should not be

34 *See, e.g.*, F.A. Hayek, *Competition as a Discovery Procedure*, Q. J. AUSTRIAN ECON., Fall 2002, at 9, 17–18 (discussing the microeconomic processes that aggregate and shape macroeconomic data).

35 JAMIE PECK, CONSTRUCTIONS OF NEOLIBERAL REASON (2000). *See also* Milton Friedman, *Neo-Liberalism and Its Prospects, in* FROM THE COLLECTED WORKS OF MILTON FRIEDMAN (Robert Leeson & Charles G. Palm eds., 2013) (1951), (providing an elaboration on Friedman's views of neoliberalism and competition).

36 Friedman, *supra* note 35, at 3. I termed this a concession, but it may also be construed as a fundamental recognition of the crucial role that the state must play if any system is to function.

37 *See id.* at 4.

38 *See id.* (highlighting social implications on the market).

39 F.A. HAYEK, LAW, LEGISLATION AND LIBERTY: THE MIRAGE OF SOCIAL JUSTICE (1976).

40 *See id.* at 74 (exploring the significance of competition in the market and the achievements of the free market).

41 *Id.* at 97 (emphasis added).

42 *Id.* at 67.

> guaranteed to all without endangering general freedom .... [T]here can be no doubt that some minimum of food, shelter, and clothing, sufficient to preserve health and the capacity to work, can be assured to everybody.[43]

Progressive Liberal Individualism

Also relevant to understanding contemporary meanings of social justice is the fact that, over the course of the twentieth century, justice has become increasingly understood in economic terms. The relationship between the individual economic well-being and the market has become central in defining the appropriate role of the state, and this is true even among progressives.[44]

In exploring this development, I use the work of left-leaning philosopher Philippe Van Parijs – who is also a staunch proponent of a basic income guarantee.[45] Van Parijs recently elaborated on his understanding of social justice in which he placed the individual – not the social – as central.[46] He begins with the caveat that "any defensible conceptions of social justice today must articulate the importance we attach to equality, freedom and efficiency."[47] These three concepts are further defined.

In regard to justice, Van Parijs continues with the assertion that any defensible conception of justice must be liberal and egalitarian, explaining that he means "*liberal* in the philosophical sense of professing equal respect for the diversity of the conceptions of the good life that are present in our pluralistic societies."[48]

43 F.A. HAYEK, ROAD TO SERFDOM 120 (1944). This labor-ready purpose for social welfare benefits reflects other neoliberal concepts, such as the language of "welfare dependency" and "moral hazard," which played an important role in undermining the extension of welfare policies. *Id.* In fact, by the nineties, President Clinton declared that the era of big government was over and that "[t]oday, we are ending welfare as we know it." *See* Barbara Vobejda, *Clinton Signs Welfare Bill Amid Division*, WASH. POST (Aug. 23, 1996), https://www.washingtonpostcom/wp-srv/politics/special/welfare/stories/ wf082396.

44 Nancy Fraser explores this tum in critical thought in the context of second-wave feminism. *See* Nancy Fraser, *Feminism, Capitalism, and the Cunning of History: An Introduction* (Aug. 23, 2012), https://halshs.archives-ouvertes.fr/halshs-00725055/document (observing how neoliberal policies affect the relationship between feminism and capitalist behavior). For a less scholarly (and roundly criticized) conservative commentator's similar assessment, *see* Ross Douhat, *The Handmaids of Capitalism* (June 20, 2012), https://www.nytimes.com/2018/06/20/opinion/feminism capitalism.html.

45 *See* Philippe Van Parijs, *Social Justice and the Future of the Social Economy*, 86(2) ANNALS OF PUB. & COOP. ECON. (SPECIAL ISSUE) 191–97 (2015). As the quote above indicates, this progressive position was also shared to some extent by Hayek. As the reader will see in the following pages, there are other points of convergence between these two theorists.

46 *See id.* at 192 (advocating that personal responsibility is a driving force for social equality).

47 *Id.*

48 *Id*, emphasis in original.

This conception of social justice is rooted in the economic and built around the individual. I do not mean to suggest that there is anything inherently wrong with concern for diversity or pluralism or, for that matter, with a goal of equal opportunity. I do, however, want to assert that such a focus is a theoretical and political problem when it totally eclipses the needs, functioning, and nature of society, and makes the individual the only relevant measure for justice. The realm of the social becomes blurred, if not completely dissolved, in what might better be described as individual economic justice.

In regard to defining equality, Van Parijs clearly explained that equality is *not* to be interpreted to mean equivalence in outcome, and this is true whether what is distributed is happiness, income, wealth, health, or power. For him, inequalities in distribution can be justified in two ways. First is the principle of personal responsibility under which inequalities do not violate an egalitarian mandate if they are byproducts of pursuit of individual actions, provided there is what he terms "*real freedom*."[49] This idea of real freedom is a central (and individually focused) theme in Van Parijs' work, although it is not fully explained. Sometimes he seems to indicate that real freedom equates with opportunity and is something to be fairly distributed: "Equality is not a matter of equalizing outcomes, it is a matter of equalizing opportunities, possibilities, real freedom."[50] One would assume that this distribution of opportunity as constituting real freedom would have something to do with state action, but it is not clear what that action is or what its objectives are.

However, it does seem clear that Van Parijs' conception of the state's proper role is a thin one and limited to the provision of opportunity, which one assumes means monitoring discrimination and exclusion. Presumably, any state interference with outcome would compromise this generalized access to real freedom, a conclusion buttressed by the articulation of his second principle, which is efficiency:

> we should not try to equalize at all cost .... [J]ustice is not about strict equality even of possibilities, but rather about the sustainable maximization of the minimum – the *maximin* – about making the real freedom of those with least real freedom as great as sustainably possible.[51]

Van Parijs' logic here exemplifies the ascendency of the individual over the social conception of justice.

This perspective on social justice boils down to two propositions. First, society's primary responsibility is to ensure sufficient opportunities for individuals to engage in productive economic activities of their own choice – in other

49 *See* Van Parijs, *supra* note 45, at 192 ("Justice is about the fair distribution of possibilities, of opportunities, of capabilities, of the real freedom to do things").
50 *Id.*
51 *Id.*

words, social justice maximizes individual choice/liberty or "real freedom." Second, if there is real freedom, then the just or equitable distribution of social benefits and rewards demands that distribution be achieved through the exercise of individual talent, initiative, and effort – in other words, end results are an individual responsibility. Fundamental social arrangements affecting the individual that are outside of the scope of access questions are not interrogated.

The valorization of the individual and its implications for the diminishment of the social are also evident when it comes to the idea of what constitutes a good life. Van Parijs rejects the idea of a socially determined, collectively enforced notion of justice, asserting that "[l]iberal conceptions of justice in this sense are to be distinguished from pre modern or traditional conceptions of justice which start from a specific conception of the good life ... in order to determine what the just society is." He equates social justice with individual economic choice, specifying one significant aspect of real freedom to be the "freedom to consume." He also valorizes the freedom to determine what one does with one's life. No consideration of individual responsibility for the generation of collective or social goods is elaborated. Real freedom thus translates into a call for allowing an individual to maximize her or his economic potential and social position as she or he defines it.[52]

Van Parijs positions the individual as a free-floating agent, not someone inevitably contained within or constrained by society (once society has provided the required opportunity or real freedom) or by personal history and experience.[53] The state is not viewed as generally responsible for the direct provision of goods and services (except, perhaps, in creating a nominal safety net), nor should it intervene in the interest of equities in outcome. The state is responsible, however, for ensuring the proper functioning of markets (and, thus, providing equal opportunity or real freedom).[54] Ironically, this progressive individualism perspective on social justice reaches the same conclusion as neoliberalism – the market is the social institution through which individuals will gain freedom.[55] It follows that the laws necessary to effect the social order advanced by this particular vision of justice are those that prohibit discrimination (a very weak notion

52 *Id.* at 192–93.

53 *See, e.g., id.* at 192–93 (considering the individual's role in the greater economy). This position is reminiscent of Hayek, although Van Parijs asserts that he is defining social justice, while Hayek rejects the term. Compare HAYEK, *supra* note 39 (calling the social aspect of social justice redundant), with Van Parijs, *supra* note 45, at 192 (defining social justice as "real freedom for all, or a liberal egalitarian conception of justice that is both responsibility-sensitive and efficiency-sensitive").

54 *See id.* at 193 (defining the state's role in developing a healthy market economy).

55 Compare Van Parijs, *supra* note 45, at 195 (concluding that public subsidies or favorable tax statuses may be justifiable because they are efficient tools in the social economy), with David Singh Grewal & Jedediah Purdy, *Introduction: Law and Neoliberalism*, 77 L. & CONTEMP. PROB. 1, 2 (2014) (describing the convergent evolution of market-based theories of individual freedoms).

of providing opportunity),[56] complemented by guarantees of political and civil rights recognizing individual dignity, autonomy, and responsibility.[57]

Moral or fairness arguments for policies aimed at redistribution based on broader conceptions of justice are easily disposed of under the logical constructs advanced by Van Parijs (and Hayek, for that matter) using two argumentative tactics. First, his adoption of a notion of relativism, or cultural pluralism, emphasizes individual choice and renders social justice a matter of individual definition. This maneuver also locates the ultimate responsibility with the individual, who must choose what is best for her or him, as well as determining how to achieve it. Second, his appeal to economic efficiency positions cost-benefit analysis as the ultimate standard for defining public policies.[58] For those of us who see social justice as inevitably inefficient sometimes, this move to market principles is perverse.

Social justice advocates need a new vocabulary – one that will set forth a logic of *social* justice that recovers the notion of a collectively determined and realized public good that both defines state or governmental responsibility and takes into account ends as well as means. This rhetoric should not only complement but also transcend individual interest.[59] In this project, the concepts of human vulnerability and resilience, as well as a recognition that we are all inevitably dependent on various social institutions and relationships over the life course, are of vital importance. The realities of human vulnerability and dependency reveal the fallacy in the conceptions of individual liberty and autonomy that lie at the heart of neoliberalism.

Embedded Implications of Human Vulnerability

Ultimately, of more significance to the development of the theory than the description of human vulnerability is a second theoretical question, one that has

56 The state monitors the point of entry into the economic sphere but not how that sphere ultimately performs. *See, e.g.*, Dinner, *supra* note 21 at 1063 (proposing that employment-discrimination law is indicative of a more efficient labor market).

57 *See id.* at 1068 (positing values espoused by Title VII). Public policy also reflects this orientation, with cities and states bidding for businesses to relocate so as to provide employment opportunities, often at the expense of public programs such as education when heavy subsidies are used as incentives. For instance, the latest notorious competition between cities was for Amazon headquarters, offering millions in tax breaks and public investment for the promise of creating jobs. *See* M. J., *How America's Cities are Competing for Amazon's Headquarters*, ECONOMIST (Dec. 5, 2017), https://www.economistcom/the- economist-explains/2017/12/05/how-america s-cities-are-competing-for-amazons-headquarters (describing the attempts by cities to lure Amazon into establishing a new headquarters in their respective cities).

58 *See* Van Parijs, *supra* note 45, at 192 (framing Van Parijs' economic efficiency argument).

59 *See* Duncan Kennedy, *Special Supplement, The Social Justice Element in Legal Education in the United States*, 1 HARV. UNBOUND J. LEGAL LEFT 93, 93 (2005) (discussing the application of a wider vocabulary to the term "social justice").

normative implications: If to be human is to be universally and constantly vulnerable, how should this recognition inform the structure and operation of our society and its institutions? To answer this question, it is necessary to reflect initially upon the whole idea of society. Margaret Thatcher, in a 1987 interview in *Women's Own Magazine,* famously proclaimed there was no such thing as society:

> They are casting their problems at society. And, you know, there's no such thing as society. There are individual men and women and there are families. And no government can do anything except through people, and people must look after themselves first. It is our duty to look after ourselves and then, also, to look after our neighbours.[60]

She was making a political, not a sociological, statement reflecting her view on state responsibility (or lack thereof). However, the idea of society and how it functions in critical theory are not always obvious, and it is important to explicitly reveal the assumptions that are made. We know societies are not all the same, but they may nonetheless have universal shared characteristics. First, any society has to be intergenerational if it is going to perpetuate itself. Every society needs a means of organizing itself and establishing the rules that will guide individual interactions with each other, as well as establishing the appropriate relationship between the individual and the state. Second, every society must, of necessity, devise social institutions and relationships that respond to the realities of the human condition, which means responding to human vulnerability and dependency.

These two assertions about society are at the heart of vulnerability theory. The social institutions and relationships that a society forms must not only transcend the specific interests of particular individuals and groups but also have concern for the intergenerational needs of society. This societal perspective defines a preeminent social justice challenge. Vulnerability theory teaches us that human beings are all inevitably embedded within the social – located throughout our lives in particular systems of social organization. The social nature of those institutions and relationships form the basis for state, or collective, responsibility. This responsibility cannot initially or primarily be understood only in terms of individual well-being. Social justice responsibility must be intergenerational and directed to the systems of institutions and relationships developed by a society to maintain general human well-being and flourishing. We cannot adequately assess what is just on an individual or group basis without considering the justice of the fundamental social order. The societal problems of general organization and order must define state responsibility in the first instance.

60 *Margaret Thatcher: A Life in Quotes*, THE GUARDIAN (Apr. 8, 2013), https://www.theguardian.com/politics/2013/apr/08/margaret-thatcher-quotes.

In defining this collective responsibility, the collective reality of human vulnerability and the physical and social dependency that it inevitably generates must be of central concern. In particular, the social implications of dependency are vitally important in defining state responsibility. Dependency is most evident when we are infants and children, but while we may be more or less reliant on care at any given stage, dependency is present in some form and to some degree throughout our lives.

Social Institutions and Resilience

While it may not be explicitly focused on the vulnerability of human beings, the current political order is not dismissive of the need for social institutions. Policy pronouncements, legislative histories, party platforms, and political rhetoric have routinely recognized and celebrated the important position and function of institutions and institutional roles in society.[61] Economic or market institutions are acclaimed as producing the economic well-being of society, with the individuals controlling them cast as wealth and job creators – entrepreneurs paving the path for economic growth and prosperity for the entire nation.[62] The family is praised for its role in raising the next generation of citizens and caring for those at the end of life. Parents are lauded for their self-sacrificing actions, and the self-sufficient (marital) family is valorized as both a moral and an economic ideal, uniquely qualified to attend to dependency and the needs of family members.

The political and policy perception is that these institutions (among others) have a central and essential role in organizing and reproducing society, as well as providing for individuals, which serves as the rationale for protecting them from state interference. While this perception that institutions are necessary is correct, we must modify the current political dogma that places these institutions within a "private sphere," distinguishing them from a public arena in which state action and responsibility are the norms. The failure to recognize the public purpose of these institutions (and the corresponding public responsibility

61 *See* JACOB S. HACKER & PAUL PIERSON, WINNER-TAKE-ALL POLITICS: HOW WASHINGTON MADE THE RICH RICHER – AND TURNED ITS BACK ON THE MIDDLE CLASS (2011) (talking about the relationship of political institutions to inequality and wealth concentration); DARON ACEMOGLU & JAMES A. ROBINSON, WHY NATIONS FAIL: THE ORIGINS OF POWER, PROSPERITY, AND POVERTY (2012) (showing the relevance of political and economic institutions for development).

62 Particularly in modern capitalist societies (*i.e.*, market-oriented economies), private corporations are the main actors in deciding what, when, and how much is produced and also serve as our main employers and taxpayers. In the words of Lindblom, they are a kind of "public officials" considering that "jobs, prices, production, growth, the standard of living and the economic security of everyone *all rest in their hands*." *See* CHARLES E. LINDBLOM, POLITICS AND MARKETS: THE WORLD'S POLITICAL-ECONOMIC SYSTEMS 172 (1977) (emphasis added).

for them) is not only misguided but also detrimental to the functioning of society and the welfare of many individuals within it.

That these constructed entities are deemed "private" institutions, even though we enact laws to facilitate their creation, determine their shape, terms, and responsibilities, and ease their functioning, is a paradox. They are creatures of law, brought into being by doctrines set out in corporate, family, property, employment, tax, trade, welfare, and other laws. The law determines the nature of the relationships between individuals within these essential social institutions, such as parent/child, employer/employee, shareholder/consumer, and so on.

Creating social institutions and relationships also involves defining the relationship between the state, the institutions it creates in law, and the individual. Laws and legal principles form or constrain the ongoing scope of state responsibility for social institutions once they have been created. In the United States, the idea of ongoing state responsibility is viewed as an exception when it comes to social institutions, particularly the market or family. For example, in the business arena the notion of the "free market" and the "efficiency" inherent in competition consistently are raised as barriers to state regulation and oversight. We have fashioned doctrines of "family privacy" and "parental rights" that deter government participation in significant and consequential decisions affecting the present and future well-being of children. This default position of the "private" ordering system for essential societal institutions must be adjusted by recognizing the necessity of ongoing public monitoring of and oversight for these institutions. This oversight and advocacy for needed adjustments should be the primary focuses of social justice scholarship.

The law, by shaping essential social institutions and the relationships within them, dictates the basic organization of society – allocating power and privilege, as well as determining the means for individual and societal well-being. Both individuals and society ultimately are dependent on the successful and fair operation of society's institutions. The relationship between the individual and society is symbiotic and mutually dependent. As indicated previously, the concept of derivative dependence is important here. If we are to fulfill the social roles we occupy within society, we must be able to rely on its institutions. If society is to flourish, it must rely on the success of the institutions and individuals who comprise it. Individual and collective reliance on social relationships and institutions mandate that the state monitor these essential social arrangements and make adjustments when they are not operating equitably. This includes those institutions that are now classified as private, as well as those deemed public. At most, social institutions can only be considered to be quasi-private.

Conclusion

Vulnerability theory, built around the recognition of our shared vulnerability and dependence, illuminates why we need to first consider general legal institutions and relationships in determining social justice. By placing the vulnerable subject at the center of its inquiry, vulnerability theory requires that critical inquiry begin with a consideration of how society structures its institutions and relationships through law and policy. In urging us to do this before looking at how specific individuals or groups are faring within those social arrangements, the theory seeks to define and apply a legislative or administrative set of decision-making ethics, rather than setting forth a cluster of individual rights to entitlements. Vulnerability theory is more focused on establishing the parameters of state responsibility for societal institutions and relationships than it is on setting the limits of state intervention.

Importantly, a vulnerability approach to social justice recognizes that the relationship between the individual and society is synergetic. Social institutions operate in integrated and sequential ways within society, and individual success depends on the successful integration and operation of those institutions. In its consideration of the role of social institutions in producing resilience, the theory also illuminates the ultimate corresponding dependence of society on the collective successes of those individuals. Just as no individual can successfully stand apart from the state and its institutions, the destiny of the state ultimately relies on the actions of the individuals within it. A social justice paradigm should encompass the whole – not just individual parts – of society. This integrated approach may require that, in some circumstances, specific interests or individual desires must be adjusted to accommodate social well-being. But this should be a process of balancing, not ignoring the respective positions of everyone involved in any situation.

Law is a primary way in which we order society and structure its synergetic relationships. It provides the rules governing individuals in their interactions with each other but also defines the relationship between the individual and the state – including the state's responsibility to the individual and the individual's responsibility to the state. Policies and laws must construct and sustain an adequately responsive state – one that is grounded in vulnerability, addresses the range of dependencies inherent over the life course, and is attentive to all stages of development and forms of need. Following that path is the route to the realization of a robust and comprehensive sense of social justice.

Chapter 19

Conclusion

Resilience is the Watchword

Lua Kamál Yuille

Vulnerability is en vogue. It may even be the zeitgeist. Some version of the idea has garnered attention and become influential in a variety of fields – international relations, ecology, feminist theory, bioethics, sociology, medicine, economics, legal theory, and so on. A multimillion-dollar wellness industry has organized itself around its power. Popular culture and social movements have raised vulnerability as a banner. Vulnerability theory, as developed in more than a decade of Fineman's writing, provides something more. Her intervention transforms vulnerability from a catchphrase and compelling concept into a coherent interdisciplinary heuristic for understanding, evaluating, and prescribing social, legal, and economic policies and procedures, which promise to be responsive to the variable needs of all people, not regardless of but reflective of, the particular realities of their physical embodiment and social and institutional embeddedness. The realization of this promise is the future of vulnerability theory and the implicit demand of the zeitgeist. Consider, for example, the rise and fall of #BlackGirlMagic.

On May 18, 2021, filmmaker Zandashé Brown apostatized the mantle of black womanhood:

> I dream of never being called resilient again in my life. I'm exhausted by strength. I want support. I want softness. I want ease. I want to be amongst kin. Not patted on the back for how well I take a hit. Or for how many.[1]

Her vision was compelling; it went viral, and a meme emerged. It was an anti-#BlackGirlMagic manifesto.

#BlackGirlMagic – itself a meme, mantra, and campaign – first cast its spell on American and then, global consciousness (or, at least, on Black consciousness) in 2013. It was a celebration of the resilience of black girls and women. CaShawn Thompson, who is credited with catalyzing its popularity, explained the motivation for #BlackGirlMagic: "[W]hat I understood to be magic was

1 Zandashi Brown (@zandashe), Twitter (May 18, 2021), https://twitter.com/zandashe/status/1394805726825099279.

DOI: 10.4324/9781003405627-25

fairytales, witches and people that could work spells and make things out of no things and make things happen that nobody else could, and that's what I saw [in Black women]."[2]

The inchoate, informal #BlackGirlMagic movement might be read as critical socio-economic praxis. Through it, Black women rewrote settlements about their social position and economic potential. It felt, and for many still feels, radical. And, indeed, unabashedly celebrating Blackness, particularly Black femaleness, is a radical rejection of the ethos of White supremacy. But #BlackGirlMagic fundamentally replicates dominant socio-political economic norms both in its aims and its method. It works to claim that Black women are ideal neoliberal subjects: independent, autonomous, entrepreneurial. Indeed, Thompson's earliest material deployment of #BlackGirlMagic was merchandising.

The resonance of Brown's anti-#BlackGirlMagic manifesto is, therefore, not surprising. Nor was it the first such critique. In 2016, for example, Linda Chavers controversially broke the spell of #BlackGirlMagic in ELLE magazine: "Black girls aren't magical. We're human."[3] Chavers saw neither celebration nor liberation in #BlackGirlMagic. Instead, she saw in it the reification of the "strong, black woman" archetype and its concomitant harms. Radiah Shabazz saw #BlackGirlMagic as delegitimizing the actual experiences of Black women; "perhaps, #BlackGirlMagic has been taken too literally. I can't wave a wand and make all my problems go away. I'm human. I will cry. I will ache. I will feel."[4] Taraji P. Henson called the meme damaging, "It dehumanized us, our pain; it belittles our tears .... we're not fairies. We don't magically rebound ...."[5]

They may not know it or adopt its heuristics, but #BlackGirlMagic spell breakers (like Brown, Chavers, Shabazz, and Henson) have embraced the descriptive core of Fineman's vulnerability theory. They depathologize Black women's capacity to experience pain, harm, and illness, as central to the nature of being human. That is, they recognize vulnerability as the universal human condition.

And, although their language belies it, spell breakers also accept the power of vulnerability theory's principal demand: resilience. When Brown asks for support, softness, ease, and community, she is asking for resilience. Just not some profoundly empty[6] notion of resilience. In the dominant socio-cultural

2 Cashawn Thompson, *Cashawn*, Black History Untold: Herstory (2019), https://www.blkhistoryuntold.com/herstory/cashawn.

3 Linda Chavers, *Here's My Problem with #BlackGirlMagic*, ELLE (Jan. 13, 2016), https://www.elle.com/life-love/a33180/why-i-dont-love-blackgirlmagic/.

4 Radiah Shabazz, *Stop Telling Me I'm Resilient: Why It's Harmful, not Helpful*, BLAVITY (Aug. 10, 2017), https://basicblackchick.com/2017/08/11/stop-telling-me-im-resilient-why-its-harmful-not-helpful/.

5 J. Grant, *Taraji P. Henson on Why the 'Strong Black Woman' Identity Damages Us*, ESSENCE (Dec. 6, 2020), https://www.essence.com/lifestyle/health-wellness/essence-wellness-house/taraji-p-henson-explains-why-the-strong-black-woman-identity-at-essence-wellness-house/.

6 P. Sehgal, *The profound emptiness of resilience*, N.Y. TIMES (Dec. 1, 2015), https://www.nytimes.com/2015/12/06/magazine/the-profound-emptiness-of-resilience.html.

imagination and rhetoric, resilience is treated as an intrinsic individual characteristic. It is what gives substance to and ranks the neoliberal subject. In this paradigm, the more resilient you are, the less vulnerable and dependent you are. The better you are. And where does one acquire this resilience? It is magic for which no person or institution bears responsibility. One cannot demand resilience any more than one can demand, for example, good health. Instead, individuals must unlock it from a store of innate metaphysical endowments. They must practice it with yogic fortitude. Or, they can be thankful to be blessed with it. Magic. It is radical and revolutionary to reject this mythic, alchemical resilience: Fuck magic. Fuck resilience.

But through vulnerability theory, Fineman demystifies and rehabilitates resilience. It is not manna from some neoliberal heaven. It is not an innate condition. And it certainly is not magic. Resilience is the accumulation–over time and within and through social institutions and relationships–of resources to allow people and communities to confront, adapt to, compensate for, cope with, and recover from the consequences of their immutable vulnerability. From this perspective, wealth is resilience. Healthcare is resilience. Housing is resilience. Education is resilience. And the support, softness, ease, and community Brown craves–these resources are resilience.

The fraught evolution of #BlackGirlMagic provides a rich basis from which to reflect on the tasks of vulnerability theory as a tool for social change as it enters its next chapter. Vulnerability theory's descriptive claim–"the fact that we are born, live, and die within a fragile materiality that renders all of us constantly susceptible to destructive external forces and internal disintegration"[7]– is logically simple and empirically irrefutable. But it is psychosocially and politically radical. So, for more than a decade, Fineman and a growing, interdisciplinary community of vulnerability scholars have been engaged in an extended intellectual project of consciousness raising. Re-examining legal, political, and socio-economic relations and policies through the vulnerability lens has occupied considerable energy. But, as the #BlackGirlMagic pushback illustrates, there is a growing implicit acceptance of vulnerability theory's foundations. Perhaps never before have the notion and implications of universal vulnerability been so palatable.

What people lack, however, is a clear notion of how to envision change in the world of constant vulnerability and how to mobilize around it. Brown *longs* for the resilience of support and kin, but she launches her plea for it into the ether. That is more than Chavers, Shabazz, and Henson, who make no claims at all beyond rejecting the notion that individuals are solely responsible for generating their own resilience. Largely absent from this #BlackGirlMagic/anti-#BlackGirlMagic story is any proactive, constructive role for the government. Resilience can be distributed through political mechanisms structured (and

7 Martha Albertson Fineman, *The Vulnerable Subject: Anchoring Equality in the Human Condition*, 20 YALE J.L & FEMINISM 1,12 (2008).

often invisibilized) by law. Or it can be generated extra-legally. #BlackGirlMagic celebrates the extra-legal generation of resilience by black girls, who are systematically marginalized from and in mainstream sources of resilience. But in so doing, it cedes those more powerful, better resources, and politically accountable sites of resilience generation. #BlackGirlMagic spell breakers do not cede; they implicitly reject the notion that resilience is the province of the hearty, entrepreneurial individual, who can will the necessary resources into existence out of nothing.

Vulnerability theory resolves the #BlackGirlMagic dissonance: There is no state of invulnerability; there is only the possibility of resilience, and generating, regulating, and distributing resilience is the primary task of all social institutions. Those institutions are, in turn, enabled, structured, and supported by the government. Ensuring the adequate, just, and equitable distribution of resilience is the primary justification for any government and the measure of what Fineman refers to as the responsive state.

The contours of resilience–as a socio-economic goal and as legal/political principle–however, remain undertheorized and under examined in vulnerability theory. What is the nature of resilience in and across institutions? How can specific institutions be structured to adjust and adapt to the changing resilience needs of individuals? What is the significance of differential actual allocation of resilience among identifiable communities? When is it appropriate for the state to inhibit resilience? How do you measure resilience and at what scale? How do specific rules and policies differentially impact resilience? These are the types of questions to which scholars of vulnerability are increasingly turning their attention. And the answers to these questions can provide generative support to the spell breakers to make demands for a responsive state.

Vulnerability theory permits a deeper and more authentic understanding of how people engage with each other and their communities. It reframes the central challenges of law, politics, and economics. And it transforms social justice into an institutional design project with resilience as the watchword.

Chapter 20

Afterword

Atieno Mboya Samandari

It is an honor to write this Afterword on the collection of Martha Albertson Fineman's published work. I first encountered Fineman's scholarship as a young, public-interest women's rights lawyer in Kenya in the early 1990s. During that period, I came head-to-head with the limitations of transplanted, liberal legal solutions for women's problems, which were acutely demonstrated by widowed or marginalized married women living in rural Kenya's patriarchal culture. The widows were typically seeking help to keep control of family property that they had usufruct access to during their husband's lifetime; access that was threatened after their husband's passing. For marginalized wives, they hoped the law would guarantee them a measure of secure property ownership which, under customary law, would all revert to the estranged husband. Land in rural Kenya is still largely controlled by customary norms and practices that privilege traditional male ownership and succession, though with the advent of neoliberalism, private rural freehold land ownership is possible for those that can purchase it. The women clients I worked with did not fall into this latter category.

The solutions that Kenya's law offered these women were to pit them against members of the nuclear and extended families in which they had longstanding relationships that they wanted to maintain, in addition to getting secure property rights. It quickly became clear that the individualistic, adversarial human rights approach that we took to these issues, which isolated the aggrieved woman from a community that she valued and depended on, would not bring peaceful enjoyment of property if a legal victory were achieved. The dilemma, then, was one of trying to help Kenyan rural women gain secure property rights – which were to be won by focusing on their individual rights, autonomy, and separateness from their marital family – while honoring their need to maintain meaningful connection to their familial and social networks. This dilemma is what led me to Fineman's work. The transplanted liberal approach to property ownership that Kenya had adopted in its formal laws did not resonate with these clients, yet they were hoping that law had the solutions that customary norms would not ensure for them.

Unlike the liberal western norms that stigmatized dependency, which Fineman critiques in her early work, dependency and interdependency of family and community in rural Kenya is an accepted way of life. As a result, the

DOI: 10.4324/9781003405627-26

autonomous, liberal legal subject, which, as a women's rights lawyer in Kenya, I was bringing as the answer to these women's insecure property rights, was not well received by most of them. The maintenance of social relationships was important to these clients, with the exception of a few cases, most were not willing to trade their social embeddedness for individual land ownership. They were looking for the law to guarantee them secure rights *within* social embeddedness, not in exchange for it. This prompted my search for legal theory and practice that grappled with such a context, and I found it in Fineman's work.

Kenya's adoption of formal equality rhetoric into the country's legal framework turned a blind eye to rural women's own recognition of their socially "gendered lives," where they experience society differently from men, within a complex web of important socio-legal cultural relationships and norms. Formal state law in these contexts is more a symbol of justice and equality that cannot deliver the solutions these women are seeking. The women's vulnerability in rural property ownership was not mitigated by Kenya's liberal, state-generated legal norms and practices. As a result, a plural legal system that consists of both state and cultural laws and practices constitutes Kenya's legal landscape. When cultural laws failed to yield justice, the women turned to state law in the hopes of securing their property rights. Individual autonomy-based state law, however, did not solve their problem and purchasing the land in question from their marital family was not a viable option when collective rural culture disenfranchised women from secure property rights.

Working with Fineman at Emory has been an invaluable opportunity to think about the limits of formal equality under state law and the importance of incorporating a shared collective welfare within liberal conceptions of social justice. Such an approach would be more useful in societies that already embrace collective welfare as a basic ethic, as is the case in many of Kenya's rural communities. Fineman's call across her work for the valuation of caretaking and the recognition of the debt owed to caretakers for their social reproduction work resonated with the lived experiences of rural Kenyan women. This role remains culturally important and respected, yet solutions proffered by the state legal system emphasized autonomous independence, which is at odds with a collective, interdependent context.

Fineman's concept of embodied vulnerability as the foundation for a new approach to state law that upholds collective well-being and achieves meaningful social justice for aggrieved parties, like Kenya's rural widows and marginalized wives for instance, is an important contribution that expands the boundaries of jurisprudence. Vulnerability theory, which is premised on the complex, sometimes messy, vulnerable subject that is embedded within state institutions that are the final arbiters and providers of resources that foster social resilience throughout the life course, opens new possibilities for legal thought and practice that can mitigate the myriad manifestations of human vulnerability found in diverse settings.

The Vulnerability and the Human Condition Initiative, through the numerous workshops and scholarly discussions it has held both at Emory and other universities, and through a variety of courses incorporating vulnerability theory, continues to push socio-legal thought beyond its current individualistic and oftentimes constricting formal closures. Vulnerability theory beckons toward a new conception of law and institutions that is responsive to the universal vulnerability that accompanies the human condition.

Index

affirmative action: and formal equality 16; and gender equality 11, 15, 17, 18; opposition to 105; and substantive equality 108, 109, 111
Allen, Anita 118–19
autonomy: and economic equality 104; and equality 105, 157; and formal equality 38, 105, 107; and gender equality 104, 110; and substantive equality 109, 110, 111, 157
autonomy, as foundational myth: in conflict with inevitable dependency 65, 105; opportunities for new foundations 88, 106; perpetuating inequalities 86, 83, 103, 109
autonomy, individual: and collective vulnerability 104, 109, 111, 113, 125, 133, 140, 153; and deviations 103; and economic considerations 91, 111, 148; as freedom 107, 108; and policy 108, 109, 163, 169, 179
autonomy, family: and caretaking 110, 120, 121, 122, 132; and children 120; and gender 104; and marriage 109; and societal dependency 103, 121; nuclear/natural 72; and privacy 6, 114, 121, 122, 149

Berry, Betty Blaisdell 10

capitalism 92, 160
caretaking: and derivative dependency 44, 65, 75, 84, 92, 131; as function of family 64, 73, 98–99, 110, 119, 122–23; and gender neutrality 59, 65, 76, 110, 121, 132; policy 111, 123, 131, 136; and social supports 87
caretaking, as unpaid domestic labor: within marriage 64, 110; to personal detriment 91, 94, 96; as societal reproduction 89, 90, 92, 93; solutions 95, 110; of women 69, 74, 104
children: child abuse 68, 74, 116, 119, 120, 122; in poverty 44, 74, 87, 139, child support 10, 39, 43, 44, 46, 56, 74
child advocacy 52, 53, 54, 55, 56, 59, 120, 122
childcare 34, 35, 38, 40, 43, 44, 64
child custody: "best interest" test 52, 53, 54, 55, 56, 57, 58; and gender neutrality 52; joint 35, 58; maternal 18, 19, 67; paternal 35; primary caretaker standard 34, 44; reform 57, 58, 59; sole 58; "tender years" doctrine 18
choice, individual 92, 104, 125, 132–33, 140; and inequality 95, 105, 109, 111; and social justice 159, 163, 164, 167, 168, 169
civil rights 11, 106, 159, 162, 169
Clinton, President Bill 89, 93, 166
collective responsibility *see* responsibility, collective
Collier, Richard 99
compassion 146, 148, 150, 159
consciousness Raising 93, 102, 176
contract: consent 64; marriage as 16, 36, 38, 63, 64, 65, 116
corporations: corporate responsibility 149, 150; corporate vulnerability 125, 126, 154, 155, 156

dependency 68, 94–96, 103–06, 171, 178; derivative 65, 79, 84, 83, 91–92, 131, 132, 172; inevitable 65, 69, 76, 79,

83–83, 84, 89, 131, 136; privatization of 72–75, 90
differences, individual: developmental 135, 136; embodied 135, 136, 140, 144; embedded 83, 135, 136, 144
distribution: equitable 10, 46–49, 85–86, 87, 96, 145, 167, 168, 177; needs-based versus contribution-based 42–43, 45–46; state responsibility for 95, 138, 145, 154
divorce: economic aspects of 10, 18, 33–40, 43, 45, 50–51; no-fault 10, 42, 59; reform 11, 18, 19, 33, 47, 48, 49, 53, 60, 74
domestic violence 68, 118
diversity 126, 166, 167

Eisenstadt v. Baird 115
embodiment 130, 134, 174
empathy 31, 90, 146, 147
employment 9, 40, 89, 137–138, 149, 161, 164, 172; as contract 130; incompatibilities with caretaking 34, 40, 98–100, 131; inequality of relationship 131, 134, 155
equality: and autonomy 105, 107, 109, 110; and dependency 46; and difference 142; formal 63, 126–27, 129–30, 132, 14–43, 163, 179; gender 9, 11, 33, 38, 63, 83, 84, 132; rule equality versus result equality 13–19; substantive 63, 105, 108, 111, 142, 152
Equal Rights Amendment 14
experts 55, 57, 58, 101

family: deviant 66, 74, 78; extended 178; natural 72–78; nuclear 43, 63, 67–68, 72–74, 84, 117–18, 178; private 72–78, 84, 90, 104, 119, 133, 149; public 71, 121; sexual family 63, 65–66, 75–77, 78; traditional 17, 68, 70, 71, 74, 75, 78, 118
family law 67–68, 74–75, 77, 84, 101, 104, 115, 132; as gender neutral 9–11, 15–16, 63
fatherhood 35, 36
feminism: discrimination, sex-based 9, 15, 105; feminist legal theory 9, 11, 12, 20–23, 26, 30, 32; liberal 11, 13, 16, 44, 47, 60, 61, 63, 83; second wave 68; theory 17, 20–23, 24, 26, 28, 32, 104, 174
freedom, individual 105, 108, 152, 161, 168
Friedman, Milton 165
Fuchs, Victor 34, 35

Geertz, Clifford 22
gender: differences 29, equality 11, 38, 63, 64, 83, 84, 132; neutrality 16, 24, 27, 28, 52, 57, 76
gendered life 23, 25, 26, 28–32, 179
gender roles 93
Ginsburg, Ruth Bader 9
grand theory 11, 20, 21, 22, 23
Griswold v. Connecticut 114, 115, 117
guardians ad litem 53, 55, 126

Hayek, Friedrich 165, 166, 168, 169
helping professionals 55, 56, 57, 58, 59
human condition 83–83, 89, 125, 150; and vulnerability 129, 133, 136, 170, 175, 180
human rights *see* rights, human

independence 38, 67, 103, 120, 150, 179; and autonomy 107–10; as cultural ideal 59, 72, 85–86, 84–83, 88, 94–95, 105, 132–33, 159
individualism 72, 148, 149, 150, 166, 168
individual responsibility *see* responsibility, individual
individual rights *see* rights, individual
inequality: economic 34, 147, 163; inevitable 130, 133, 140; *see also* equality
injury: individual 139, 147; social 143, 144, 150; state inaction as 83, 140, 151, 152, 153
intimacy 67, 68, 69, 74, 75, 76, 117, 118

joint custody *see* custody, joint
judicial discretion 16, 36, 41
justice: collective versus individual 132, 133, 150, 159, 162, 163, 168; social *see* social justice

labor: unions 10, 15, 46, 106, 109, 137, 149; wages 10, 34, 37, 49, 73–74, 91, 94, 113, 155
legal subject: liberal 84, 153, 179, vulnerable 133–34, 136, 140, 144, 153, 157, 159, 179

MacKinnon, Catherine 23, 118, 119, 121
maintenance (alimony) 10, 39, 40, 41, 78, 116
market 147; and autonomy 103–04, 107–08, 112–13, 121; and caretaking 64,

68, 73–74, 91–96, 132; participation by women 10–11, 16–19, 43, 73–74; responsibility 138, 145, 148–50, 153, 161–69, 171–72; vulnerability of 155
marriage: abolition of 64, 65, 75; egalitarian 18, 45, 51, 157, 167; as solution to poverty 74, 94, 160; state regulation of 64
McGuire v. McGuire 116
mediation 13, 56, 84, 88
meritocracy 85, 109
Merton, Robert 11, 22
moral hazard 155, 156, 166
morality 54, 104
motherhood: deviant 74, mother/child dyad 65, 76, 84; natural 18, 101; single 71, 74
myth: 74, 176; of autonomy 65, 103, 105–06, 108; foundational 83, 88, 103

National Organization for Women 10, 33
neoliberalism 140, 158, 162, 164, 165, 168, 169, 178
neutered mother 63, 64, 67, 78, 84
neutrality of law 32, 61
nurturing ideal 67, 76

parental roles 120, 136
Parents Involved in Community Schools v. Seattle School District No. 1 126, 142
partnership metaphor (for marriage) 10, 16, 36, 39, 41–43, 45–46, 48–49, 69, 109
patriarchy 28, 65, 74, 91
poverty 31, 138, 139, 153, 164; and inequality 85, 95, 160; traditional family or fatherhood as solution 74, 94; of women and children 44, 74, 87
pregnancy 29, 105
privacy: family 68, 72, 114–23, 136, 172; individual 123, 149, 152,
private sphere 13, 164, 171
privilege 31, 85–86, 108–11, 136, 157, 178; conferral by institutions 7, 104, 126–27, 134, 138–40, 144–45, 154, 172; of marriage or nuclear family 68, 70, 75
property 153; children as 53, 119–20; distribution at divorce 10, 37; impact on custodial parent 40, 45, 49–51; law ordering family 67–68, 75; rhetoric of 50–51; rights to private 154, 163, 178–79
public sphere 13, 18, 71, 91

Reagan, Ronald 162
religion 31, 75, 93, 109, 138, 140, 144, 147
reproduction 29, 71, 72, 87, 117, 119; rights 114–15; of society 63–64, 84, 90, 103–04, 131–32, 171, 179
resilience 71, 156, 169, 171–73, 174–77, 179; inequality of 138–39, 144; resources for 137; state responsibility for 83, 125–27, 129, 145, 154, 157
responsibility, collective/state 78–79, 148–50, 157; and autonomy 104, 111, 112–13; and dependency 84–83, 87–88, 90, 120, 121–23, 170–71; and derivative dependency 91–92, 93–95, 132; for human vulnerability 136, 145, 153–54; and inevitable dependency 72, 131; ror social institutions 125, 129, 145, 152–54, 172–73
responsibility, individual 83, 90, 103–04, 131, 133, 139–40, 148–50, 155, 167–69
rhetoric 22–23, 71, 74, 120, 171, 176; of divorce 45–47, 54; of gender equality 13, 17, 27, 33, 60–61, 68–69, 73, 179; of individualism, autonomy 72, 83, 87, 107–08, 149–50, 164, 169
rights 68, 87, 90, 121, 152; children's 43, 53, 117–20, 136; civil 11, 159, 169; father's or men's 10, 118; human 135, 159, 162–63, 178; individual 106, 107–09, 114–115, 148, 153, 173, 178; parental 39, 56, 65, 76, 136, 172; privacy 114–115, 123; women's 13–14, 48, 49, 178–79
Roe v. Wade 2, 118
Roosevelt, Franklin Delano 161

Same-sex marriage 64–65, 70
self-sufficiency 94–95; and autonomy 107–109, 110–11; as cultural ideal 72, 85–86, 84–83, 88, 92, 103, 132–33, 140, 170
sexual affiliation 39, 64–66, 70–72, 75–77, 117, 121–22
sexuality 30–31, 76, 103, 114
shared parenting 48, 58–59
Smart, Carol 23
social contract 152–53, 157
social debt 84, 87–95, 104, 131, 179
social goods 85–86, 108, 113, 150, 152, 161, 168
social identities 134, 144–45
social institutions: and dependency 83–84, 90, 104–106, 131–33; family as

"assumed" institution 68, 70–73, 78–79, 131–33; and gender equality 14, 17–19, 60–63; and inequality 144–45, 149–150; role in providing resilience 125–127, 137–39, 149–150, 171–73, 176–77, 179–80; state responsibility for 94–96, 125–127, 129–30, 134, 147–48, 164, 170; vulnerability of 125–127, 154–57
social justice 90, 103, 133, 140, 143–44, 150; and equality 130, 141–42; origin and history of term 159–169; and vulnerability theory 170–73, 177, 179
social relationships 130–40, 144, 172–73, 176, 179; and dependency 83, 110, 148; and vulnerability 125–26, 159, 169–70
social roles 131–32, 134–35, 148, 154, 172
Social Security 10, 37–38, 44, 86, 149
subsidy 64, 85, 92–93, 104; of caretaking 75–77, 84, 90–91, 111, 121–23, 131–32; corporate welfare 154–55; stigmatization of 88, 110
symbolism 18, 38, 42, 53, 71, 92, 99, 149; of gender equality 38, 47–50, 61, 75; of law 179

taxation 41, 85, 90, 93, 95, 140, 155, 160
Thatcher, Margaret 170
Thornton, Margaret 100

Uniform Marriage and Divorce Act (UMDA) 10, 40
U.S. Constitution 53, 108, 114–16, 118, 142, 143, 148, 151–52; equal protection clause 9, 133, 135, 141–43

Van Parijs, Philippe 166–69
victimization 13–14, 45, 47–48, 53–56, 60–61
vulnerability: and dependency 140; and difference 134–37; human 125–27, 129–30, 133, 139–40, 144–45, 150, 154–56, 169–71; institutional 125–26, 154–56; and resilience 137–39, 174–77; of state 156–57; universal 133, 139–40, 144–45
vulnerable subject 83, 133–34, 136, 144, 153, 157, 159, 179

welfare assistance 75, 83, 88, 131, 161–163; reform 11, 74, 89, 94; stigmatization of 90, 93, 153
White, James Boyd 22–23
Woodhouse, Barbara B. 120

For Product Safety Concerns and Information please contact our EU
representative GPSR@taylorandfrancis.com
Taylor & Francis Verlag GmbH, Kaufingerstraße 24, 80331 München, Germany

www.ingramcontent.com/pod-product-compliance
Ingram Content Group UK Ltd.
Pitfield, Milton Keynes, MK11 3LW, UK
UKHW020003200926
475702UK00015B/2454
* 9 7 8 1 0 3 2 5 2 2 2 1 0 *